FREEDOM
of the
PRESS

A Da Capo Press Reprint Series

CIVIL LIBERTIES IN AMERICAN HISTORY

GENERAL EDITOR: LEONARD W. LEVY

Claremont Graduate School

FREEDOM
of the
PRESS

By

GEORGE SELDES

DA CAPO PRESS • NEW YORK • 1971

A Da Capo Press Reprint Edition

This Da Capo Press edition of
Freedom of the Press
is an unabridged republication
of the first edition published in
1935. It is reprinted by special
arrangement with the Bobbs-Merrill
Company.

Library of Congress Catalog Card Number 73-146159

SBN 306–70125–1

Copyright, 1935, by the Bobbs-Merrill Company

Published by Da Capo Press, Inc.
A Subsidiary of Plenum Publishing Corporation
227 West 17th Street, New York, N.Y. 10011
All Rights Reserved

Manufactured in the United States of America

FREEDOM OF THE PRESS

By GEORGE SELDES

You Can't Print That!

Can These Things Be?

World Panorama

The Vatican—Yesterday—Today—Tomorrow

Iron, Blood and Profits

FREEDOM
of the PRESS

By

GEORGE SELDES

THE BOBBS-MERRILL COMPANY
Publishers
INDIANAPOLIS   **NEW YORK**

PRINTED AND BOUND BY
BRAUNWORTH & CO., INC.
BOOK MANUFACTURERS
BROOKLYN, NEW YORK

This book is dedicated to fellow newspaper men and women, some of whom helped me beyond repayment many years ago and others in the preparation of this book, and especially, to: Miss Sigrid Schultz, Miss Dorothy Thompson, Mrs. Stan Harding, Miss Beatrice Baskerville, Messrs. John S. Steele, Hiram Motherwell, Percy Winner, Thomas B. Morgan, Fred Hollowell, Harry Greenwall, Vernon Bartlett, Samuel Spewack, John L. Spivak, William Bird, Floyd Gibbons, M. R. Fodor, Constantine Cazana, Karl von Wiegand, Carl Groat, Lowell Mellett, Ed Keen, Jim Howe, William Bolitho, Lincoln Eyre, Ray Sprigle, Warren Christman, Ferd Reyher, Herbert Corey, Frank Sibley, Eugen Szatmari, George Slocombe, Cal Lyon, Fred Smith, Peter Guldbrandsen, Frazier Hunt, Spearman Lewis, Joseph Shaplen, Arno Dosch Fleurot, David Darrah, Don Levine, A. R. Decker, Larry Rue, Vincent Sheean, John Clayton, Henry Alsberg, Fritz Voigt, Jay Allen, Guido Enderis, Camillo Cianfarra, Robert Hammond Murray, Jack Starr Hunt, Carleton Beals, H. J. Phillips, Silas Bent, Ernest Gruening, Charles Erwin, Dr. Karl Lahm, Webb Miller, John Gunther.

The best Things, when perverted, become the very worst: So Printing, which in it self is no small Advantage to Mankind, when it is Abus'd may be of most Fatal Consequences. —ANONYMOUS PAMPHLET, 1712.

The press is a mill that grinds all that is put into its hopper. Fill the hopper with poisoned grain and it will grind it to meal, but there is death in the bread.—WILLIAM CULLEN BRYANT.

Our liberty depends on the freedom of the press, and that cannot be limited without being lost.—JEFFERSON.

CONTENTS

CONTENTS—*Continued*
APPENDIX

FOREWORD: REPORTER TO READER

THERE is a growing suspicion that the press is no longer what it claims to be, the "Tribune of the People," the "Voice of the Public," the "Upholder of Truth," the "Defender of Public Liberty," as thousands of newspaper mastheads daily proclaim it.

In the 1920's millions undergoing disillusion vaguely realized that they had been deceived by newspaper war propaganda. In the 1930's the myths of cyclical depressions and prosperity-around-the-corner again shook the confidence of the public.

"You can't believe a thing you read in the papers nowadays" has become a commonplace.

In the early days of 1935 mass meetings and conventions attended by thousands of persons have applauded general attacks on the press and specific charges against certain newspaper owners as agents of Fascism and breeders of war. There has been popular resentment against certain editors in the past but never to my knowledge as general an indictment against the press of the nation as we have today.

Meanwhile the radio is being employed more and more to reach the public mind and emotions. Censored as the radio remains, it permits, perhaps as retaliation to press antagonism, a considerable amount of criticism of the newspapers. The immunity of the press is over.

That there has always been a mixture of curiosity and suspicion in the layman's mind is known to every newspaper worker. For twenty-five years I have been asked for the "inside" story, for the "lowdown," the "true facts," the "suppressed feature" of world events and dramatic local episodes. Laymen suspect all newspaper men have good stories to tell which have never appeared in print and they are rarely disappointed.

A part of a reporter's life is made up of adventures. These may appear romantic not only to the layman but to journalists

ix

who write plays and books about the trade. But a large part of it is made up of writing about unromantic people and events, from divorce suits to a world war, and the forces which shape our lives and our civilization. To get the facts, to present them as truthfully as human frailty permits, becomes a newspaper man's problem as deep and as wide as the world.

Unfortunately, there are powerful forces which do not want the facts, from a millionaire's divorce to a war scare, presented truthfully. There are corrupting influences. Many newspaper men are subject to them without ever realizing it. And although laymen keep on repeating great phrases which have become platitudes—that the bulwark of our liberties is the free press; that freedom springs from uncensored printing; that war and peace and a new deal for all men depend largely on public opinion and information; that our daily lives and the future of international relations are ordered by the new estate, the Fourth, which has become more important than State and Church and armed forces,—they remain ignorant or indifferent to the power which shapes their destiny.

In the first chapter of this book I have done little more than tell a few adventures from a reporter's life. But I have chosen the adventures that have a meaning, the clues upon which the explanatory and critical chapters are hung. As a reporter, for instance, I turned in the story of Andrew Mellon's divorce, stories of strikes, interviews with politicians and statesmen and news items concerning large corporations; eighteen months in the American Army and ten years among the dictators of Europe made the newspaper game for me something like the thrilling thing it is in fiction. But from the first day to the last there was censorship, there was suppression of news, there was distortion and there was coloring of news, there was always an attempt by someone to mislead the public, and these things I should like to explain.

I do not say that the integrity of the world press has broken down completely: I do insist that attacks upon it are stronger than ever in the history of newspaper printing, and although this statement becomes self-evident when it is known that ten large nations, the dictatorships of Continental Europe, no longer have a free press, I want to go further and show the attack upon its integrity in the free nations, France, Britain and the United States especially, where, *Deo volente,* dictatorship may be avoided but where, unfortunately, another oligarchy, dictatorial big money and big business of the public utilities and the Teapot Dome kind, is always trying to destroy the foundations upon which free government is built.

Throughout this book I have tried to show the way in which forces are working against our free press. The most important, I think, are:

Financial.
Political.
Social.
Advertising.

I have also tried to show the human elements which are in conflict. I think that the objectives of the editors and publishers in the non-dictatorial countries can be summed up as follows:

Idealism.
Profits.
Power or influence on public opinion:
    a.   personal power.
    b.   power in group or organization or political party.
    c.   power in super-patriotic or dictator movements.

I have tried to show the operation of outside forces on the press. I agree with Walter Lippmann who a decade ago wrote that the crisis of democracy is a crisis in journalism, and again I agree that "those who think the sole cause is corruption" are wrong. "There is plenty of corruption to be sure," continued Mr. Lippmann in his *New Republic* days, "moneyed control, caste pressure, financial and social bribery, ribbons, dinner parties, clubs, petty politics." Truer today. In the decade which has passed, this crisis of democracy has been followed by decadence instead of recovery. Notably in the new dictatorships. The free press has died there and freedom with it. As for France, read the list of newspapers controlled by the munitions makers and the war fomenters of the *Comité des Forges*. And in the United States, for example, the fifty-two-volume report of the Federal inquiry into public utilities, completed in December, 1934, tells a miserable story. When a propaganda agent in Missouri can boast and prove that he has corrupted not one but hundreds of papers, in fact the entire press of the state with one or two exceptions, and when twenty more propagandists report similarly in other states, a more dangerous situation can result than most crises in our peacetime history as a republic.

Notable events and crises in my quarter-century of experiences have been:

The era of political corruption of the first decade of the century, the "shame of the cities," the Chicago Stockyards Jungle, Frenzied Finance, the pure food and drug investigation, etc.

War propaganda while America was neutral.

The Mexican war scares.

The World War.

The rise of Bolshevism and Fascism.

The Red scare, strikes and unrest in the United States.

Wars, Revolutions, Dictatorships in Europe.

Teapot Dome.

The Prosperity Boom.

The wrecking of the peace conference of 1927 by the munitions interests, agent Shearer claiming the "credit."

The Depression and the Panic.

The Insull Plan, or public utility propaganda system.

The NRA, the New Deal, the new labor unrest, the new danger of dictatorship.

Several chapters will be devoted to certain aforementioned subjects. The writer asks readers to approach them by posing this question: Did the press play fair with us on any or all of the above matters?

Before attempting an answer, read the canons of journalism which the American Society of Newspaper Editors adopted in 1923 and use it as a yardstick to measure the integrity of the press. Compare it with the code of ethics of the American Newspaper Guild. No criticism in the following pages goes beyond that legitimately based on the editors' code and there are no strictures more severe than those written by the organized newspaper men of America.

Whether or not I have succeeded in my intentions to remain objective I cannot judge. To keep error out I have asked for and received the co-operation of at least a hundred fellow newspaper men and women.

Throughout the book, which tells of the suppression of news by business organizations and dictators, political factions, department stores, drug manufacturers, oil, steel, coal, other ruling groups as well as occasional friends of small editors, I have also stressed the magnificent service of the press in exposing and defeating these very same corrupting powers. It has been my aim to emphasize the fight for a free press which I still consider the most important fight in the world today. If the impression is given in the early part of this book that the situation is quite hopeless, I suggest that the reader turn to the chapter called "Roll of Honor" which lists some of the great and little papers that are still successfully waging the war, not to employ child labor or to pay mean wages, but for the real freedom of the press as Milton and Mill, Jefferson and Paine and the true patriots who made America, defined it.

Whether or not the press in the free countries is a free press cannot be answered yes or no. Nor can I predict victory for that part of the press which is represented on the honor roll. I have asked, as I hope the reader will, the following questions:

Is the press meeting its responsibilities today in telling us the truth, keeping us intelligently informed on important issues, the great and minor problems of the world, such as:

War and Peace. Is the press leading us into another war or working for international accord?

Bolshevism and Fascism. Has the press told us and is

it telling us the truth about new systems of government which we may have to choose some day?

The great labor unrest. Does the press report labor troubles, strikes and violence honestly? Is it capable of being impartial in labor disputes?

Child Labor. Why is the American press in favor of this relic of uncivilized days?

Pure Food and Drugs. Why did the press fail the public in the first fight, 1906, and help kill the Tugwell Bill, 1934?

The Economic System. Has capitalism broken down or merely suffered an eclipse? Around which corner is what sort of prosperity? Is the machine age to affect our daily lives? Can it enslave or deliver us?

I cannot answer all these questions, but using the experiences of hundreds of newspaper men, I can offer an opinion as to the part the press plays in forming public reactions to vital questions.

I do know this, that years late, tragically late sometimes, we can say truthfully that certain things were propaganda and certain things were intended lies; that, for instance, the wartime "atrocities" were both propaganda and lies, that neither the elder Lindbergh nor LaFollette was a traitor or a Bolshevik, that the nationalization of women in Russia was a newspaper lie, that the Mussolini march on Rome remains a newspaper myth, that despite denials from most upright newspapers, there really was a Teapot Dome scandal and that the prosperity-around-the-corner campaign, while partly propaganda and wholly untrue, was merely the wish fulfillment of politicians and editors. And so on, indefinitely.

In discussing newspaper truth and untruth the point to make, it seems to me, concerns integrity, and intentions, and human frailty. One man makes an honest mistake but another may repeat the falsehood either because a propagandist pays him or because the propaganda fits the views or prejudices to which he is pledged. Newspaper truth is not a question of how many angels can stand on the head of a needle, or how many are dead in a wreck or a battle, but it remains a question of the intentions of all the men and women who have to do with the presentation of news.

The suspicions of laymen have never been answered by the press. Newspapers, upholding the right of criticism as a road to freedom, oppose all criticism of themselves. Almost universally they suppress mention of libel suits, which are of course a sort of layman's criticism. Newspapers, like kings, pretend they can do no wrong. I wish they were right.

*   *   *

Einstein to Tagore: I cannot prove that scientific truth must be conceived as a truth that is valid independent of humanity; but I believe it firmly. . . . We attribute to truth a superhuman objectivity; it is indispensable to us, this reality that is independent of our existence and our experience and our mind, though we cannot say what it means . . .

PART ONE
ROMANCE AND REALITIES

From the Canons of Journalism of the American Society of Newspaper Editors:

(3) *Independence*—Freedom from all obligations except that of fidelity to the public interest is vital. . . .

    B. Partisanship in editorial comment which knowingly departs from the truth does violence to the best spirit of American journalism . . .

(4) *Sincerity, Truthfulness, Accuracy* . . .

Resolution adopted at first convention of the American Newspaper Guild:

". . . Reporting is a high calling which has fallen into disrepute because news writers have been too often degraded as hirelings compelled by their employers to serve the purposes of politicians, monopolists, speculators in the necessities of life, exploiters of labor, and fomenters of war. . . ."

FREEDOM OF THE PRESS

CHAPTER I

ONE MAN'S NEWSPAPER GAME

MY FIRST morning in a newspaper office—the *Pittsburgh Leader*, February 9, 1909—was spent in shifting from chair to chair. Reporters rushed in, yelled their hot news to the city editor, and motioned me away from their desks. The copy boy, taking me for a rival, also intimidated me. He passed the fresh papers, damp and pungent with ink and gasoline, to everyone in the city room but sneered at me. I was timid and scared, but I was also happy. At nine that morning I had been hired as a reporter.

At noon, with two evening editions gone to press, the city editor rose for lunch. "I want to talk to you," he said and began immediately. "What's your idea of being a reporter? What are you after? Do you want to make money, do you want to play politics, do you want to write novels, or what?"

Before I could stammer, he continued. "Because," he said, "this is the lousiest profession in the world—that is, if you stick in it. It's all right for a couple of years. But you'll never make money. You'll get nine dollars a week now and if you're good you'll be making twenty at the end of three years and if you're an ace it will be twenty-five. Do you know that there isn't a man in town, with the exception of the political reporters, making more than that, but the men in the composing-room, who belong to labor unions, are making double?"

His mind was on money. He was an old-timer. I was eighteen, it was a noble era, and my thoughts were elsewhere. I abhorred the idea of even discussing money. "My view of journalism," I began with all the enthusiasm of my virginal eighteen years, "is that it is the finest profession on earth. On the freedom of the press all our liberties are built." I

19

quoted Carlyle's report on Edmund Burke and the Four Estates, and Thomas Jefferson, Washington and the other
founders of the nation, and Dana and the great editors. I
spoke of Liberty and Truth. In fact, I said everything except
that Journalism to me meant the Greek ideal of the Good, the
True and the Beautiful. I didn't quite say that.

"Rats," replied Houston H. Eagle, city editor of the *Pittsburgh Leader*. "Do you know what this [sneering] 'profession' is? It's prostitution. Prostitution! Journalistic harlots,
that's what we all are, and that's what you'll be if you stay
in this lousy business, so if you've any other ideas, can 'em."

"Now, Mr. Eagle——" I began.

"Listen, boy," he replied with a bitter vehemence which
distorted his face, "if you want to earn a living go into some
other trade. Then you'll make it honestly, that is compara-
tively honestly, but in this business you'll not make a living,
and what you do make you'll make whoring for the crooked
politicians, and the crooked bankers, and the crooked street-
car company, and the crooked department stores . . ."

"But," I protested, "I came to the *Leader* because the *Leader*
is the People's Paper; I didn't ask for a job on the *Gazette-
Times* or any of the other papers. . . ."

"Then you're a bigger fool than I thought you were,"
replied Mr. Eagle, "and you'll find that out for yourself. A
newspaper needs a lot of young fools—foolish enthusiasm
and foolish ideals. We love ideals. And we love enthusiasm.
At nine dollars a week."

That afternoon I wrote my first piece for the papers:

"Stanislas Schmidt, aged 32, of 1811 Center Avenue,
driver of a Silver Top Brewing Company delivery wagon,
was slightly injured at 10 o'clock this morning at Penn
Avenue and Liberty street when his wagon was struck
by a street car."

Who can describe the trepidation of the ensuing hours waiting for the first final edition? I had watched Thirlkeld,
assistant city editor, read copy on my masterpiece, watched

the copy boy take it across the bridge to the composing-room, watched the clock minute by minute. At last the boy made his rounds. Again he passed me up. Everyone in the office was reading carefully for typographical errors. Someone threw his copy on the floor. I got it. The item was not on the front page. I was depressed. At last under the heading Local, a collection of a dozen paragraphs, I found my own. It read:

"Stanislas Schmidt, 32 years old, of 1811 Center Ave., driver of a beer delivery wagon . . ."

Silver Top was not mentioned; Silver Top was a large advertiser.

My education had begun. It increased amazingly toward evening when the staff retired to the Hotel Henry bar for a round of beer. How proud I was when permitted to buy drinks for the city editor, the assistant city editor, star and other reporters, and the foreman of the composing-room, and ten-cent beer at that, the round costing me my day's pay. Everyone hazed me.

"Here's a kid believes in the Freedom of the Press," announced Houston Eagle, and everyone roared heartily.

"Tell it to Andy Mellon," shouted someone, but that meant nothing to me.

Apparently I was promising. In my cubhood years I was sent to interview William Jennings Bryan, to report a banquet speech of Governor Woodrow Wilson, to accompany Theodore Roosevelt for a day, to cover William Howard Taft's Pittsburgh visit, to write a four-column story of Robert La Follette's declaration in favor of woman suffrage. But perhaps I was not as important as I thought I was. The Bryan stunt, for instance: Eagle said, "Ask him if he is going to run for President again," and I did, and I was promptly thrown out of the hotel room when the massive candidate rose in his underwear and insulted pride and shoved me. I came back to the office, and like the legendary reporter who told his city editor that there was no ascension story because the balloon had blown up and killed everyone, I said there was nothing to write because Bryan had put me out.

Eagle said nothing. But an hour later the *Leader* appeared with its usual three streamers, the middle one in red, devoted to the main sensation of the day, the other two in black, the bottom one reading:

BRYAN ASSAULTS LEADER REPORTER

In this way I learned empirically that we were a Progressive Republican organ and that Democrats were ungodly poison.

As for the La Follette interview, it was a scoop. Neither the Democratic nor regular Republican papers would touch it. (I did not know, of course, that the conspiracy of silence and defamation by the press against the Wisconsin leader had begun.)

The big moment of my cubhood came when I was assigned to cover the Mellon case.

Andrew W. Mellon was to us a banker about whom we knew nothing. There were of course the Mellon bank and the Union Trust Company and a few other enterprises, but generally speaking no one suspected we were harboring in our smoky midst one of America's three richest men and one of its ten real rulers. Mellon, like Zaharoff, always preferred the role of mystery.

In the middle of September, 1910, suit for divorce had been filed by Banker Mellon against his wife *née* Nora McMullen, whom he had married in 1900. The employees of the prothonotary's office hid the papers. "For seven months," Mellon's unwelcome biographer, Harvey O'Connor, wrote years later, "not a paper appeared in the court record. Not a word leaked out in the well-disciplined Pittsburgh newspapers, on some of which Union Trust held underlying mortgages. News agencies in the city also clamped on a censorship, and even the telegraph agencies were summoned to aid. The publishers, all wary men trained in the Pittsburgh tradition, assigned a crack reporter to the case and were kept informed on every

minute detail of the charges, counter-charges and proceedings. . . . Attorney Ache [Paul S. Ache, representing Mrs.
Mellon] finally broke through the ring of silence and interested the *Philadelphia North American* in the Mellon case."

I was not a "crack reporter," neither were several of my
colleagues; the crack reporters were the gentlemen who came
from Philadelphia and later from New York, but otherwise
O'Connor is right. And there is much more to the story.

On April 20, 1911, a bill was introduced, passed by the
legislature of Pennsylvania and signed by Governor Tener.
"This act," telegraphed the *North American* man, while all of
us in Pittsburgh kept our mouths shut, "robs a wife of her
constitutional right of a jury trial in a divorce suit. Whose
powerful influence obtained this astonishing bit of legislation
is not known, but nothing could have been designed that would
be more useful to Andrew Mellon, the master money-maker
of Pittsburgh, who has some $100,000,000 to wage his fight
against his young and handsome English wife. Friends of
Mrs. Mellon . . . fear the new law is another demonstration
of Mellon's skill in noiseless, effective methods in all his un-
dertakings."

I do not here, nor elsewhere for that matter, intend to discuss the details of the divorce suit, which shocked me at the
time—shocked me despite a year in Magistrate Jimmy Kirby's
central police station court where all the terror and misery in
human nature was spread before his Honor and the police
reporters to make a column holiday. An endless procession of
pimps and prostitutes, drunks, panhandlers, yeggs, dope ped-
dlers and dope victims, all the inhabitants of the cesspools, the
gutters, the poverty-stricken alleys of the metropolis, passed
in terrible review before us every morning to the accompanying drone of "Ten dollars or thirty days," "Ten dollars or
thirty days" from the pink, sleek and fat Republican interpreter of the city's laws.

I lived in this atmosphere of human filth and degradation
for a year. I found it again in the divorce courts. And now
in the impressive Superior Court the accusations, spy testimony and servants' gossip produced by the leading lawyers of

Pittsburgh in the employ of the leading banker, I found again the same foul atmosphere. The human animal, I thought, is pretty low.

There was one important difference I did not then realize: all the others, men and women, would get into the papers and would be stigmatized, while Mellon was safe.

With my many hastily scrawled sheets of copy paper I rushed back to the *Leader* office and began typing. "Hot stuff?" asked Eagle. "Hot stuff," I said. He laughed. In my mind's eye were page headlines, screaming newsboys, thousands running to pay their pennies for my story, half a million citizens discussing it that night. I pounded page after page.

The story completed, Eagle glanced at it carelessly, and walked out of the city room, up the corridor, into the office of Alexander Pollock Moore, the Big Boss, our awesome editor-in-chief. And that is the last the news department ever saw of the Mellon case.

The next day it was the same, and the day after. I did my work; I wrote thousands of words; not one of them appeared in the *Leader,* and the same was true of my colleagues of the six other papers. The "conspiracy of silence" was complete. A German language paper, perhaps intentionally, perhaps by oversight, carried one discreet report; this report found its way to the *Philadelphia North American,* and the next time the Mellon case was in court the *North American* representative was present. We gladly gave him all our previous notes.

Again we watched anxiously for publication. The *North American* arrived, but there was nothing about Mellon in it. It was our turn to laugh. "Mellon's bought you too," we shouted in the court corridor. "You wait," he replied.

What had happened? Probably for the first time in our fair city's history the telegraph companies had also suppressed the news.

The next day the *North American* appeared on the streets of Pittsburgh—appeared and disappeared. The newsboys shouted, the papers were snapped up, the police set about beating the newsboys, and soon all was quiet. The next day the

North American sent out still larger bundles and the New York papers also arrived with the story. Neither Mellon nor the police could suppress it completely.

"Gold and politics appear to have combined against me," said Nora McMullen Mellon to the reporters. "I hope the voters of Pennsylvania and the sons of Pennsylvania who have mothers whom they love will realize that the law just adopted in this state, abrogating the right of trial by jury in divorce cases, is not only directed against me but is also a blow to every mother in Pennsylvania."

Our most prominent churchman, Bishop Cortlandt Whitehead of the Episcopal diocese, denounced the changes in the divorce law; civic bodies voiced a protest against abolition of trial by jury, but not a word appeared in the newspapers printed in Pittsburgh.

It was at just this time that Will Irwin in *Collier's Weekly* began a series of articles on "The American Newspaper: a Study in Journalism and its Relation to the Public." Irwin had gone from city to city, honoring the honest newspapers and telling the truth about the others. He had undertaken, he said, to answer the following charges laymen generally were making against the press (two decades ago):

That the newspaper has grown venal.
That advertisers and great financial interests control it.
That it has grown sensational.
That it has lost its power in public causes.

No one more than the reporters of Pittsburgh awaited the number devoted to our politically purged city. I cannot begin to describe the fury, the enthusiasm, which pervaded the journalistic corps the day *Collier's* arrived telling our sundry citizenry the fact that Pittsburgh's Prostituted Press was about the worst in the nation. It was a harlots' holiday.

It was also a surprise. Mr. Irwin was telling us facts about ourselves which were news. He told us for instance that the *Gazette-Times* and the *Chronicle-Telegraph,* owned by Senator George T. Oliver, were the errand boys of the steel and

coal and munitions interests; that the *Post* and the *Sun* had
borrowed money from the Farmers' National Bank, "a city
depository involved in the graft cases"; that the Oliver papers
were indebted to the Frick-Mellon banks; that the *Press* was
bought by Oliver P. Hershman whose friends were Chris
Magee and William Flinn, the bosses of the town. "Gang-
established, gang-favored, unwilling in any event to take the
first step—the *Press* was of no use for the purposes of reform," Irwin wrote. Of the so-called liberal *Despatch* and its
editor, Colonel C. A. Rook, he said they played "the gang
game of silence," and of my own dear *Leader,* that "William
Flinn, the old joint-boss with Chris Magee, a contractor grown
rich on city jobs, backed Alexander P. Moore, in its purchase."

Salaries were abominably low; as a result employees were
permitted to do press-agent and propaganda jobs and take
tips from the outside; political reporters got civil service jobs
additionally, and places on the registration commissions, paying fifty dollars a week. The owners knew of these corrupting
forces but preferred them to paying wages.

The Pittsburgh graft cases had been front-page stuff for
more than a year before I got my first job, and the splendid
vehemence with which the press, notably the *Leader,* attacked
the malefactors of great wealth had given me the impression
the press was a noble defender of the public good and that the
Leader's name led all the rest. In Will Irwin's story of
Pittsburgh I learned that the exposure of municipal corruption
had been made despite a conspiracy of silence among the seven
newspapers; that, in fact, the Voters' League had been forced
to issue pamphlets and bulletins for a long time because the
press individually and collectively had refused to publish a
line about the city's corruption until the League forced them
to do so. "Is this true?" I asked the reporters on all the papers.
"Of course it is," they replied. Some of them had secretly
helped the League.

The individual reporters whom Irwin named as getting
money from political jobs were very angry. They said, "Irwin
is also a newspaper man, he is fouling his own nest, he is

disloyal, he is just a muckraker," but the majority helped spread *Collier's* through the town, made it town talk, hoping both to clean up the rotten situation and shame the publishers into paying decent wages. But naturally nothing happened. So long as Pittsburgh remained geographically about half-way between Chicago and New York there would always be a stream of good reporters to be exploited. Why pay wages?

The Mellon case and the Irwin story, I believe, educated me out of my naïve cubhood; the former also taught me a financial lesson: there was money to be made selling suppressed news to outside papers, and a five-dollar bill shone magnificently beside a twelve-dollar-a-week salary. In fact, the business of dealing in suppressed news became so good that several reporters opened an office especially for that purpose; they called it the Pittsburgh News Bureau, I believe, and they did better than working for regular wages. But there was also news, mostly labor news, crimes committed by the first Fascist army in America, the coal and iron police, privately organized by the Pennsylvania corporations, the Black Cossacks who rode workingmen down on the sidewalks in strike towns, crushing them because they were strikers and foreigners; scandals involving national advertisers, deaths from patent medicines, financial crimes committed by leading citizens within the law— all these news items were not fit to print in most of the newspapers of America, but they were news for a Socialist organ published in New York. The *Call,* however, was not in a position to pay. To the honor of several Pittsburgh newspaper men it must be said that they frequently supplied the *Call* and other publications with the news their own editors were suppressing.

I was sent one day to copy an indictment for rape against the son of one of the owners of a large department store, and the next day to interview the girl. When I turned in the story I asked Eagle what he was going to do with it. He said:

"Turn it over to the business office; they will blackmail that store for the next twenty years; you'll see larger ads from now on."

"May I make a copy to give to the *Call?*" I asked.

"Sure thing," Eagle replied, "I'd like to see it published."

I made the copy and gave it to a man named Merrick who represented the *Call*. But the *Call* arrived and didn't carry the story.

I chased after Merrick. He said, "Do you mind if I use it locally? I'm planning a paper in Pittsburgh."

Saturday was a sensational day. A new weekly called *Justice* appeared; it was devoted entirely to the rape case. In addition to my story, which covered the entire first page, there were socialistic diatribes on justice and injustice, the exploitation of the poor by the rich, and the suppression of news in Pittsburgh, covering the entire second page, except for a coupon asking for subscriptions. The newsboys appeared on the street that morning, shouted the story, and within a half-hour were being clubbed by the police who had been asked to do so by the department store and its allies, the business managers of the daily press. The position of the latter was that the venders of *Justice* were not regularly accredited newsboys and therefore violated the honored and sacred freedom of the press.

Next Saturday Merrick reprinted my story, with the story of the police, the department-store owners, the publishers of the seven Pittsburgh dailies, and again newsboys were clubbed. And so it went on week after week while *Justice* established itself with a considerable circulation. Again the journalistic fraternity was secretly pleased.

Another big story that came my way was an investigation of the labor situation in the Pittsburgh zone. Eagle had obtained, he never told me how, a sheaf of forty or fifty pages which read like this:

Name	Address	Occupation	Cause
John Adamovich	131 Carson Street	Laborer	Union agitator
John McGinley	4432 Penn Avenue	Roller	Unionizer
William Stuart	42 Plum Street	Puddler	Socialist
George Hoffman	McKees Rocks	Roller	Trouble maker

There were more than two thousand such items. Eagle told me it was the black list of the steel corporations. Its publication would be a nation-wide sensation. We had caught the steel companies in a conspiracy.

Ever since the Homestead strike, the iron, coal and steel interests of Pittsburgh had employed an espionage system to prevent the unionizing of their industries. Whenever a workingman was heard talking unions or uttering socialistic phrases he was immediately discharged and his name added to the black list which was circulated from company to company in violation of every moral and legal code. I had a hard time finding the men; they were either out of a job or employed in other trades, and each one expressed amazement when I showed him the black list which explained months or years of wandering from town to town in Pennsylvania, West Virginia and Ohio in search of work.

Then came the Stanley Steel Trust Investigation. One morning while I was still asleep, a United States marshal came into my room and read a summons to appear before the congressional committee. I went to Washington. Congressman A. O. Stanley received me in his office, showed me where he kept an assortment of the finest Kentucky whisky—some of the bottles were marked "Laid down by my grandfather in 1858" or "Laid down by my father in 1875"—and then asked me, not about the black list, but about an earlier job of work, my investigation of the racial change in Pittsburgh labor.

Some months earlier I had worked on that story. I found that since the time of the Homestead strike the employers of the Pittsburgh area had decided to rid their plants of American labor. They wanted unlimited immigration, cheap labor, ignorant labor which would work for low wages and not talk unionization. I had not only obtained this evidence, but also advertisements reading:

"Wanted: Balkan workmen, Rumanians, Serbians, Hungarians, etc., for steady jobs in the steel plants."

"Have you got the photographs of these newspaper ads?" asked Mr. Stanley. Paul Reilly had taken them for the *Leader*. I had them.

"And," I continued, "I've got a good story." And I told him about the black list.

That afternoon I signed my name two or three lines below that of Andrew Carnegie, the philanthropist, and went into the committee room. Congressman Stanley presided. Mr. Reed, of Pennsylvania, was the attorney representing the steel interests. I was questioned and cross-questioned. I told all about the steel trust's effort to drive out American labor, replace it with the cheapest European labor, and as I testified I watched the Associated Press man and the other reporters taking notes.

The afternoon wore on. And still no one asked me about the black list. I grew impatient. I was young. I was also suspicious. So, when the committee and Mr. Reed were about to dismiss me, I concluded my statement about labor with a voluntary disclosure about the black list on which I had been working.

Mr. Reed leaped to his feet. The members of Congress gasped. "I protest," shouted Mr. Reed. The press stared at me.

"Let the clerk read the last reply," said Mr. Stanley.

The clerk read. Mr. Reed protested. But I insisted on speaking, and I did so amid shouts and murmurs. Mr. Reed moved that my black-list testimony be stricken from the record, and this was done. I was dismissed.

None of the reporters present spoke to me. That was puzzling. If I knew anything at all about newspaper values, I knew that I had supplied them with a sensational front-page story, and I had indicated in my testimony that I had a wealth of corroborative detail. I also knew that the official order to strike the testimony from the record did not ruin its news value. For that I had the proof next morning, for the press did in fact mention my statement.

Two tiny items on an inside page: one stating that I had testified that a black list existed, the second, a "follow" from Pittsburgh, a single paragraph under the heading: "Editor admits having black list," the whole written in an incredulous and disparaging manner and "buried" almost universally on the back advertising pages.

Thus ended another chapter in my education. I learned that there is news that can be killed—and there is news that can be buried alive.

But all newspaper work, literally and figuratively, is not running to a fire. There were strange interludes of another sort in the *Leader* office.

Alexander Pollock Moore, as I have said, was our editor-in-chief; he wore a velour hat and we regarded him as a well-dressed Napoleon. The city room was in the rear of the building, Mr. Moore's office up a corridor, some fifty feet away, but his rare visits to our department were thrilling. He might ask, "Who wrote that story?" and you could not tell by the tone whether he was going to say, "That's fine, very fine," or "It's lousy." The first year he never noticed me. In the second year I was chosen, thanks to an interest I had shown in the theater, to visit the boss's office once in a while to write interviews with stage folk.

As a rule there would be some flashy petite chorus-girl sitting on the couch; the boss would mumble her name and say, "Write about two columns." The first time it happened he said: "Give her a big break—say she's undiscovered talent—wants to play Shakespeare—Juliet, of course—or that new man, Isben."

"Nora, in *The Doll's House,* by Ibsen," I said, showing off.

"Yeh, that's the guy," the famous actress interpolated.

Still showing off, I would ask questions about the lady's noble ambitions, bringing in the names of all the playwrights I was then reading, Shaw and Ibsen, Brieux and Wedekind and Strindberg, until the editor-in-chief would say:

"Beat it, kid, you've got enough. Two columns. Two-column cut. Here's the picture."

So I would invent a two-column story about the latest talent and the undiscovered Nora or Juliet or Countess Julie up on the couch of the front office.

When Lillian Russell came to town, not I but the chief editorial writer was chosen to do the interviewing. The result was placed on the front page. That front page today is worth a fortune. There occurred an error, the shifting of one letter in a four-letter word—and we had in print a major catastrophe.

Like the great majority of newspapers we had what Maxwell Anderson calls a son-of-a-bitch list and what others call the roll of sacred cows. In fact, we had everything. One we called the S . . . hook, the blank being a fine old Anglo-Saxon word common to Joyce and Lawrence but hardly suitable here. On this hook we literally spiked stories which contained the names of personal enemies of the bosses, Flinn, Magee, Moore and Mellon and others. Our sacred cows were persons, advertisers, department stores, theaters about whom favorable notices were to be printed frequently. And in addition to all these we had the universally famous B. O. M. or "Business Office Must," the press-agent stuff sent upstairs from the business office, the unearned increment of the advertisers. Every "must" item appeared.

These were the conditions under which freedom of the press flourished in Pittsburgh.

After working hard for several years I was able to save six hundred and seventy-six dollars, with which I entrained for Harvard. After listening to Copeland and Baker and Taussig and Wendell and George Herbert Palmer in his final lectures on philosophy, and selling to the *Boston Transcript* two stories, which the *Harvard Illustrated Magazine* thought too critical of the football and tutoring systems, I returned to Pittsburgh and to the morning *Post*.

When the war began I was night editor; there was only one person above me in command, Warren U. Christman, managing editor, who retired at midnight. Usually it was I who wrote the war headlines and put the city edition to bed.

Of the first war years I will say just this: I made a total fool of myself when I accepted as true the news reports from New York and Europe which by their volume and repetition overwhelmed what little objective intelligence I had. In those days I regarded the Associated Press as Cæsar's wife and when in doubt favored it by spiking all other copy.

For example, there was the story of the sinking of Britain's greatest warship, the *Audacious*. Britain denied; the A. P. sent the denial, but the International News Service insisted on this victory for a German submarine. I spiked the Hearst story. Two or three weeks later one of the Hearst organizations supplied a photograph of the *Audacious* actually sinking. (Many years later, in London, I learned the truth: the *Audacious* was torpedoed, but in shallow water, and the British Admiralty denied the episode because it hoped to float the superdreadnought in a few weeks.) Then there was the *Lusitania*. All the Allied reports told of a "dastardly" and "heinous" crime against civilians, but the German news bureau said the ship carried munitions. Today the sworn statement of the former Collector of the Port of New York, Dudley Field Malone, gives the exact character and tonnage of these munitions, but in 1915 I played the Allied side. I used all the stories of German atrocities including the Baltimore preacher's "unimpeachable" account of the crucifixion of Canadian soldiers by the enemy. In short, in common with about ninety per cent of the American press, I had become a blind but willing agent of the powerful and finally victorious Allied propaganda machine.

My night off was Wednesday; on Thursday morning the *Post* usually carried news of a German success. Christman and I had argued over the war daily; he rightly judged the news we received as unfair to Germany, and to counteract daily Allied victories and German atrocities, he gave Germany Thursday. (It was not until December, 1918, when I came into Coblenz with the American Army that I realized how fooled I had been by all those years of poisonous propaganda, and in the ten years I worked in Germany I think I did my honest best to repair the damage—to myself if not to others—by writing news which gave Germany a square deal.)

In October, 1916, I went to England on the steamer *Adriatic* which also carried some twenty thousand tons of munitions for the Allies. My first job in London was expanding a two-hundred-word skeletonized cable from America into a resounding story of at least one thousand words which was sold to the *London Daily News*, the *Cork Examiner*, and the leading papers in Birmingham, Leeds and other important provincial cities, each of which labeled the item "From our own correspondent." Later I skeletonized the United Press cable to *La Nacion* in Buenos Aires.

The propaganda department of the British Government at that time arranged trips to the front for sympathetic journalists. I went to the front. The Ypres salient, Mount Kemal, the hospital base at Etaples, a visit to the trenches, an airplane base, tea with General Plumer and dinner with the Prince of Wales' regiment was our program, and our residence, the Château of Trammecourt. Our group was composed of French, Italian and American correspondents. At that time we considered ourselves the most favored and on our return we found ourselves the most envied of mortals, and the journals which printed our stories boasted of the fact their own representatives had been at the fighting front. I now realize that we were told nothing but buncombe, that we were shown nothing of the realities of the war, that we were, in short, merely part of the great Allied propaganda machine whose purpose was to sustain morale at all costs and help drag unwilling America into the slaughter.

In 1917, when the United States answered the call of Democracy, Freedom of Oppressed Nations, and more important than these (although known only to the Embassy in London, the bankers in Wall Street and the President) the necessity of safeguarding the war loans, my brother and I went patriotically to the Embassy and registered for war service. Gilbert went back to America and became a machine-gunner.

In July, 1917, Joe Pierson of the *Chicago Tribune* established the Army Edition of that paper and Floyd Gibbons, whom I had met in London, gave me the job of being the entire reportorial staff. One morning the managing editor disappeared and that afternoon Pierson appointed me managing editor.

But meanwhile the press section of the army—G.-2-D., G. H. Q., A. E. F.—was being organized. Edward Marshall, the famous war correspondent who had been with Theodore Roosevelt at San Juan Hill and who had left a leg in Cuba, now asked General Pershing for my appointment as a member of this outfit and within a few weeks after landing in France

I was at Neufchateau. Here I found Will Irwin, Irvin S. Cobb, Heywood Broun, Edwin L. James, Wilbur Forrest, Herbert Corey, Cal Lyon, Damon Runyon, Martin Green, Major Frederick Palmer, Major Bozeman Bulger, Lieutenant Grantland Rice and other famous or soon-to-be-famous war correspondents.

We all more or less lied about the war.

On Armistice Day four of us took an oath on the battlefield that we would tell the truth the rest of our lives, that we would begin telling the truth in time of preparation of war, that we would do what was humanly possible to prevent the recurrence of another such vast and useless horror. Then we all went back to prosaic reporting in America.

The war had made our country conscious of Europe and our relations with the rest of the world. Foreign news had up to then been almost a monopoly of the Associated Press with its exchanges, the official or semi-official bureaus, such as Reuters, Havas, Wolff, Stefani, etc. Now the *New York Times,* which had had two or three branch offices, began to cover all of Europe and the *Philadelphia Ledger,* the *New York Herald,* the *New York Tribune,* the *Chicago Daily News* and the *Chicago Tribune* instituted or enlarged their foreign services. In 1919 I was assistant to the London correspondent of the *Chicago Tribune,* then Dublin correspondent, and in 1920 I was in Italy for the Fiume adventure; in 1920 in Germany for the Kapp Putsch, and although nominally head of the Berlin bureau for almost ten years, I was assigned to Italy for the so-called Red uprising in 1920, to Moscow in 1922 and 1923, to the French Army in Syria in 1925 and 1926, to Vienna for the revolution of 1927 and to the capitals in the Baltic and Balkan States for wars, uprisings, peace conferences, assassinations and coronations of kings, and I reported the dictators. on the march to power in many lands.

These ten European years were a continual struggle with censorship.

The suppression of news in America and its corollary, **the** dissemination of propaganda, to which a large part of **this** book is devoted, are the pragmatic necessities of **our social** and economic system. Some of the powers which control the press are known to everyone, others are secret and their work is subtle, and there is, moreover, an atmosphere in every newspaper office which defeats all the high hopes and idealism of the young reporter. It breaks him and brands him as a colt is broken and branded on the prairies. But this much must be said for the American reporter in Europe: whether he is or is not so in fact, he at least feels himself a free man.

He has escaped from the pusillanimity of the ordinary newspaper office. He need never in his foreign lifetime stop to consider the local advertiser, the public utility man and the cheap politician who control his town, the quack-medicine man, the president of the First National Bank, the Steel Corporation, the department store, the host of friends and enemies of the publisher. If, on the other hand, his dispatches regarding American entry into the World Court and the League of Nations, or the progress or failure of Fascism, Communism, Nazism, the European co-operatives and other great and vastly more important subjects are aligned with the editorial policy previously set by his editor and publisher, he generally does not realize this influence and boasts that he is superior to the helot in the home office.

Speaking for myself I can say that on only one occasion did I receive an order about what and how to write: I was told by the Paris bureau to cable the facts about "the failure of government ownership of railroads in Germany." I cabled that government ownership was a great success. My cable was not published. The correspondents of those bureaus which replied affirmatively made the front page.

I believe I was the first to report that Mussolini was the military arm of the chambers of commerce and the manufacturers' associations of Italy and that he personally was implicated in the assassination of the leading rival politician. These dispatches were published. I smuggled news out of Italy and out of Russia, where as usual and with the encouragement of my editor, I defied the censorship. Naturally enough I was asked to leave both countries. I did the same in Fiume, Hungary, Rumania, Syria and wherever I found censorship and suppression of news. Most foreign correspondents do the same. If one uses "diplomacy" one can usually remain in the country. Its use, however, depends on whether or not the home office prefers your dispatches or the glory of having its representatives deported by a dictator. Scores of correspondents have been deported in the past decade of dictatorship. A few have also been imprisoned. It was not until Hitler took over power that the actual risk of limb or life was taken by a newspaper man, and here and now I pay my respects to a score of Berlin colleagues for taking this risk.

It was sometime during my first European years that the press reported the demise of my first newspaper, and it was then that the facts of its real ownership were revealed. With great interest I read the list of its bondholders:

Union Trust Company*	$188,000
Union Savings Bank*	172,000
S. H. Coleman Estate	41,000
Col. J. M. Schoonmaker	50,000
J. K. Mellon	8,000
Safe Deposit Trust (Greensburg)	5,000
Various small holdings	39,000
	$503,000

Colonel Schoonmaker, whom we praised highly on all occasions, interviewed every time "leading" citizens were in demand, was the vice-president of the Pittsburgh & Lake Erie Railroad.

The Mellon banks were associated with the Pennsylvania Railroad, the United States Steel Corporation, the Fricks, the coal and iron and steel interests which own Pennsylvania.

The *Leader* did nothing with the steel trust black list. Despite its authenticity, despite the fact it was sensational, a scoop, despite my "human interest" stories of the lives of the blacklisted workers, we never mentioned the black list in our columns. One thing I do know: one of our editors that same

*The Union Trust and the Union Savings were Mellon banks.

winter was subsidized to write a series of articles in praise of the steel companies. It appeared in a subsidized magazine— now happily defunct. That was the last of the black list episode.

The *Leader,* of course, may not be a typical example. Not all newspapers are so completely controlled by the big-money interests of the world. There are many sorts of journals and many kinds of control, some of which are obvious, some of which are mild, some sinister, some of which I have known for twenty-five years and some of which I first came upon in making the investigation which follows.

PART TWO
THE CORRUPTING INFLUENCES

CHAPTER II

THE POWER OF ADVERTISING

> . . . good advertising [is] an economic and social force of vital importance.—PRESIDENT F. D. ROOSEVELT.
>
> Advertising is one of the vital organs of our entire economic and social system.—PRESIDENT HOOVER.
>
> Advertising (rather than competition) is the life of trade. Advertising ministers to the spiritual side of trade.—PRESIDENT COOLIDGE.
>
> (The annual advertising budget in the United States is $1,500,000,000.)
>
> The publication of fraudulent advertising costs the American public about $500,000,000 annually.—W. E. HUMPHREY, Federal Trade Commissioner.

As A reporter my first hate was the advertiser. Every reporter hates the business office with its sacred cows, its son-of-a-bitch list, its business-office-musts. Every newspaper man in America, it is safe to say, hates the advertisers.

The advertisers supply the money with which the newspapers are run. Our bread comes from them. But we daily bite the hand that feeds us, and we hate, as the German war hymn had it, with a hate that shall never die. It is a hate to be proud of.

What is the reason for it? The newspaper advertiser, in the eyes of the honest newspaper man, stands for everything that is low and filthy and degraded in this world. Everything that is wrong with newspapers is usually laid on the golden

41

doorstep of advertising. "If we could only do without advertising we could have a free press." So say we all.

How true is this expression? Is it largely emotional, or is it a reasonable statement of fact? Let the reader judge for himself. Herewith, and in the following chapters of this section, will be presented the following subjects with documentary evidence:

The part advertising plays in suppressing news.

How advertising in the newspapers corrupts the public, social, economic and political action.

How many patent-medicine advertisers sell vicious worthless products.

The activities of governments and big interests in influencing the public through the press.

How the propaganda machinery works with the cooperation of the press.

In the first part of the evidence I will give briefly a number of instances of suppression of news by advertisers. The range is many years. For those who think that things have changed for the better, examples during 1933 to 1935, the time of the writing of this book, are included. In addition to considering the influence of the advertiser on the news there is also considered the viewpoint of the advertiser, and still more important, the attitude of editors and publishers toward the utility corporations, the patent-medicine men, the department-store owners, toward big business—in short, toward the sources of their money.

Is news suppressed by the advertisers? Here is a mild statement from a questionnaire about the newspaper business which Marlen E. Pew recently published in the house organ of the American press, *Editor & Publisher:*

"Q.—There is a belief that much news is colored or suppressed on order from the business office. Is this true? Can you recall incidents in support of your belief?

"A.—It happens once in a while in many offices. The publisher is a weakling, or is out playing golf while some

narrow-minded henchman is riding the staff. An advertiser calls up demanding that some scandal story be
suppressed and invariably contacts with the business office,
for obvious reasons. Some editors are independent enough
to throw ink-wells at publishers' assistants or tell even the
boss he doesn't know the butter side of his own bread and
sometimes convince him of the fact. Other editors compromise or wiggle out of unpleasant situations of this
sort."

"It happens once in a while in many offices" seems to me
too half-hearted a confession from an editor who while engaged in daily newspaper work was known as a fearless fighter
against the corrupting influences of the advertisers. Mr. Pew
knows as well as I do that every newspaper man he has talked
to in his whole lifetime has had some evidence of advertisers
suppressing news.

The case of the entire press of Pittsburgh suppressing the
news of a rape case in which the son of a department-store
owner was the defendant is not unique. The entire press of
Philadelphia suppressed the news of a charge of immorality
against one of its leading department-store officials and the
suicide of the accused. The New York papers published the
story.

But the *New York World* went to a ludicrous extreme when
it rejected O. Henry's famous *The Unfinished Story* because
it dealt with a department-store girl who got seven dollars a
week and who planned to sacrifice what in those days was
euphemistically known as "her virtue." This story, the supposedly fearless *World* thought, might harm its relations with
all department stores.

Suppression of news by the department stores is the most
frequent and flagrant story. The department stores are the
largest local advertisers; almost all newspapers live on this
sort of advertising, and a boycott by the stores is frequently
fatal to the publisher. Department-store owners are no better
or worse than other business men. The fact to be noted is that
they insist that their peccadilloes and their crimes, their di-

vorces, their minor scandals and their violations of the law, be suppressed. Usually their insistence wins.

The *New York Times* reported that United States Commissioner Manley issued warrants for the arrest of members of the firm of a department store in Philadelphia, in violation of the Lever Act. The government accused this store of charging unreasonable prices for sausage, tea, cocoa. But the morning after the *Times* brought this information, there was no mention of the facts in the *Philadelphia Public Ledger*.

When an alumnae committee of Bryn Mawr accused the same store of failure to conform to the fire laws, the papers were silent; when the fire marshal filed suit against the store, the *Ledger,* according to Oswald Garrison Villard, could not see that there was any news value in the fact. But when the store denied the charge which the *Ledger* had never printed, the *Ledger* had space for it.

Then there were strikes of clothing workers, upholstery workers, and the picketing of department stores. The *Ledger* remained anti-union to the extent of refusing paid advertisements merely setting forth the claims of the workers. An indictment of the United Gas Improvement Company was either suppressed or hidden on inside pages by several Philadelphia papers. The lapses of the *Ledger,* which Curtis once said he would make the *Manchester Guardian* of America, Mr. Villard concludes, "are utterly unworthy of it and are a treachery of journalism itself."

With great frequency persons are caught shoplifting in department stores. According to a recent report this happens almost every day at Klein's in New York. Usually such arrests are not news. But when the *New York Times* reports the arrest of two fashionably dressed persons who lived at the Hotel Vanderbilt and who posed as members of upper society, it is apparently news. It is news for many papers. But the *Times* mentions the store as James McCreery & Company, the *American* reports a "Thirty-fourth street department store," and the *Tribune* does not mention the episode.

In Chicago the vice-president of a department store is indicted for bribing city aldermen to obtain passage of an ordinance permitting him to bridge his two buildings. The press of Chicago obliges. For five days the trial goes on sensationally; for five days the newspapers of Chicago are silent. One German language newspaper brings the story.

The big sensation in all the Boston newspapers one day was the collapse of two hundred employees just after the noon hour. All had been poisoned by the food in their box lunches. Not a single paper mentions the name of the purveying restaurant; it is "a local chain restaurant."

In Boston a board fixes the minimum wage in the women's clothing industry at fourteen dollars a week, but is powerless to enforce it. It is authorized, however, to advertise the names of those who refuse to pay. The *Globe* runs the board's advertisement with an offending firm's name, but the *Transcript* refuses, although the law imposes a fine of one hundred dollars for such refusal.

Keith's Theater is a Boston advertiser. For ten weeks, at practically every performance, a maniac throws missiles, severely injuring persons in the audience. Every Boston paper knows of this but not until the maniac is caught is there any mention of his activities. "And," comments the *Springfield Republican,* "there are still journalists to declare that Upton Sinclair's strictures on the press were exaggerated and there are still innocent souls who believe that the Boston dailies are faithfully serving the city that supports them."

When the press in Ohio attacked the Standard Oil Company and the Rockefellers, their so-called "fixer," Dan O'Day, made out a series of new advertising contracts for a Standard by-product, Mica Axle Grease, which Ohio papers accepted. Perhaps it was a mere coincidence that the attacks ceased the same day.

Not alone is Will Rogers among newspaper critics to call humorous attention to the way California papers play up Florida hurricanes and the way Florida papers play up California earthquakes, each paper playing down the local lamentable acts of God. The situation is not alarming. Exaggerations and vice versa will not do much harm to the general public.

But there is the subject of disease and plagues. They affect life and death. Has it always been the role of the newspapers to suppress such unfortunate news? I have been much amused by the following quotation from the "Latrobe Journal" of 1819 which Ruth Boyd has so kindly sent me. The subject is yellow fever. "By the beginning of August," wrote the contemporary historian, "it was a matter of notoriety that the disease did exist. Every notice, however, of the calamity was carefully kept out of the newspapers. I asked one of the editors from what motive this omission arose; his answer was that, the principal profit of a newspaper arising from advertisements, the merchants, their principal customers, had absolutely forbade the least notice of fever, under a threat that their custom should otherwise be withdrawn; thus sacrificing to commercial policy the lives of all those who believed from the silence of the public papers that no danger might come to the city. From the beginning of August to the 19th of September the deaths increased from 10 to 12 a day to 46. . . . But no exact register is anywhere kept of deaths and burials."

About a century later, when the bubonic plague reached San Francisco, the big-business advertisers of that city asked the newspapers not to publish the fact. There was a midnight conference of editors, publishers and business men. With the exception of the Hearst representative all agreed to suppress all mention of the plague. Government experts announced it was spreading and causing death. The newspapers attacked the government experts and did everything to hamper their work. The quarantine was made ineffective. The plague lasted until 1911, ten years. Lives were lost, millions of dollars were lost. "In this case," says Will Irwin, "no one directly threatened the withdrawal of advertising; the fact that the financial powers, including department stores, were strongly on one side was enough for publishers and managing editors trained in the modern commercial school."

Then in 1933 there was an epidemic of amoebic dysentery in Chicago. It was the height of the World's Fair season and not a word appeared in the press. The newspapers, accused later of suppressing the news, laid the blame on the Department of Health.

In March, 1934, the scandal at last was aired. The Chicago Medical Society adopted a committee report censuring Dr. Herman N. Bundesen, the health commissioner. In reply he showed that on August 16, 1933, he traced two cases of amoebic dysentery to the Congress Hotel and discovered fifteen clinical cases among three hundred and sixty-four persons who handled food. In October he submitted a report to the American Public Health Association convened in near-by Indianapolis, and the *Indianapolis Times* (Talcott Powell, editor) scooped the country. With the aid of the local Health Department the *Times* traced eight cases which originated in the Congress Hotel, Chicago. The other Indianapolis newspapers took up the sensational story. These papers are for sale in Chicago. But not a word in the Chicago papers. Doctor Bundesen heard of these reports in the Indianapolis newspapers although no Chicago newspaper did. October nineteenth he made a new investigation, finding one hundred eighteen additional infections among hotel workers. In November he sent out sixteen thousand questionnaires to persons who had been guests in the hotel and by November eighth he received thirty-five replies indicating infections. He then issued a general warning through the press. The first item to appear in a Chicago paper was under a three-line head November ninth saying the situation was "entirely under control, and there is no need for any alarm whatsoever." The Fair was to close in three days.

"The wool trust suppresses opinion by the force of its advertisements," said *Collier's,* and quoted from a letter of Wood, Putnam and Wood to *Collier's* agent, Brockholst Mathewson: "It is up to the advertiser, in a way, to decide whether to use *Collier's* or not. . . . I don't want to cancel the American Woolen Company's order. . . . I am very much inclined to say we will run a half page with you in March rather than a quarter page. Mr. [William M.] Wood of the American Woolen Company is particularly sensitive. . . . It would be a great source of gratitude to me if I could learn through you just how far Mr. Mark Sullivan proposes going in this matter. . . ."

The matter was Sullivan's exposure of the influences in Washington on Schedule K of the tariff. "Mark Sullivan," *Collier's* replied editorially, "has achieved a hitherto unaccomplished feat. The city of Washington reeks with society glamour, money prestige, special favors, ignorance of common life, and indifference to the common man. The journalist who can tell the whole truth about congress must be above the lure of gold and the glitter of social favor. He must see the hidden springs and obtain the inside news without paying with his soul. Mark Sullivan's mind is beyond the contagion of wealth or flattery. . . .

"Mr. Wood wishes us to practice the principle of deference to a powerful advertiser. . . . This attempt of the wool manufacturers to prevent the press from telling the truth about a necessity of daily life, affecting the struggles and the happiness of the poorest citizen, is a wide and calculated policy with especial bearing on the congress soon in session. . . . The time may come when the Wool Trust, or some other trust, is able to put *Collier's* out of business, but the time has not come yet."

William Winter was "forced to resign" by the *New York Tribune* for unfavorable criticism of plays presented by an advertiser.

Walter Pritchard Eaton, of the *New York Sun,* attacked dirty plays and the theater syndicate withdrew its advertising. Eaton was discharged within six months and the advertising came back.

Contrast the cases of William E. Corey and C. W. Post. Corey, a multimillionaire, wanted to divorce his wife and marry Mabelle Gilman. The press grew sentimental in powerful support of the abused wife.

Post divorced his wife and married his stenographer. Almost no newspaper in the country mentioned the case. Post was not only a large advertiser but the author of full-page paid ads attacking the labor unions. He is also the author of an article boasting of how he wrote letters to newspapers threatening to withdraw his advertising if they continued their attacks on big business, and how the newspapers complied.

In *My Own Story,* Fremont Older says, "The [San Francisco] *Bulletin* was on the payroll of the Southern Pacific Railroad for $125 a month. This was paid not for any definite service, but merely for 'friendliness.' . . .

"Crothers [owner] felt that the influence of the *Bulletin* was worth more than the Southern Pacific had been paying. He insisted that I go to Mills [W. H. Mills, 'who handled the newspapers of California for the railroad company'] and demand $25,000 from the railroad for supporting Gage. . . . the railroad paid Crothers $7,500. . . ."

After Upton Sinclair had exposed the horrors of the Jungle in Chicago, it was testified before the committee on agriculture and forestry of the Senate that "Frank Heney showed that to defeat a bill regulating the packing industry now before Congress, Swift and Company alone are spending a million dollars a month upon newspaper advertising. Heney testified that he has had an examination made of every newspaper in California, and every one has published the full-page advertisements of this firm. Senator Norris testified that he had an examination made in New York state, and has been unable to find a single paper without the Swift advertisements—which, it is pointed out, are not in any way calculated to sell the products of Swift & Company but solely to defeat government regulation of the industry. Armour & Company were paying over two thousand dollars a page to all the farm publications of the country—and this not for advertisements, but for 'special articles'!"

Again, thanks to William Randolph Hearst, the venality of a part of the press was indisputably proved in the publication of the Archbold letters. Planned as a bomb against Hearst's political enemies, the series showed how Standard Oil certificates of deposit and enormous sums of money in the form of subscriptions were sent to editors so that public opinion could be bought.

In mid-summer 1934, the New York regional labor board informs me, a decision was handed down against a bread company. No mention of this fact appeared in a majority of the newspapers.

The *Editor & Publisher* of February 11, 1933, exposed a campaign of the Bond Bread Company to enlist the newspapers in Connecticut. Ten kinds of co-operation were asked in a contest to which advertising was attached: "To receive all entries, to handle judging in the local contests, and to appoint judges; to announce the contest and later to announce the winners, in the news columns; to have the subject of Vitamin D discussed by food experts without special reference to Bond Bread or to the contest; to furnish reprints of advertisements for grocery stores; to have merchandising displays in the newspaper office; to write the grocers announcing the contest; and to offer further support through other individual ideas of the papers."

In reply to a question from *Editor & Publisher,* George R. Gould, director of advertising, *New Haven Register,* said "the same work has been done by many newspapers time and time again. . . . Here in New Haven we want more newspaper advertising and we feel that if we make a success of the contest advertising we will be aiding other newspapers in securing the campaign. . . ."

In July, 1932, Proctor & Gamble, soap manufacturers, canceled their advertising contracts with all newspapers which had used a syndicated article telling women how to make soap cheaply at home.

There are sins of commission and sins of omission. Has the press as a whole ever given any information to the American public about cigarette smoking?

When I was in Berlin I interviewed the greatest authority on that subject, Prof. Dr. Johan Plesch of the University of Berlin. Doctor Plesch is not an anti-nicotine fanatic. He is a smoker. But he has studied nicotine, written an exhaustive book on the subject, and is well acquainted with its dangers. He gave me a list of the deadly poisons contained in tobacco. He did not argue against cigarettes but he laid down this law: inasmuch as all tobaccos contain poisons, the continued use of certain brands of cigarettes is dangerous. We all know that temperance in tobacco as well as in alcohol is to be desired. But to escape danger to one's health the tobacco user must continually change the kind of tobacco he uses, so that the minute amount of poisons the different varieties contain may not affect him. American tobacco contains more of certain kinds of poison than Turkish, and vice versa. One should change kinds, not brands, frequently.

This mail article was sent to my paper which syndicates to more than thirty others, but no clipping ever came back showing that a single one had published it. This, of course, is not documentary proof. But the wager can safely be made that not more than ten per cent of the press of America publishing cigarette advertising will use an article of this kind.

In the midst of the Lucky Strike campaign, "Reach for a Lucky instead of a sweet," my friend Dr. Ben Jablons, authorized by the Medical Association of New York, made a public statement that "excessive use of tobacco to kill the appetite is a double-edged sword, for nicotine poisoning and starvation both leave dire results in their train." This, apparently, was not news.

In 1934 the Camel Company advertised that its cigarettes gave one a "lift." The New York Academy of Medicine, the *Journal* of the American Medical Association and medical meetings discussed this new stunt. Was it news or not? The newspapers thought not. But *Time,* which also runs Camel advertising, thought yes. It quoted doctors saying "the evidence seems to indicate that nicotine is at least one of the toxic factors in cigarette smoking," and "other toxic factors, ammonia, pyridine and pyridine derivatives, cyanides and sulphocyanides, arsenic," a list of poisons which tallies with that Doctor Plesch gave me several years ago.

In Europe the munitions makers frequently place full-page advertisements for guns or shrapnel or submarines in the press. The reader is not expected to buy a submarine. If he is intelligent, he understands that the ad is merely a bribe.

In the United States such advertising is confined to the technical press. It never reaches the lay reader. But this does not mean that the munitions makers of America do not influence the press by advertising. The Du Ponts, for instance, manufacture millions of dollars' worth of peacetime goods, including cloth for dresses, and advertise them extensively.

However, there have been, as there are at present, campaigns to take the profit out of war, to nationalize the war industry. At such times the power of the merchants of death makes itself felt.

On one occasion the Bethlehem Steel Company, faced with a public demand for a nationally owned armor plant, ran a series of full-page advertisements in 3,257 publications, at a cost of millions of dollars. It later issued them in pamphlets which the reader will find in the New York Public Library. Bethlehem was exceedingly pleased with the results its advertising money obtained. It reprints the favorable editorials and news items from the daily and weekly newspapers. Notable, it points out, is the two-column editorial published April 13, 1916, by Editor McLean in his *Washington Post*:

> "Where private capital can and will serve the people well at reasonable and fair prices, the *Post* shall at all times oppose the entrance of the government into competition with such private enterprise.
> "The Bethlehem Steel Company can serve the country well. No one doubts that. . . .
> "Every patriotic American should be gratified that our country has secured such an offer . . . as proposed by the Bethlehem. . . ."

The Bethlehem advertising helped defeat the project for a national armor-plate works. In the advertising the American public was told the company was prepared to make armor "at any price which the Federal Trade Commission may name as fair"; under the signature of Charles M. Schwab himself appeared the statement that "no representative of the Bethlehem Steel Company is seeking or has sought to influence legislation as to the size of naval or military expenditure." Under the signature of President E. R. Grace a letter to Senator Tillman, of the Naval Affairs Committee, stated: "It is said that a government plant should be built 'to take the profit out of war.' Our Company has no inclination to make capital out of the military necessities of the United States. In the event of war or threatened war, all the facilities we have for any purpose are at the disposal of the United States Government upon its own terms. . . ."

So much for advertising. Three congressional investigations have proved that the Bethlehem made hundreds of millions surplus profits out of the United States, that it set prices secretly in combination with its rivals, that it raised prices whenever it could, and that it was one of the three munitions companies which financed Shearer, who boasted of his lobbying in behalf of a large navy in Washington and was "credited" with defeating the Genoa conference to limit naval construction. The part the press played in the Shearer case is notorious.

Does advertising play a part in the political alignment of the press? We need not speak of the Communist Party, which is naturally anathema to about ninety-nine per cent of the American press, nor even the Socialist Party, which is merely tolerated as good-natured Christian political reform; the issue becomes clear when a "regular" party, that is, one which is not pledged to destroy the status quo, begins its campaign. Where is the press when a third party arrives? What does the press do to Progressive, Farmer-Labor Party, Non-partisan League and a hundred state and local independent party candidates?

The answer is that the press almost always helps destroy all but the Republican and Democratic Parties. The reason obviously is that the interests of the publishers of the majority of newspapers of the United States coincide with the interests which control the Republican and Democratic Parties.

Does advertising play a role? In New York, Chicago, Boston, Philadelphia, in fact the major cities of the nation, there is little or no political advertising, certainly not enough to buy up the editorial policy of the newspapers, but throughout the country the smaller press is fed this advertising by the Democratic and Republican machines.

Take the case of the *Pittsburgh Leader,* for example. We had the courage to support La Follette and Theodore Roosevelt. But our main campaign at every election was the office of sheriff. We usually elected our sheriff. In return we got the advertising of Allegheny County which this office controlled, many pages of official notices, paid at high rates.

But more important still: although nominally "Progressive," we maintained our link with the regular Republican organization, just as the other Pittsburgh newspapers which owed money to the Mellon banks remained tied to the Democratic organization. For us it meant that members of the Republican National Committee would visit Editor Moore once in a while to discuss mutually profitable market tips, also that bankers and brokers would let Moore and other owners in on the "ground floor" when new corporations were floated. No one can dispute the fact that it was profitable for the editor and publisher of the *Leader* and other publishers to remain linked to either the Republican or Democratic machine.

A large part of the small press, however, is bought outright. It was not until recently that some facts concerning the 1920 presidential campaign came to light showing how this is done. There was at that time a defunct advertising agency which was bought for a mere four hundred thousand dollars. Its specialty had been advertising in four hundred foreign-language newspapers which had a circulation of about four million and could be counted to influence some eight million voters.

Under the guise of the "Americanization" of these foreign-language paper readers, a committee was formed to purchase this agency. Among the members were Secretary of the Treasury Mellon, John B. Farrell, William Boyce Thompson who had been vice-president of some of Harry Sinclair's oil companies and chairman of the Republican Finance Committee, John T. Pratt, New York capitalist now deceased, Francis Sisson of the Guaranty Trust Company, Senator T. Coleman du Pont, Samuel Insull, the Armour, Swift and Libby packing companies, the American Smelting & Refining Company, the Continental and Commercial National Bank of Chicago, the First National of Chicago, Don S. Momand, Mrs. Cabot Ward, Frank D. Gardner, and other business interests. Among the contributions received was thirty thousand dollars in Liberty bonds from Mr. Pratt who, it was later testified, had received fifty thousand dollars' worth of the Sinclair Liberty bonds from Will Hays.

This subsidized advertising bureau functioned from 1919, through the successful election of Harding, to 1924, when the equally reliable Coolidge was making the world safe for business. ("Profits and civilization go hand in hand"—Coolidge.) It then ceased operations. But, "where were the fearless Washington correspondents while this was going on?" asks a fearless Washington correspondent, referring to the Liberty-bond scandal and the confession from Mr. Mellon that he knew about the bonds, and once handled them. "Were they too dull and incompetent to obtain this important story, or was it the old familiar business of 'laying off' a secretary of the treasury who has been singularly generous in the matter of making tax refunds to influential newspapers? . . . What will such newspapers say when their editors read the foregoing list, and observe the cream of the 'lily whites' in the business world, including Mr. Mellon himself, deliberately engaged in an enterprise to control the editorial policies of 400 newspapers through their advertising—the ultimate goal being to accomplish the election of Warren G. Harding and the Ohio Gang?"

Is the situation better today than it was a score of years ago when the first pure food bill was passed, or ten years ago, or a hundred years ago? Many persons think so. F. P. A., famous columnist of the *New York Herald Tribune,* thinks so. To prove his contention he reprints the following address which Mrs. Dwight Morrow (Smith '96) made to the college alumnae:

"Our colleges have striven to prepare us for just this task by giving us inner resources of pleasure not dependent upon money or society. They have insisted, all of them, out of their own plain living, whether set down in cities or among the green hills of the country, that good clothes, fur coats, movies, orchids, champagne, fine houses, servants, theaters, fast motors, modern plumbing, gold mesh bags, all the magazines and strawberries in March are not necessary for happiness."

"Everything listed in Mrs. Morrow's speech," comments F. P. A., "is advertised in the issue of the paper that carried it, or is for sale by at least one advertiser. If Mrs. Morrow, or somebody else, in 1896 had said those words, listing all those salable advertised articles, many newspapers—maybe all of them—would have been afraid to print them. This comment is made for the benefit of those cynical persons, like the *New Yorker's* Mr. Clifton Fadiman, who think that newspapers are dominated by The Gate, or advertisers. . . . The old editorial disease, advertisophobia, does not exist in these parts. . . . Newspapers are honester and more fearless than they used to be."

To F. P. A. and Mr. Fadiman: On February 26, 1934, at a time material for this book was being collected, and at a time the Tugwell Bill for pure food and drugs was not yet dead, Mrs. Roosevelt, wife of the President, whose views as given at her press conferences are reported in the national press, made the following statement regarding the Tugwell Bill: "I think all goods sold to the public should be labeled as to their grade and quality. Without this the consumer cannot know what he is buying. This is the only way the consumer can intelligently have a hold on the market. I mean authentic government grades and standards."

Was this news? Was it news fit to print? All the newspaper women sent out Mrs. Roosevelt's statement. All of them said later they could find no trace of the statement ever having been printed.

Among those who leaped forward to attack the National Recovery Administration codes because they were producing restrictions on advertising, was Howard Davis, business manager of the *New York Herald Tribune*. The Associated Press sent to its more than one thousand newspapers the following excerpt from his address before the Inland Daily Press Association:

"Great changes are taking place. Whereas a few years ago business men were encouraged to advertise, now by governmental restrictions in many codes and marketing agreements they are being restrained in their efforts to acquaint the people through advertising with what they have to sell. If advertising is destroyed, a free press will be destroyed."

[But this last sentence was too much for the *New York Times:* It ran the item verbatim but cut these splendid words out.]

"Newspaper publishers do not want dishonest advertising, but the time has come when they should demand that no further restriction be placed on honest advertising. Those restrictions already placed should be removed at once.

"A tax on advertising was one of the favorite Old World methods of destroying a free press. In fact, the press of England did not become free until advertising taxes on newspapers were removed a half century ago.

"The United States is now threatened with such taxes in various States. If taxes are to follow restrictions on advertising, the free press of this country will be a thing of the past."

Forward to battle the plumed knight of the free press, Elisha Hanson, counsel of the Publishers' Association, counsel of paper and power companies, bitterest enemy of the Newspaper Guild. In his attack on the NRA, he said:

"Legislation and codes have had a really restricting effect on advertising.

"If you don't believe that statement, take a look at your financial pages of the last year. The Securities Act nearly finished them. And as for codes, more than one hundred—the most important in so far as volume of sales is concerned—contain various restrictions on advertising. More are proposed in amendments now pending before the NRA.

"The restrictions already accomplished, whether proper or improper—and many of them are improper—are nothing as compared with some which have been proposed but thus far defeated."

The Department of Agriculture, where Tugwell functions, was accused of making "the greatest drive against advertising of any agency in the history of the government" because it asked an amendment to the old Federal Pure Food Act which Hanson opposed.

The mind of the advertising man is a fearful and wonderful thing. Many ad-writers are merely newspaper men who, having grown tired of talking about "prostitution" at twenty-five dollars a week in the city room, go out for the big money that the profession of advertising pays, and remain immune, cynical and ironic. But that profession, like the oldest trade in the world, has its enthusiasts.

Here, for example, we look into the economic mind of Gilbert T. Hodges, chairman of the Advertising Federation of America. Before the American Home Economics Association convention he mentioned the charge that advertising is eighty-five per cent emotional and only fifteen per cent rational, and replied by saying that an emotional stimulus for buying is the only one that can promote the mass selling necessary for economic recovery in this country. Moreover:

> "The advertising industry will lead us out of this depression as surely as the automobile industry led us out of the panic of 1907. As for the claim that it is the consumer who pays for advertising, I can only say that advertising pays for itself."

Another leading economist and philosopher is Albert D. Lasker, chairman of the board of Lord & Thomas, advertising agents. To the *New York Times* he writes that there are low standard countries, like Mexico, where "consumers let their habits dictate their purchases," but America is different: "Largely through advertising we have created desire . . . stimulated production by stimulating consumption. It has done it on so vast a scale as to bring about a higher standard of living among the American people than could have possibly existed without advertising under any system of government."

(The date is September 27, 1934: on the front pages of the

press is the announcement that one-sixth the population of the United States, twenty million persons, is living on money handed out by the government. There are more than ten million unemployed. But perhaps our economist refers to the standard of living on Park Avenue?)

Mr. Lasker takes the opportunity to discuss freedom of the press also. "No more vicious calumny has ever been put forth," he declares, "than the suspicion that the press, in any major or important way, can be influenced editorially by its advertising patrons." Mr. Lasker is herewith referred to the later chapter dealing with the public utilities.

There are also other types of advertising men. Lee H. Bristol, vice-president of a medicine company, sensing the public challenge to the entire profit system, believes that "advertising will be the focal point of the attack" upon it. And, he continues, "We've got to pledge ourselves to reform. We ourselves have been to blame for violations of good practices in the past. . . . They are a blot on all advertising. . . . What we have to do is clean house."

C. B. Larrabee, managing editor of *Printer's Ink,* one of the first to lead the attack on the Tugwell Bill, reminding the Advertising Federation of America that there has always been a good-natured skepticism toward advertising, adds that "today this skepticism is based on some pretty logical arguments by opponents of advertising. We must also face the rather unpleasant fact that a certain number of our advertisers are not ethically decent enough to conduct their business advertising fairly and honestly. . . . I think it is time to kick the crooks out. . . . John Public is gradually coming to believe in the faulty syllogism 'Crooks advertise. Therefore, all advertisers are crooks.' . . . Eliminate those shabby, shoddy, unethical gentlemen who do more by their unethical tactics to destroy advertising than Jim Rorty and the entire Communist Party."

But the most alarming statement about advertising does not come from Rorty or Communists, but from a colleague of Messrs. Lasker, Hodges and Larrabee. It is dated August, 1933, and refers to our own age, the golden age just ended:

"1. Advertising played a deplorable part in the era of greed. It was the willing tool of avaricious business.

"2. Advertising supinely submitted to practices and impositions that destroyed the foundations on which the theory of advertising is built.

"3. Advertising catered to the violators of all the codes in the decalogue. It co-operated in its own pollution and prostitution. It descended to a racket.

"4. Advertising was used for the purpose of establishing false value standards. Time-honored institutions, tried mediums, did not hesitate to lend themselves to schemes that were perhaps within the law, but far beyond the bounds of decency. A revelation of the facts would make our people gasp, inured to rackets as they are.

"5. Advertising by its attitude indicated an absolute contempt for public intelligence. In the opinion of advertising, and we can only judge by its methods, tone, approach, and the character of its appeal, we are a nation of suckers and morons.

"This outburst may be termed ill-tempered and ill-advised, but certainly not by those who are correctly informed. A revelation of the facts would be helpful and not harmful. Does anyone imagine that the suppression of the facts in the Harriman Bank helped this nation? Does the fact we were all guilty cover up the flagrant violations of public confidence?"

The author of the foregoing is a highly placed advertising counselor, Louis Blumenstock by name, who speaks of "the black record of advertising," says his indictment cannot be challenged, who goes beyond his indictment when he mentions "crooked businesses, prosecuted and convicted, still buying space in publications; new crimes being hatched against readers; fraud written on the face of advertisements," and concludes with the statement that "advertising may also be blamed for most of our distress during the past four years." Could any advertising-hating newspaper man go further?

The attitude of the advertiser toward the editor was well expressed by George Frank Lord, when he directed the advertising of the Du Pont interests: to him editors and publishers were merely appendages of the advertising game. Said he:

"Time was when publishers were editors who endeavored to mould the opinion of their readers along this line or that. Then the circulation and influence of the publication was in proportion to the popularity of the editor's ideas, but nowadays the *real publishers are the advertisers,* since their financial support of a publication is in most cases all that keeps it alive.

". . . they (advertisers, the *real* publishers) must see to it that the publication renders a real service, that it is constructive, sound and clean, rather than destructive, irrational and immoral.

"The claim that the withdrawing of financial support from a destructive (i. e., in the opinion of the advertisers) publication is a mischievous use of advertising patronage to curb the power of the press, seems pure sophistry to me.

"If he (the advertiser) stops demanding or using that kind of circulation (circulation gained by publishers who approve policies and measures that advertisers disagree with) it will quickly go out of existence."

Now let us see just what some big advertisers—the medicine men—have done to our free press.

CHAPTER III

BAD MEDICINE

No ONE but a fool would deny today that the pure food and drug law of 1906 was a necessity. But the press of America, with notable but few exceptions, opposed that law.

Today an attempt is being made to clean up fraudulent advertising of foods and drugs. The main difference between 1906 and 1934 is this: in the old days newspapers individually supported the medicine men; in 1934 the organized newspaper owners' associations of America fought and defeated the original Tugwell Bill.

In 1933, when the fight had just begun, Heywood Broun concluded a report with the following conversation between himself and a cynical gentleman he met in Washington:

"You are wasting your time getting excited about the Tugwell Bill," said the cynical gentleman. "It hasn't a chance on earth of passage in any form whatsoever."

"But it's a good bill, isn't it?" Broun the believer replied.

"Of course it is, but the newspaper owners won't have it, and you will find when you have been around as long as I have that anything newspaper owners don't want never has happened in America and never will."

Broun did not reply, but still idealistically hopeful, he recalled the old line which dramatists once used for the second-act curtain—"I wonder."

The Tugwell Bill is dead. An emasculated Copeland Bill, cut to the bias of manufacturers and publishers, is under consideration at the moment of writing, but its passage is of no great importance. What is important for consideration here is the part the press and the advertisers have played in this little drama affecting the health and pocketbooks of the American people.

In 1933, and more recently, patent-medicine men and the newspapers raised the cry "freedom of the press," but in

November, 1905, it was *Collier's* which came forth with this headline: "The Patent Medicine Conspiracy against the Freedom of the Press."

As first proof it gave the "contract of silence," a copy of which was supplied by William Allen White, of the *Emporia Gazette,* an editor and a newspaper always considered by newspaper men as representing the highest ideals in world journalism. The notorious clause which the medicine men had inserted in all advertising contracts was:

It is mutually agreed that this contract is void if any law is enacted by your State restricting or prohibiting the manufacture or sale of proprietary medicines.

That the object of this clause was to silence the press and buy its support for the medicine men was openly admitted by Frank J. Cheney, president of the Proprietary Association of America, which *Collier's* called "an organization of quack doctors and patent medicine makers." Cheney manufactured a catarrh cure. The organization paid about forty million dollars to the newspapers annually for advertising. "By means of this organization and its force the newspapers of America actually became lobbyists for the patent-medicine manufacturers whenever any public health legislation threatened to expose these medicines."

Addressing the association, President Cheney told his colleagues how to influence the press. He said in part:

"We have had a good deal of difficulty in the last few years with the different legislatures of the different states. . . . I believe I have a plan whereby we will have no difficulty whatever with these people. I have used it in my business for two years, and I know it is a practical thing . . . I, inside of the last two years, have made contracts with between fifteen and sixteen thousand newspapers, and never had but one man refuse to sign the contract, and by saying to him that I could not sign a contract without this clause in it he readily signed it. My point is merely to shift the responsibility. We to-day have the responsibility of the whole matter upon our shoulders. . . . There has been constant fear that something would come up, so I had this clause in my contract added. This is what I have in every contract I make: 'It is hereby agreed that should your State, or the United States Government, pass any law that would interfere with or restrict the sale of proprietary medicines, this contract shall become void.' . . . In the State of Illinois a few years ago they wanted to assess me three hundred dollars. I thought I had a better plan than this, so I wrote about forty papers and merely said: 'Please look at your contract with me and take note that if this law passes you and I must stop doing business, and my contracts cease.' The next day every one of them had an article. . . . I have carried this through and know it is a success. I know the papers will accept it. Here is a thing that costs us nothing. We are guaranteed against the $75,000 loss for nothing. It throws the responsibility on the newspapers. . . ."

One of the first of the large newspapers to defy the medicine men was the *Cleveland Press*. The association then sent a letter to its members warning them to stop advertising. Later, it boasted, "Because of that letter which we sent out the *Cleveland Press* received inside of forty-eight hours telegrams from six manufacturers canceling thousands of dollars' worth of advertising and causing a consequent dearth of sensational matter along these lines. It resulted in a loss to one paper alone of over eighteen thousand dollars in advertising. Gentlemen, when you touch a man's pocket, you touch him where he lives; that principle is true of the newspaper editor or the retail druggist, and goes through all business."

In 1911, five years after the Harrison Pure Food and Drug Bill was passed, *Collier's* offered a reward for a list of the firms backing the Advertisers' Protective Association which "exists for the purpose of trying to suppress newspaper comment on pure food and drugs, and for the purpose of attacking Dr. Wiley." One letter from this organization, which claimed it represented a four hundred million investment, said: "Write to each newspaper, magazine, and journal in which you advertise, and ask them to protest against Wiley's ruinous and irresponsible methods. Impress upon the editor's mind that when Wiley forces you to take your advertisement out of his publication, he is taking money out of the newspaper's pocket, as well as out of yours."

The medicine men also formed a League for Medical Freedom to fight state legislation. B. O. Flower, one of the nine founders, was also president of the R. C. Flower Medicine Company. "R. C. Flower," *Collier's* reported, "is the notorious quack and general humbug whose latest arrest was as late as 1908."

Among the discoveries which followed the passage of the drug bill was the use of opium in soothing sirups administered to infants.

Thirty years have passed since *Collier's* first exposed the patent-medicine makers and their attack on the freedom of the press. "Truth in Advertising" was adopted as the slogan of the advertising industry and the American newspaper publishers discovered "ethics." "Honesty" and "Integrity" and "Responsibility to the Public" and above all else, the word "Truth" appears in their codes. Advertising has grown into a billion or a billion and a half dollars a year business.

Have the advertisers quit their intimidation of the press? Have they stopped making harmful medicines? Has the press published nothing but the truth in advertising? The negative answer to all these questions was contained in the Tugwell Bill.

One drug manufacturer dared to support the reform measure: E. R. Squibb & Son.

Typical of the medicine men's recent method of obtaining press support is the following letter which the Creomulsion Company, of Atlanta, Georgia, sent to the editors who received its advertising money:

"Gentlemen: You are about to lose a substantial amount of advertising revenue from food, drug, and cosmetic manufacturers. Your pocketbook is about to be filched, and you will see how if you will personally study . . . the inclosed copy of the Tugwell Bill. This bill was introduced by *two doctors*. . . . You publish your paper for profit and as a service to your community. In most virile business organizations the altruistic policies in the final analysis are means to the primary end, which is profit. . . . An isolated editorial or two will not suffice. . . . You need to take an aggressive stand against this measure. You need to bring all personal pressure you can upon your Senators and Representatives. You need to enlighten and thereby arouse your public against this bill that is calculated to greatly restrict personal rights. If this bill should become law we will be forced to cancel immediately every line of Creomulsion advertising."

Another example: Avron Spiro, of Lake, Spiro, Cohn, Inc., advertising agency, sent a telegram suggesting a campaign in the newspapers to influence the public against the Tugwell Bill. To the United Medicine Manufacturers of America he suggested that, after all, "newspapers will stand with you because they are vitally affected. . . . Self-preservation is the first law of nature and self-medication is one of the first laws of self-preservation. . . . The newspapers are vitally concerned for this bill hits directly at them. It establishes a government censorship on advertising directed by non-advertisers."

Through *Editor & Publisher* Frank A. Blair, president of the Proprietary Association which claims eighty per cent membership of the package medicine industry, said to the newspaper owners of America:

"According to eminent authorities the Tugwell Bill is an attempt to take away from the people the right of self-medication and to restrict or destroy industries that pay a large portion of the government expense and a good part of the national advertising, amounting to about $345,000,000 in 1932. . . .

"All large newspapers today and many small ones publish health columns. . . frequently refer to proprietary medicines with approval. . . . Many publishers have already gone on record against the Tugwell Bill. . . . [Its] loose phraseology . . . constitutes a real threat to the

business of advertising as well as to the industries. . . .
The manufacturers look upon the Tugwell Bill as a
nuisance measure . . . one that will increase unemployment and 'upset the apple cart' of business improvement."

Writing to the White House the president of the United
Medicine Manufacturers of America, Inc., informed Mr.
Roosevelt that the mere introduction of the bill had, by the
first of November, 1933, already curtailed newspaper advertising lineage and slowed down the drug industry.

This same organization—the facts can be found in the *New
Republic* because they did not appear in the daily press—held
a meeting in the Hotel Sherman, Chicago, September 11 to
13, 1933, and adopted a "fighting program" of seventeen
points, of which the most important is: "To secure co-operation of newspapers in spreading favorable publicity [against
Tugwell and the administration] particularly in papers now
carrying advertising for members of the association."

Now let us see how the subscribers to the code of ethics,
the defenders of the free press, and the upholders of "Honesty," "Integrity" and "Truth" repaid the medicine men for
their advertising. Editor Frederick Sullens, of Michigan, for
example. Having heard that an appeal had been made to the
Mississippi members of Congress to oppose revision of the
old pure food and drug bill, he wrote in his *Jackson Daily
News,* "Frankly I am interested in this because many of these
products are extensively advertised, in fact, they form at least
ten per cent of our advertising revenue."

Tugwell wrote Sullens asking whether he was willing to
sacrifice public health to advertising profit.

Sullens replied:

"The inclination is strong to tell you to go to hell. . . . Just
consider I was correctly quoted."

Frank E. Gannett was first to offer his newspapers to the
advertising and drug associations. In a full-page signed statement he said:

"That public opinion might be better informed the Gannett Newspapers secured for the American Newspaper

Publishers Association, the American Advertising Association, and the Proprietary Association a place on the program of the New York State Federation of Women's Clubs annual convention at Elmira, N. Y., November 16 [1933]. The address was by Dr. C. H. Goudiss, a nationally known authority [?] on foods and nutrition and at one time associated with Dr. Harvey W. Wiley.

"Through the facilities of the *Elmira, N. Y., Star-Gazette-Advertiser* the text of Dr. Goudiss' address was transmitted to the Associated Press, United Press and Universal News Service, and carried on those wires.

"The Gannett Newspapers are opposed to un-American legislation that jeopardizes the future of thousands of manufacturers, retailers and millions of employees. The Gannett Newspapers believe in and will fight for the principles of the Tugwell Bill which protect against unscrupulous and fraudulent merchandising and advertising, but oppose the methods and machinery by which this bill seeks to accomplish that much-to-be-desired result.

"The Gannett Newspapers
Albany Evening News. Albany Knickerbocker Press. Olean Times-Herald. Hartford (Conn.) *Times. Elmira Star-Gazette-Advertiser. Elmira Sunday Telegram. Newburgh Beacon News. Ithaca Journal-News. Malone Telegram. Ogdensburg Journal. Rochester Democrat & Chronicle. Plainfield* (N. J.) *Courier-News. Rochester Times-Union. Utica Observer-Dispatch.*"

Paul Block, chain newspaper owner, under whose Foundation at Yale the present writer had the ironic experience of delivering a lecture including many facts given in this volume, raised the frazzled but effective red flag in attacking Tugwell. In his *Newark Star Eagle* he published a two-column page editorial *Time To Drop "Brain Trust."* He called the Securities Bill "evil"; the Wagner Labor Bill "unhealthful," suggested by "certain radical young lawyers"; said the Tugwell Bill "threatened to bring chaos to industries"; concluding, "We reiterate our faith in President Roosevelt's Americanism. We are confident that he, personally, is opposed to a Socialistic state and the Communistic life into which some of the juvenile 'Brain Trust' would like to lead us. . . ."

Block went further with his later editorials which he inserted at advertising rates in the *New York Times* and other papers, one of them entitled *Eliminate the Washington Dream Walkers*. Of Tugwell:

> "The writings and speeches of Professor Tugwell, now assistant secretary of Agriculture, are clearly Socialistic if not Communistic and he should be asked to resign."

And in conclusion: "Come, Mr. President; come, gentlemen of Congress, cleanse the administration of ultra-socialists and communists before it is too late. America does not want them. This is still the country of Washington, Jefferson and Lincoln. A free America. A democratic America, where free speech, a free press, religious tolerance and freedom of dictatorship are desired. Paul Block, Publisher."

Even Mark Sullivan, famed Mark Sullivan who for many years initiated and fought *Collier's* battles against corrupt business, took a crack at the newspaper's profit enemy No. 1. August 2, 1934, his *Herald Tribune* had his usual two-column story with this headline:

MAGAZINE WITH TUGWELL ON STAFF ACCUSED OF INCITING CLASS FEELING

MARK SULLIVAN QUOTES 'NEW REPUBLIC,' SAYS MEMBERSHIP OF A FEDERAL OFFICIAL IN SUCH A GROUP MAKES HIM THINK OF RUSSIA.

Mr. Sullivan quoted the *New Republic's* editorial on the Dillinger case, saying there were curious undercurrents, some people saying Dillinger only robbed banks, murdered one man; "think of all the suicide and all the starvation caused by the Wall Street guys." The magazine concluded that "We do not approve these clearly immoral reflections; we simply report them."

To Sullivan this editorial showed a "subversive" spirit. "It is an incitement to angry class-consciousness, of the sort which in other countries has been used to bring about overturn of the social order.

"The reason for reprinting the editorial here," continues Sullivan, "is that on the list of those who direct and write *The New Republic* the name of Rexford Guy Tugwell appears each week in the rank of contributing editor." This could only happen in Russia, continues Mr. Sullivan; he adds that there are no radicals high in government office, "Tugwell is the only one among them having a position as high as undersecretary. . . ."

The 1934 convention of the American Newspaper Publishers' Association opened with the adoption of a resolution favoring the freedom of the press and immediately turned all its forces to destroy Tugwell.

With rising enthusiasm the A. N. P. A. listened to its general manager, Lincoln B. Palmer, "expose the philosophic and economic fallacies" of the common enemy. The Tugwell Bill was, he said, "the most offensive measure ever introduced in Congress insofar as proper advertising was concerned. . . . During the past year there has been marked evidence of efforts on the part of administrative officials and others to change the existing philosophy and practices relating to advertising and to substitute punitive and tyrannical legislation to harass manufacturers and advertisers; in fact, to prohibit any advertising that is not literally true. Probably the most offensive measure which was ever introduced, insofar as proper advertising is concerned, was the first one of the series of the so-called Tugwell Bills, S-1944, regulating advertising of foods, drugs and cosmetics, one paragraph of which read in part as follows:

" 'An advertisement shall be deemed to be false if, in any particular, it is untrue, or by ambiguity or inference creates a misleading impression.' "

The speaker then quoted from *Our Economic Society* by Tugwell and Howard C. Hill, in which the social waste of five hundred and forty thousand out of the six hundred thousand men engaged in the advertising racket is pointed out; in which it is shown that advertising tends to make people buy one instead of another kind of soap, not necessarily better; in which it is said advertising may ruin one and enrich another manufacturer, not because better or worse goods are offered but because of advertising; in which the Veblen theory of the closed market is explained, etc. The speaker quoted all these things but he did not explain them. He did not answer a single accusation. He merely held them up to view and mentally shuddered at the fact that such things can be uttered and printed in this great advertising age. What Mr. Palmer did say in refutation of these "false economic and social theories" of Tugwell, Chase, Hill and Veblen, was just this: "It is our opinion that the attempt to use our school system for this or any kind of propaganda is reprehensible and should be condemned."

The publishers of America then adopted a resolution urging extensive revisions in the Tugwell Bill, to ease restrictions on advertising, and to create a review board to consider appeals of advertisers.

Another great service from the publishers to the advertisers was the objection to the inclusion of the paragraph, "We subscribe to the principle of truth in advertising, and to this end shall not knowingly accept or publish an advertisement that is false or misleading in any particular," which the pure food and drug division of the Department of Agriculture sought to have inserted in the newspaper code.

During these months and years of excitement the publishers' weekly organ, *Editor & Publisher,* found itself in a tender spot. Immediately after the announcement of the new drug bill Editor Pew had said:

"If the bill is enacted, there will undoubtedly be less medical advertising, for many of the drug and cosmetic nostrums now being advertised would command no market if limited to an honest exposition of their intrinsic merits. They flourish on misrepresentation, and only the medical profession has any comprehensive idea of the vast damage they have done. The economic waste involved in the futile chase of health and beauty is estimated in the

millions annually, and the loss in newspaper revenue will
be trifling in comparison."

This sentiment, it soon proved, was about ninety per cent
opposed to that of a majority of Mr. Pew's subscribers and
supporters.

When the commotion reached a climax at the end of 1933,
Mr. Pew continued to print the economic and social views of
Secretary Tugwell. From *The Industrial Discipline* he quoted
the paragraph which had so aroused editorial fury throughout
the country:

> "Those industries which are faced with the necessity
> for lowering prices come to the point of trying various
> other alternatives for expanding the market and still
> maintaining the price level. A good deal of our elabora-
> tion of distributive processes is attributable to this kind
> of activity. Branding, elaborate packaging, inflated
> claims to special quality, with exaggerated ballyhoo, are
> all, more or less, attempts to escape the necessity of honest
> market expansion through decreased prices. *It is doubtful
> whether nine-tenths of our sales effort and expenses serves
> any good social purpose.*"

From Washington, Pew published reports of the activities
of the Federal Trade Commission in forcing discontinuance
or revision of false and misleading advertisements, chiefly
nostrums and beauty preparations, and the resultant saving of
millions of dollars a year by the public. In one year, 1932, it
was estimated by the commission that more than twenty thousand false and misleading advertisements had been discontinued entirely or revised "to check fairly with the truth."
The worst frauds were "perpetrated by those who prey on
the suffering of those of their fellows who are willing to try
anything to get relief from pain or the handicap of illness.
Millions of dollars are spent annually for preparations worthless or of doubtful value but advertised as being effective for
such uses as reducing flesh or building it up; removing

wrinkles, age lines, freckles, moles, warts, and the footprint of time; tinting or bleaching, and the like."

Frequently Mr. Pew published the names of newspapers which had been convicted, as, for example, the *Wichita* (Kansas) *Beacon,* fined five hundred dollars on each of five counts for printing false advertising, nor did he hesitate to name the makers of poisonous nostrums or their products.

In the gold-boom years advertisers were selling thirty-four million dollars' worth of face creams and rouge annually, twenty-five million dollars' worth of dentrifices, twenty-one million dollars' worth of talcum and other powders, twenty million dollars' worth of perfumes and nine million dollars' worth of hair tonics. The beauty business amounted to about one billion eight hundred million a year. A large part of its claim was fraudulent, a large part of its output was poisonous, but it flourished, thanks to advertising in the press, and silence in the press.

Psychology was raided for its useful commercial information by the advertising men. They learned how to capitalize fear and stimulate the battle with the inferiority feeling (wrongly called complex) of the millions whom they intimidated into buying advertised goods by threatening them with pyorrhea, athlete's foot, bad manners, halitosis, mispronunciation, abysmal ignorance, loss of memory and body odor.

It is a vicious business and the press is party to it. No newspaper, and very few other publications, have been willing to serve the public when it means the loss of money. The American Medical Association in its two periodicals, the *Journal,* which is intended for doctors, and *Hygeia,* for laymen, gives space every month to exposing this criminal assault upon the health and pocketbooks of the American people. The Association has also published *Nostrums and Quackery,* by Dr. Arthur J. Cramp, wherein "a fraud is called a fraud" and seven hundred products, many of them nationally advertised, are discussed; it has published nineteen complementary pamphlets priced at ten to thirty cents.

The reader who is interested in knowing the names of poisonous or harmful or useless patent medicines which our famous newspapers sponsor by accepting advertising, should purchase these publications. He should also buy the books *100,000,000 Guinea Pigs,* by Arthur Kallet and F. J. Schlink, *Skin Deep,* by Miss M. C. Phillips and *Your Money's Worth,* by Stuart Chase and F. J. Schlink, but after he has read them he had better subscribe to the Consumers' Research reports which are confidential and which grade all products made in the country, from lip sticks to automobiles, and show the worthlessness of a great part of all national advertising. Being confidential they go the limit within our libel laws. Messrs. Kallet and Schlink make this statement, which every investigation having the consumer, not the advertiser or newspaper in mind, has also reached, that "advertising is well known to be the mainstay of sales of fraudulent and dangerous drugs and adulterated and substitute foods."

What does it all amount to—in money? Millions of dollars a year. According to *Editor & Publisher* it affects forty-five per cent of the general advertising of the press. From this authority I give the following figures:

"Something like 45 per cent of the national advertising in city newspapers is for products covered by the provisions of the Copeland Bill, if one may judge by 1933 figures for ten cities from coast to coast, as measured by Media Records. Compilations for these ten cities show that 25.5 per cent of the general advertising was for groceries, which would be least affected by the bill. Medical advertising accounted for 9.9 per cent, and toilet requisites for 9.4 per cent of the general advertising.

"In addition, quantities of retail lineage placed by drug stores, department stores, groceries, toilet goods and beauty shops would come within the purview of the bill.

"Compilations of the Bureau of Advertising, A. N. P. A., on the amount of advertising done by leading firms only, showed the following expenditures in 1932 in fields covered by the measure:

"Druggists' sundries—45 firms spent $9,000,000 in newspapers, $2,908,596 in magazines, and $1,903,612 in broadcasting.

"Toilet goods—36 firms spent $9,705,000 in newspapers, $10,434,943 in magazines, and $3,472,536 in broad-casting.

"Foods—62 firms spent $17,460,000 in newspapers, $13,153,156 in magazines, and $7,344,764 in broadcasting.

"Soaps and cleaners—9 firms spent $2,845,000 in newspapers, $4,842,107 in magazines, and $691,677 in broadcasting.

"Soft drinks—9 firms spent $2,555,000 in newspapers, $866,995 in magazines, and $581,526 in broadcast time.

"The compilation, while not pretending to completeness, listed 342 advertisers of all kinds, who spent $116,200,000 in newspapers, compared with $52,301,139 in magazines, and $25,321,984 in broadcast time."

James Rorty, author of *Our Master's Voice: Advertising,* estimates the newspaper income from advertising at seventy-five per cent, and its total turnover at two billion dollars or more, making it one of the twelve large industries of America. He is of the opinion that truthful advertising generally does not sell goods as well as crooked advertising; that truthful advertising would mean the disappearance of nine-tenths of the traffic. Reviewing this book which he suspects may be the epitaph of advertising, Stuart Chase says of advertising, "The whole show is a rotten show; gaudy, costly, and rotten. The advertising business is inseparable, culturally, from the newspaper business, the magazine business, the movie business, the radio business. Together they spread a gigantic screen of misinformation, propaganda, half-truths, and plain loud lies on behalf of manufacturers, merchants, and financiers who have a plethora of goods and services to unload. There is little utility, comfort, art, beauty, integrity, or nourishment for the human spirit to be found anywhere in the picture."

To dismiss Rorty and Chase by calling them liberals or raising the red flag would not answer their strictures nor change the growing opinion of all intelligent people in America. Meanwhile there is still a feeble fight for a little reform—as much reform as the recipients of advertising money think good for the country. The Tugwell Bill was superseded by the

Copeland Bill. Of this event the Emergency Conference of Consumer Organizations published the following opinion: "The Fleischmann Yeast Company, probably to an extent greater than almost any other national advertiser, would be affected adversely by the original Tugwell Food and Drug Bill. This bill has been twice revised by Senator Royal S. Copeland, who is employed by the Fleischmann Yeast Company at a high fee in connection with its weekly advertising broadcast.

"The original Tugwell Bill was far too weak to afford adequate consumer protection, and the Copeland-revised Bill is so much weaker from the consumer viewpoint that it should be thrown out entirely and new legislation substituted. . . ."

Of course nothing can be done without a free press, and the free press is too busy looking after its freedom to fight the battle for the consumer.

So much for impure food and poison for the body; let us now consider the poison for the body politic—the propaganda machine of the public utilities of America.

CHAPTER IV

THE UTILITIES CORRUPT PRESS AND PUBLIC

> "The electric power industry has con-
> spired to corrupt the public mind. . . . The
> biggest news story since Teapot Dome has
> been played down by news services and
> newspapers."
>
> "The very wealthy and very dull *Wash-
> ington Star* with 36 pages that day, carried
> not a line. . . . Throughout the . . . Federal
> investigation . . . only a few papers have
> consistently covered these vitally important
> disclosures."
>
> "Most startling news since Teapot
> Dome . . . high priced efforts to suppress
> them . . . feebleness or venality of the
> newspapers. . . . It breaks my reporter's
> heart to see such a sizzling story going to
> waste."
>
> (The foregoing are newspaper men's
> stories not in newspapers but in liberal
> magazines; the following is from an ad-
> dress by a public utility director:)
>
> "There we are, brothers under the skin,
> utility and newspaper battling shoulder to
> shoulder. Our most important contact
> is . . . the American Newspaper Publishers'
> Association. . . ."

THE President of the United States is the author of the
charge that the privately owned utility corporations have
engaged "in a systematic campaign of misinformation, of
propaganda . . . of lies and falsehoods."

How and where was this campaign waged? In the press.
All the official testimony, all the confessions of the propaganda
chiefs agree that the press of the United States was the chief

means of spreading misinformation, propaganda, lies and false-hoods, as Mr. Roosevelt charges.

Whether the report made to me by a friend of the President will ever be published officially, is therefore of no matter; the report was, that as originally written, Mr. Roosevelt's charge did not end with the word "falsehood" but continued with several lines mentioning the press as its chief agency.

There were many other agencies, radio for instance, bill-boards, women's clubs, patriotic societies, the universities and the public schools, the subsidization of authors, notably Rich-ard Washburn Child (who had previously been accused by the *World* of being Mussolini's publicity boy)—in fact, every agency except skywriting.

But money talked loudest in the press: the propaganda and advertising fund used to corrupt the American mind was twenty-five million dollars to thirty million dollars a year. This amount was spent on our press.

The Federal Trade Commission has published fifty-two volumes of evidence, in a large part devoted to the newspapers of America. Not one but thousands are named. Is it any wonder then that throughout the hearings of the Federal Trade Commission and in November and December, 1934, when the findings were made public in six reports, they were "played down" or suppressed, that honest reporters' hearts were broken, as they themselves have written? Thousands of newspapers in the past five years failed to publish the testi-mony and many which published a little of it hid it in the back advertising pages. Neither man nor institution cares to confess "lies and falsehoods."

Yet this investigation has disclosed one of the biggest scandals in the history of the United States and certainly the greatest scandal in the history of the American press.

The investigation was originated by Thomas J. Walsh, Sen-ator from Montana; the subject of propaganda in the press was brought up by George W. Norris, Senator from Nebraska, and the plan to expose the suspected corruption was resisted by George H. Moses, Senator from New Hampshire. Robert M. La Follette, Jr., of Wisconsin, and Burton K. Wheeler, of

Montana, supported Walsh and Norris. The American Manufacturers' Association did its best to kill the investigation. Naturally enough the International Paper and Power Company, which several years later was exposed as owning a whole string of newspapers, also opposed.

But more important than this attempt by big business and certain senators to keep the facts from the American public was the opposition shown by the American Newspaper Publishers' Association.

When the Federal Trade Commission announced that one of the purposes of its investigation would be to show the practices of manufacturers of newsprint which allegedly tend toward monopoly and discriminate against publishers of small daily and weekly newspapers, the National Editorial Association announced its support. Said Senator Schall when he heard of this and the announced opposition of the all-powerful publishers' organization:

"The authorized spokesman for the newsprint manufacturers was present and ready to oppose the measure. The record of the hearing of Saturday, Feb. 9, contains the statement of Elisha Hanson, who appeared as the attorney for the International Paper Company in opposition to reporting the resolution. Mr. Hanson had previously appeared before the Committee on Agriculture as attorney for the American Newspaper Publishers' Association. At that time he declared: 'We think this particular investigation is unnecessary.' At this hearing, in response to my questions, Mr. Hanson denied that either former Senator Lenroot or himself represented the newsprint organization."

Preliminary to the taking of testimony, Senator Walsh characterized the electric light and power lobby as "the most formidable lobby ever brought together . . . representing capital to the amount of nearly $10,000,000,000."

In the opinion of Senator John J. Blaine, of Wisconsin, it was "the most powerful lobby in the history of the nation . . . both Republican and Democrat," headed by former

Senator Irvine L. Lenroot, of Wisconsin, and former Senator Charles J. Thomas, of Colorado. Senator Walsh feared that no action would follow the investigation "because it will dry up the source of campaign funds for the next election."

One of the greatest sensations sprung by the commission was the purchase of newspapers outright by the International Paper and Power Company. Immediately some editors demanded that the American Publishers' Association do something. But the investigation also showed that of ten or a dozen dominating publishers, two are directors of this corporation and four or five are also paper mill owners, several publishers are financed by the International, and a large number are tied up to banking interests which are part of the paper and power industry.

One of the powerful bankers—Albert H. Wiggin, chairman of the board of the Chase National Bank—was a director of the I. P. & P. The House of Morgan, the Bankers' Trust Company and other great banking institutions are connected with the power industry. Owen D. Young of this group was allied to the Mohawk-Hudson Power Company. Altogether it was shown in the hearings that connections exist between bankers, industrialists, power magnates and publishers.

The power interests divided the United States into twenty-eight districts and set up that many propaganda bureaus. The parent association was called NELA—National Electric Light Association—with George F. Oxley director of publicity. The money to corrupt the public mind was taken from the public. M. H. Aylesworth, managing director of the NELA, addressing a public relations conference said: "All the money being spent is worth while. . . . Don't be afraid of the expense. The public pays the expense."

The press was "reached," as one agent put it, by propaganda, paid and unpaid: paid advertising, "canned" editorials, clip-sheets, cartoons, photographs, boiler plate, news bulletins, but chiefly by the advertising millions. About one newspaper in ten refused utility money; every newspaper knew what the utilities expected in addition to advertising space. Very few newspapers were involved in the filth of Teapot Dome but a majority of the fourteen thousand or fifteen thousand dailies and weeklies published in America, according to evidence now published, took utility money.

The words blackmail and bribery, always alarming and open to challenge, were frequently used by the public utility officials and their propaganda and advertising agents in dealing with the press. Where publicly they made speeches about the "co-operation" of newspapers in "educating" the public to appreciate the "service" which the power and light companies were giving the American public, in their private correspondence and conversation they accused many newspapers of using blackmail to extract advertising and called many of their investments bribery.

With the Hearst and Scripps-Howard press the public utilities could do nothing: they realized that advertising in these fifty newspapers was purely advertising and would not get them very far, but with thousands of newspapers which were "on the fence" concerning public or private ownership, the case was different. Here it was purely a matter of money. If you paid the owners of the press they favored private ownership. If, on the other hand, you refused to pay, the newspaper most likely would favor public ownership.

But the papers which were considered as "blackmailing" the utilities were that portion, large or small, which, having the evidence of corruption of politicians, of exploitation of the public through high rates, of crookedness in watered stock, and other legally punishable crimes, would proceed to launch a campaign "for the benefit of the common people" unless the local power company and the national power trust came across with liberal advertising.

This will explain why, in many cities, newspapers frequently attacked the public utilities one year, and shut up the next. Once the "contact" was satisfactorily made, the newspaper which was in the springtime the champion of the "peepul," became by winter the upholder of rugged individualism of the private interests. The propaganda written in New York headquarters or in any one of the twenty-eight publicity bureaus appeared in these "converted" newspapers as editorials or news items. With them went beautiful photographs illustrating the benefits of private ownership, articles and pictures delivered as paper mats, as boiler plate, pamphlets, speeches, mimeographed releases, all in all millions of words and thousands of inches of illustrations favoring big business. Naturally, when the cost was out of proportion to the benefits, but based on fear of exposure or attack, business called this method blackmail and considered its expenditures bribery.

The greatest success in this magnificent field, James Rorty rightly points out, "was practical only with respect to the smaller and less powerful newspapers, just as it was only the less eminent professors who accepted fees. . . . Integrity, as Stuart Chase has pointed out, is a luxury in our civilization. It is, with certain qualifications, one of the privileges of wealth and power. No evidence was produced to show that the NELA had bribed the *New York Times.*"

In Missouri, however, the utilities claimed they got their propaganda into six hundred and ninety-nine newspapers, failing only in the *St. Louis Post-Dispatch,* according to the Federal Trade Commission's investigation.

The first ten of the fifty-two volumes of exhibits and testimony published by the Federal Trade Commission deal largely with the press. It would require a year to read and organize this evidence. On the first ten volumes my wife and I spent a full month. From the reports of the state propaganda committees we found that in addition to the six hundred and ninety-nine Missouri papers "reached," the propagandists also reported as follows from other states:

In Georgia, of two hundred and fifty newspapers, only four printed news or editorials favoring public ownership.

Four newspapers in Alabama held out against utility advertising and propaganda.

In North and South Carolina the *Raleigh News and Observer* was the only paper among three hundred unfriendly to power propaganda.

"Practically every daily uses some of the news stories," the Wisconsin bureau reported.

After years of propaganda and advertising the utilities obtained from two hundred and twenty-three Illinois editors a vote of one hundred and ninety-one against government ownership.

In Boston newspapers were bought by the power trust.

In New York City the owner of three big papers is listed as a mouthpiece for the utilities.

In reply to a questionnaire a majority of North and South Dakota editors agreed to run propaganda as editorials if paid for.

In Ohio, six hundred and twenty-five of seven hundred newspapers were "reached."

And so on through the forty-eight states. Summed up, the twenty-eight agencies claimed four-fifths of the American press used their propaganda. Allowing for exaggerations and reading the evidence, it is plain that the industry, capitalization seventeen billion dollars, with annual gross income of three billion dollars and thirty-three million clients, got, by the use of good-will and straight advertising, the support of the major portion of the press of the nation. This is what the testimony shows the papers did in return for money:

Attacked the federal power policy.
Attacked Muscle Shoals and Boulder Dam bills.
Attacked senators, representatives and other opponents of private power corporations.
Attacked state bills regulating the power companies.
Published false and misleading information concerning the operation of municipal and national plants.
Created a red scare whenever private corporation profits were menaced.

What was the ultimate purpose of the propaganda campaign? It was not merely to secure local support but to "change the public consciousness" as one of the agents reported. The reason was this: the owners realized long before a minority of the public became aware of it, that the great and inexhaustible source of power of the country is water power. When the first government plant was projected years ago Newton D. Baker, who oddly enough in 1934 appeared as a corporation attorney, said of hydroelectric plants:

"Whoever owns them in a large sense may be said to own the United States. If I were greedy for power over my fellow men I would rather control Muscle Shoals than be continuously elected President of the United States."

And that was exactly the plan of the utilities: to own the United States by owning its water power; to possess more power over their fellow men than the presidents; to obtain this business dictatorship over America by creating a favorable public opinion; by using every means, especially the press, to create this opinion.

In town and city, year after year, press and politicians debated public or private ownership of public utilities. Sometimes the enlightened public voted municipal ownership despite the opposition of the press. In the large cities where the Scripps-Howard or Hearst organization had a representative, that newspaper was usually the only one which presented the claims of public ownership truthfully. Rarely if ever was the public made aware of the fact that thousands of newspapers presenting the cause of private ownership were in the pay of the private corporations.

In the state of Washington the utilities and their big business allies spent more than one hundred and seventy-five thousand dollars to defeat the Bone Bill which gave municipalities the right to "sell and dispose of electric current to any other city or town, governmental agency or municipal corporation, or to any person, firm or corporation, inside or outside its corporate limits, and to purchase electric current therefrom."

In Washington, during the Nye-Vandenberg munitions hearings I talked to Senator Bone. He said: "I believe in public ownership. When I ran for the Senate the corporations and the newspapers, with the exception of the Scripps-Howard paper, were against me. I had two ways of getting the truth to the public: by mass meetings and by radio. At every meeting and through the small radio owned by a friend, I informed the voters of the state why the press opposed me. I was elected."

A large part of the utility ads placed nationwide is known as "good-will advertising." Its purpose simply is to obtain the good will of the publisher. In several states laws have been passed against this form of advertising because it is considered bribery. The utilities at numerous conventions held that editorial good will was a great asset. But good will may mean public corruption; through good will the propagandists hoped to change the public economic and social thought of America and direct it. These objectives, it was generally admitted at the hearings, were reached.

Specifically, the propaganda bureau obtained from the press support for its campaign against the American Government's policy of supplying power and light at a low price; it inspired the campaign against public ownership of all power plants, from that in the smallest town to Boulder Dam or Muscle Shoals.

Generally it was a campaign to uphold the big-business interests of the United States, the well-known trusts which since the time of Theodore Roosevelt have been subject to criticism and attack, the powers known as the capitalist system or Wall Street, or the Money Trust, or Plutocracy, or Special Privilege, the System, the Beast, or what you will by any other name. One need not be a radical or even a liberal to lend credence; a minimum of intelligence in reading the fifty-two-volume report shows the fact clearly.

Let us now look more closely at the machinery of public corruption and its action. It is not possible here as in Somerset House, London, for plain citizens to inspect the books of corporations, to find the ramifications of industry, the press, universities, the munitions makers, bribed authors, etc. In America it requires the powers of a Nye committee to open such books and even then it frequently meets Gibraltarian difficulties.

In the utilities-press connection sometimes there is a frank public announcement. Henry L. Doherty, president of Cities Service Company, for example, openly purchased the control of the *Journal-Post* of Kansas City for the purpose of defending his gas rates. In the federal inquiry, however, there were two extraordinary newspaper sensations, which—need one add?—got relatively little sensational publicity in the national press.

First, there was the case of Colonel Ira C. Copley who was known as a public utility man in Illinois and owner of the *Aurora Beacon,* the *Elgin Courier* and the *Joliet Herald-News.* Between January 1 and March 26, 1928, Copley acquired the following newspapers according to Exhibit No. 139 in the Federal Trade Commission publications:

"*Illinois State Journal,* acquired in December, 1927, and taken over by Colonel Copley on January 1, 1928.

"*San Diego Union* and *San Diego Tribune,* taken over on February 1, 1928. A corporation was formed, known as the Union Tribune Publisher Co., all the stock of which is owned by Colonel Copley.

"*The Independent,* of San Diego, was purchased by Colonel Copley on January twenty-fourth and he took possession thereof on January thirtieth and immediately merged it with the Union Tribune Co.

"On February sixteenth, announcement was made by the *Glendale Press* of the sale of itself and fourteen other southern California newspapers to Colonel Copley. The papers involved in this sale were owned by F. W. Kellogg and W. S. Kellogg and included:

Alhambra Post Advocate
Pasadena Evening Post
Monrovia Evening Post (edition of *Pasadena Evening Post*)

Glendale Daily Press

Eagle Rock Daily Press (edition of the *Glendale Daily Press*)

Burbank Daily Press (edition of the *Glendale Daily Press*)

Hollywood News

San Fernando Valley News (edition of the *Hollywood News*)

Santa Monica Outlook

Sawtelle Tribune (edition of the *Santa Monica Outlook*)

Venice Vanguard

Culver City Star News

Redondo Daily Breeze

Hermoso Daily Breeze (edition of *Redondo Daily Breeze*)

San Pedro Daily News

"Colonel Copley also purchased from W. C. McClure, the *Glendale Daily News* on February 14, 1928, and through Mr. McClure, the *San Pedro Pilot*. The *San Pedro Pilot* was merged with the *San Pedro Daily News*. The *Glendale Press* and *Glendale News* also were merged.

"Colonel Copley directed the organization of the Southern California Newspaper Association, of which Mr. McClure will be the president. This association will take in all of the papers in Los Angeles County as above named.

(Signed)   "John Callan O'Laughlin."

Exhibit No. 140 is a clipping from the *San Diego Evening Tribune,* the headline across the entire front page:

COL. IRA C. COPLEY BUYS UNION AND TRIBUNE.

It is followed by this statement from Colonel Copley: "I have no connection with any public utility anywhere and no connections with any other business than the newspaper business anywhere. . . ."

The Honorable Robert E. Healy, chief counsel for the commission, placed Colonel Copley's attorney, B. P. Alschuler, on the stand, who being duly sworn, on oath stated as follows:

"In January, 1928, the class B common stock of Western United Corporation, same being the majority of the stock of the company, was, through the transfer of the trustees' certificates under said voting trust, sold to Insull, Son & Co. . . .

"At the time of said sale and reorganization said Ira C. Copley exchanged preferred and common stock previously held by him for preferred stock of Western United Gas & Electric Co. and class A common stock of Western United Corporation. The said Ira C. Copley is at present in Europe . . .; to the best of this affiant's information, the said Copley is owner also of $1,000,000 in bonds of Western United Gas & Electric Co.; so far as this affiant knows, the said Ira C. Copley holds no stock or bonds of any other utility, nor has this affiant ever known of said Copley owning any such stock or securities.

"Question. Now during the year that Mr. Copley had those other papers here in Illinois it is true, isn't it, that he was interested in utility companies?

"Answer. Yes. . . .

"Question. Now to-day Mr. Copley owns certain interest in the Western United Gas & Electric Co., which is an operating company?

"Answer. Yes. . . .

"Question. But at the present time you know, don't you, that Mr. Copley owns 24,000 shares of the 6½ preferred stock of the Western United Gas & Electric which is the Electric Co.?

"Answer. Yes.

"Question. Having a total par value of $2,400,000?"

But the largest sensation of the investigation (1929) was contained in Exhibit No. 4270 which follows:

"International Paper and Affiliations' Interests in Newspapers.

Chicago Daily News: $250,000, preferred; 5,000 shares common.

Chicago Journal: $1,000,000 debentures of B.T.N. (Inc.) (Bryan-Thomason Newspapers); $600,000 preferred; 10,000 shares common, *Chicago Journal*.

Knickerbocker Press and *Albany Evening News* (both owned by Frank Gannett): $450,000 preferred; 3,000 shares common.

Boston Herald-Traveler: 10,248 shares common.

Brooklyn Eagle: $1,954,500 notes; 400 shares common of Brooklyn Daily Eagle Corporation, (another Gannett paper).

Hall & Lavarre: $855,000 notes (secured by stock of *Augusta Chronicle, Columbia Record*, and *Spartanburg Herald-Journal*). Contingent interest in *Ithaca Journal-News*: $300,000 notes.
April 30, 1929."

In addition, Exhibit No. 4328 showed that a holding company was proposed for the purchase of the *Cleveland Plain Dealer* "at a price in the neighborhood of $21,000,000, or such price as we may hereafter agree upon," but this paper refused to sell itself. Agents for the paper and power company apparently tried to buy up a number of the larger newspapers of the country, testimony being given that the following were also approached but refused to sell out:

Columbus Dispatch	Chain of "Booth" papers in
Kansas City Star	Michigan
Milwaukee Journal	Chain of "Star-League"
Detroit Free Press	papers in Indiana
St. Louis Globe-Democrat	*Minneapolis Star*
Boston Globe	*Buffalo Times*
Boston Post	*Dayton Herald*
Indianapolis News	*South Bend News-Times*
Cleveland News	*Atlanta Constitution*
Charlotte News (N. C.)	*Asheville Times* (N. C.)
	Macon Telegraph (Ga.)

To Mr. Hearst's *Boston American* goes the credit for first

reporting the case of the Boston newspapers. "Around the necks of the *Boston Herald* and the *Boston Traveler*," it said, "are two brand new brass collars bearing the stamp of the Power Trust."

Forty-eight hours after the federal exposure, Mr. Frank Gannett returned his loan of two million seven hundred thousand dollars. More recently the *Brooklyn Daily Eagle* passed out of his control.

The International Paper and Power Company, which said in self-defense that its purpose for buying the press was to secure outlets for its paper, was shown to be more a power than a paper company. In 1929 power was sixty-five per cent of its activity and in other years it was as high as seventy-five per cent.

After the scandal it sold out all holdings.

The *Nation* thought it strange that the American Newspaper Publishers' Association did not voice its protest and suspected that Mr. Thomason, the chairman of its paper committee, and Elisha Hanson, its lawyer who also represented the I. P. & P., had something to do with that. *Editor & Publisher*, however, demanded that Thomason and Hanson "resign connections with the newsprint organization."

A resolution condemning the paper and power company, presented by Colonel Robert Ewing, publisher of the *New Orleans States* and president of the Southern Newspaper Publishers' Association, at the convention of the American Newspaper Publishers' Association, was tabled. An amendment was offered by Mr. Thomason requesting all members to make known any financial connections with power and paper companies, banks or other outside institutions. "This amendment," reports *Editor & Publisher*, "was quickly tabled amid roars of amused laughter from the assembly."

The rest is silence.

Stephen Raushenbush was one of the first to take the place of the daily newspapers in informing the public about the hearings in Washington. In magazines, books and pamphlets he exposed corruption and the dereliction of the press. He also pointed out that the General Electric Company, Insull, the United Gas Improvement Company, Electric Bond and Share and the American Telephone and Telegraph Company directors subsidized a rural press service which reached fourteen thousand rural newspapers.

From the summary of the Commission's report we learn more about subsidized bureaus. It says in part:

> "In addition to direct contact with the press, the report shows so-called newspaper news and editorial services were given financial support by the utilities and that generally there was no disclosure to the public of this support. The list included:
> E. Hofer & Sons, Portland, Ore.
> Utilities Publication Co. and Public Service Magazine, Chicago.
> Public Utilities Reports, Inc., Rochester, N. Y.
> Darnell's Newspaper Service, Florence, Ala.
> National Industrial Conservation Board, Inc., Chicago.
> Dixie Magazine, Little Rock, Ark."

The Hofer bureau was in touch with Electric Bond and Share Company. Its purposes, as expressed by its head, were: "First, to reduce the volume of legislation that interferes with business and industry; second, to minimize and counteract political regulation of business that is hurtful; third, to discourage radicalism by labor organizations and all sorts of agitators; fourth, a constant fight for reasonable taxation by state, city, and county government; fifth, a scientific educational campaign against all socialistic and radical propaganda of whatever nature."

The amount of money supplied by the power companies, according to Mr. Hofer, was eighty-four thousand dollars a year. With that sum about fourteen thousand weekly and daily newspapers were propagandized.

The Darnell Newspaper Service supplied six hundred newspapers, mostly in Alabama, Georgia, Mississippi and Florida, with "news" attacking Boulder Dam, Muscle Shoals and government interference in private business. Although Darnell objected to the statement that he was employed by power companies, evidence was given that his bureau was heavily supported by the Alabama Power Company.

Now let us consider briefly some examples of editors, publishers and newspaper men in their relations with the propaganda fund. One of the most remarkable documents deals with the secretary-treasurer of the Republican Editorial Association of Missouri. Here is one of the letters to the head of the Missouri propaganda bureau found in the files seized by the government:

"Dear Friend Sheridan. . . . Have not had any advertising from the Missouri Power and Light Company . . . for two months now.

"When this aggregation wanted a franchise they promised me support and advertising if I helped them. I did help them and now they have a fresh upstart who says he knew nothing about our helping the company and that they have no advertising for our paper. . . .

"If you can do anything to line this bunch up for our paper, wish you would help me. Would hate to have to prove that I was wrong in supporting their franchise move, but I can show up conditions which will look bad if I must.

"Incidentally, I wish you would furnish me with any data you have regarding rates for lighting . . . electric power, and gas . . . in each city of Missouri. . . . I want to start an educational campaign on the rates. . . ."

The letter is signed by Charles W. Fear, editor of the *Missouri Trades-Unionist*. Editor Fear was doubly useful to Mr. Sheridan: he was obviously publishing a paper which represented the views of labor, and labor is generally on the side of city or government ownership; and as the executive officer of the editorial association he was in touch with and could influence every Republican editor in the state.

And here, for example, is the case of the president of the National Editors' Association in deadly parallels:

Statement by Walter M. Harrison, President of the American Society of Newspaper Editors, managing editor *Daily Oklahoman* and *Oklahoma City Times:*

"No editor who uses his newspaper to promote his own interests or the interest of a public utility, private corporation or politician, from which he receives bribes in money, jobs or favors, is worthy the name. . . . I am not afraid of your propaganda. . . . I know propaganda when I see it. . . . The public utilities of the nation spent $25,000,000 in advertising in 1927. I hope every dollar of it was purchased on a business basis. If you spent a dollar for advertising copy to sweeten a local editor in the hope of getting him to help your local franchise on his editorial page you were a sap and you offered an insult to the whole newspaper profession. Editors are not bought with advertising. This statement goes for 95% of the metropolitan press. Any suggestion to the contrary causes me to question the intelligence of the man who makes it. . . ."

Statement by Carl D. Thompson, fighter for public ownership, based on the first reports of the federal investigation into the corruption of the press by the public utility advertising and propaganda fund:

"The news letters of the (Oklahoma Public Service) information bureau were often used by the local newspapers as editorials. Their leading items often appeared in the larger newspapers as, for example, in the *Oklahoma City Daily Oklahoman* and the *Tulsa Daily World,* the largest papers in Oklahoma." (From Thompson's "Confession of the Power Trust.")

But the best "human interest story" revealed in the fifty-two volumes concerns reporters who quit their jobs for propaganda work. They make ten to twenty-five thousand a year and the twenty-five-dollar-a-week reporters envy them. "If," they say, "we are going to be journalistic prostitutes, why not get paid for it?" Well, this story shows the struggle in the mind of at least one highly paid "journalistic prostitute." It concerns J. B. Sheridan, whom we have already met in the Missouri NELA bureau. Mr. Sheridan had been reporter, editorial writer, dramatic critic. An intelligent, sensitive, superior type of newspaper man who had had ideals. But fifteen thousand dollars is a lot of money. Mr. Sheridan took it.

But, whereas my own experience as a police reporter taught me that the street-walker has little or no moral conscience left, the journalistic ditto, in the words of General Johnson, is always afflicted with ants of conscience. Every reporter I know dreams of editing a really free newspaper some day.

Mr. Sheridan did his corporation work but hated it secretly. To the Insull bureau he wrote that "my great ambition is to get rid of all municipal plants in Missouri," but to a fellow newspaper man he wrote, "The man who invented private ownership was a mortal enemy of the human race."

Here are more extracts from the letters between Sheridan and his friend John W. Colton, editor of *Aera,* the magazine of the American Electric Railway Association. In the first Sheridan quotes the Biblical injunction which many another journalist has used: "What profiteth it for a man to gain the whole world if he loses his own soul" (the phrasing is his), and concludes by stating his renewed courage and faith in government by the people.

Mr. Colton replies that he feels very much disillusioned, that it is fear that makes hypocrites of men; he has found among his associates "cheap, lying politicians," and he too repeats the lost-soul expression.

Still more radical and Christ-like is Sheridan's next letter, which states that "possession of property breeds liars and cowards." For thirty years on the St. Louis newspapers Sheridan felt he was a free man; of the five years' work for the public utilities, he says "I held my tongue." But he is going to resign. "Now I mean to resume the greatest of human rights—that of free speech."

Mr. Colton then speaks from his heart about the big-business corporations of America. "The thing about the utility industry that disgusts me," he writes, "is the lying, trimming, faking and downright evasion of trust, or violation of trust, that marks the progress toward enormous wealth of some of the so-called big men in the industry. When I see some of these fellows waving the flag, I am filled with not only disgust but rage, for they are anything but patriots. I do not know whether I am going to stay in the utility industry or not. I would thoroughly enjoy fighting some of these faking patriots through the editorial page of an influential newspaper. . . ."

Whether Mr. Colton resigned or not I do not know. But in April, 1930, the newspapers carried the story of the death of J. B. Sheridan, public utility propagandist, ex-newspaperman. He had hanged himself.

And here is another confidential letter which tells exactly what the propagandists think of the men who take their money and sell out the public: "Gee, Mr. Buck," wrote one of the agents to his chief, "what the country press is worth to people who are honest and use it honestly is beyond calculation. I have spent as much as $300 in three years 'entertaining' editors. . . . All of them are God's fools, grateful for the smallest courtesy. . . . If we could stimulate a little local advertising for some of the leading newspapers, I think we will have the newspapers and the operators so closely associated that it will be impossible to split them in the near future."

In the newspapers of the United States there has been almost no mention of the fact that the Associated Press has been dragged not once but dozens of times into the investigation of the public utilities. The jig-saw picture of this great organization made up of all these references is not a pleasant one. But it is the same picture you get when you put together the facts that the Associated Press has employed ultra-Fascists to report on Fascism, strike-breakers to report on strikes, army and marine officers to report on the "traitors" they were fighting in Nicaragua and Haiti, and reactionaries to report movements for political justice and freedom throughout the world.

Yet it is a surprise even to newspaper men to hear the officially hired propaganda agents testifying that they are also on the pay roll of the great, free, independent and infallible Associated Press. It is no doubt also a shock to the honest members of that organization.

"The Associated Press sends out practically everything we give them," reported Missouri propaganda agent (Exhibit 2962). "I am still connected with the A. P." wrote his Texas colleague (Exhibit 2021) who added he could help to put things over for his pal in New Orleans. The Detroit correspondent of the Associated Press not only handled the propaganda from the Michigan bureau but was careless enough to write a letter acknowledging the fact (Exhibit 3184). "Whenever we have had occasion to use the Associated Press our material has gone over with a batting average of 1.000 . . ." wrote H. Lee Jones, director of the Kansas bureau. "The Associated Press here has often taken stories from the Utilogram, our news bureau, and sent them throughout the state without any suggestion from this office." And so on.

On February 15, 1933, the greatest propaganda machine in the history of the United States was officially dismantled by the decision of the fifty member-directors assembled in convention. The NELA ceased to exist.

George B. Cortelyou, president of the NELA, president of the Consolidated Gas Company of New York, was immediately elected president of the Edison Electric Institute, which replaced the NELA. The Edison institute's constitution specifies it must not engage in propaganda. Its publicity statements "shall be accurate and clearly indicate their source."

According to the *New York Times* the new association was formed "with the purpose of purging the industry of evils that have grown up in some companies, such as the looting of operating companies by holding companies, the publication of inaccurate and obscure financial statements and the use of questionable propaganda and lobbying methods."

In November and December, 1934, the President of the

United States, Mr. Frank Walsh, chairman of the New York Power Authority, and the Federal Trade Commission, in the press of the country, brought the power issue to the people. The President and Mr. Walsh spoke for public ownership; the federal commissions exposed the corruption paid for by the utilities. How did the press react to these moves?

November twelfth and thirteenth all the New York papers carried the report that the people of the state were paying double what was fair for power and light. The liberal papers carried page lines; the conservative *Times* carried a one-column head on the front page as follows:

SURVEY CONTENDS
RATES FOR POWER
COULD BE HALVED

The first paragraph read:

"Washington, Nov. 12.—The cost of distributing electric power in New York State warrants rates only slightly above half the average now prevailing there, according to a voluminous report, representing three years of research, by the Power Authority of New York State, made public at the White House today. . . ."

Almost immediately thereafter came an editorial saying in part:

"Mr. Walsh's Latest.
"Frank Walsh . . . loves to sit in a golden chair and 'splash at a ten-league canvas with brushes of comets' hair' . . . cynics will be inclined to lump that $194,000,000 of promised savings with the 18,500 men the sanguine Mr. Walsh once hoped to have at work on the banks of his favorite river by Christmas, 1931."

November fourteenth the *World Telegram* published under a three-column head on page one, the story beginning:

"In the first section of its report to Congress on utility publicity and propaganda activities the Federal Trade Commission described today a nationwide campaign which, according to the testimony of a utility chieftain himself, included practically every known means of publicity except 'sky writing.'

"Censorship of school books, contacts with the press . . . etc."

The *New York Post* likewise had a large story on the front page.

The *Times* ran its story on page thirty-one, November fifteenth.

Cautiously it said that "a statement·that a campaign of 'propaganda' [in quotes] has been carried on by gas and electrical companies, rivaled in magnitude only by that of governments in wartime, was made today by the Federal Power Commission in a report to the Senate. . . . For the years 1928 to 1932 inclusive, its [the NELA] budget and expenditures were each in excess of $1,000,000, the commission declared. . . ."

November twenty-third the *Times* again placed the news of the publication of the second part of the report in its back pages. However, it did mention the thirty million dollars a year spent for advertising and quoted the following conclusions of the investigators:

"The press leads in its direct effect upon the present adult population. The schools lead in molding the opinions of coming generations. Accordingly we find the most widespread and thorough planning and attention to the publicity given to these two greatest opinion-making factors.

"When it is understood that the newspaper or magazine is practically a by-product of advertising, and that inherently advertising expenditures therefor frequently carry a certain element of good-will response from recipients, the large total spent by utilities for advertising is relevant.

"To carry out its intentions and assist in preparation of material, many prominent writers and speakers were engaged by the joint committee. Among this number, Richard Washburn Child received $7,500 for preparing two books on Boulder Dam, which were edited and published by Dr. Frank Bohn of the *New York Times*. Sixteen copies of this work were printed.

"(Editor's Note—Frank Bohn is not a member of the staff of the *New York Times*. Previous to 1928 he contributed articles to the Sunday *Times* occasionally.)

"Among many articles reprinted for distribution the report mentioned one in *The Annalist* entitled 'Why Government Fails in Business,' by Arthur S. Dewing, Professor in Finance in the Harvard School of Business, of which it said 15,000 copies were made available to the mailing list, except newspaper syndicates, the Investment Bankers' Association and Congress."

But on November twenty-sixth the *Times* had a front page item telling its believers the big news that the Edison Electric Institute had opened up war on President Roosevelt! Heading:

UTILITIES OPEN WAR
ON POWER PROGRAM
OF ADMINISTRATION
Edison Institute Threatens Court Attack on
Roosevelt Projects as Illegal

The *World Telegram* had a two-column head reporting the third part of the committee's report and the *Post* carried a full-page streamer on page two describing the shower of gold for propagandizing in the schools.

Again, on December 6, 1934, the section of the report dealing with the holding companies, showing profits "running over 100 per cent in relation to the cost of the service rendered," explaining that this money came from the ultimate consumer and contending that the corporations defended their enormous profits by the publicity campaign, was placed by the *Times* on page thirty-three.

On December eleventh the final report was filed. It stated

that billions of dollars were lost by American investors due to the public utilities securities sales methods.

Of course the utilities have made a few reforms. Reforms or no, the national government and the governments of states, notably New York, have taken the offensive. Only a very small part of the American press has shown itself on the side of the public. The majority remains the friend of the corporations which official testimony proves mulct the public. But it is more than a matter of light prices; it is, in the view of Governor Pinchot of Pennsylvania, the control of the destiny of the country through the "control of political assembly from the Congress to the smallest town meeting: their power reaches to the national government itself."

Nor is there any new reason for optimism. The journalistic cheers for the "reform" of the Edison bureau are either premature or propaganda in themselves. It is apparently playing the NELA game with variations. It still hires professors to write "factbooks" for colleges. In 1935 the flood of utilities propaganda against the holding company bill surpassed almost everything in NELA history.

In 1935, also, the Hearst press began the publication of editorials denouncing the government-sponsored bill. Mr. Hearst gave the signal by signing the first, and after that all the Hearst hired men echoed the thoughts of the sage. From now on the Hearst press can no longer be listed among the "protectors of the public interests" and the advocates of public ownership which Hearst made part of his reform program some four decades ago.

President Roosevelt has denounced the lies and falsehoods of the utilities. The many-million-dollar lie and falsehood and advertising fund is still functioning today. And we have learned two lessons: that the majority of the American press disregarded its duty and its code of ethics when it took utility money, and that when President, governors, the Federal Commission, exposed the failure, little or no change in the attitude of the press toward the utilities followed.

CHAPTER V

A SMUDGE OF OIL

Sure. I'm a crook! I'm a blackmailer.
What are you going to do about it?—H. H.
TAMMEN (half-owner of the *Denver
Post*).

LOCALLY the Pittsburgh graft cases were, in my time, considered the biggest exposures of corruption; nationally, older generations knew that the Tweed Gang gave America a measuring rod for public graft, and now Teapot Dome holds first place in this unfortunate classification. This last was a much more dramatic affair than the recently ended public utilities investigation; it involved big names, public officials, women; it had all the elements of good newspaper stories. It was much more satisfactory.

In Pittsburgh the names of reporters, publishers and newspaper owners were dragged into the hearings frequently but there was not a single mention of these facts in the seven newspapers. In the Tweed case the *Times*—being then a crusading newspaper—earned journalistic immortality by initiating and winning the fight against corruption. In Teapot Dome another situation was created: newspapers figured prominently in both actions, exposure of corruption and suppression of the news; they were both the champion of the readers and the betrayer of their duty.

First honors must be given to Carl C. Magee. Whatever his personal interest may have been, no matter what local feuds he had in hand, the fact is that Editor Magee took the initiative in exposing that well-known ex-convict then member of the Harding Cabinet, Albert B. Fall, and the robbery of the American public by the Ohio gang.

In 1920 E. L. Doheny and Leo Stack asked Secretary of the Navy Josephus Daniels for a lease of some wells between

101

Naval Reserve No. 3 and the Salt Creek field, in Wyoming. Daniels refused. His successor, as navy head in the Harding Cabinet, was Denby, but one of the first tricks of the Harding administration was to transfer the oil reserves to the Interior Department, presided over by the man who had tried in 1920 to bring the United States into war with Mexico so that his commercial interests might flourish. Secretary of the Interior Fall leased the oil fields to Harry F. Sinclair.

Mr. Stack, who had had an agreement with the Pioneer Oil Company and who was now out in the cold, remorseless commercial world, enlisted the aid of the Denver czar and people's friend. Mr. Bonfils, who two years earlier had told an assistant editor who had the first tip on the subject to "forget all about it," now utilized his famous "So The People May Know" column to declare that "Sinclair and his associates have received a gift . . . of oilfields . . . through trickery that verges . . . on the bounds of crime."

The reader will probably remember that Fall's exposure came about through the discovery that the impoverished Senator's New Mexico ranch was found one day transformed into a land flowing with milk and limousines. Gene Fowler claims it was Bonfils who made the first investigation, who learned the truth, and who kept it to himself and used it for blackmail. But it was Magee who got the tip which started everything. He was then editing the *Albuquerque Morning Journal.* His local political enemy for years had been New Mexico's Senator, Fall, who was also in control of one of the most corrupt state political organizations in our history. Magee began his attack by showing up the mishandling of the permanent school funds obtained from the sale of public lands and given the state by the Federal Government. This money, instead of being deposited in banks drawing interest, was placed in political banks drawing none.

Magee soon found that instead of paying interest the school-fund banks contributed large sums to Fall's party treasury. He also exposed the fact that the copper companies paid no taxes but contributed their money to the Fall machine. This publication at last roused Fall.

Up to then he had had no fear from the free press. When Bronson N. Cutting, editor of the *Sante Fe New Mexican,* had had his fight with the Fall gangsters, the latter instituted a civil libel suit for thirty-five thousand dollars against him and obtained a thirty-day sentence for contempt of court. Several editors of Spanish language papers also ventured to criticize Fall, were indicted for criminal libel in the district court of San Miguel County and informed they must either take jail terms or cease attacking the gang. They accepted the latter and were heard no more.

Fall now came to Magee with a demand to "lay off." Magee laughed at him. Immediately suits were filed on all of Magee's notes held by the same political banks which had the school funds. Despite the fact Magee arrived in court with the full amount of cash in his hands a receivership was asked for the *Journal.* The attorney for the bank said:

"We still ask for receivership. We admit that it will do us no good, but it will do the defendant harm."

Magee then appealed to the readers of the *Journal* to buy the bonds of this newspaper and in twenty days sixty thousand dollars was subscribed for the purpose of fighting the Fall gang.

One day Harry Sinclair visited Fall. Very soon money began to fly around the Fall ranch. Magee was suspicious. When Senators Kendrick and La Follette voiced their suspicions in the Senate about the drilling Sinclair was doing on the Teapot Dome naval reservation, Magee went to Senator Walsh and gave him the information he had. He then went to Washington and told his story to the Senate Investigating Committee.

Fall meanwhile obtained Magee's conviction on the charge of criminal libel. Judge Leahy tried and convicted him before a jury of Spanish-Americans not one of whom, according to Magee, spoke or understood English. Leahy sentenced Magee to a year in jail and a fine of four thousand and fifty dollars. But the readers of the *Journal* came to his defense in an appeal to Governor Hinkle. Hinkle pardoned Magee. Judge Leahy then tried Magee on one after another of the old contempt cases, sentenced him, and had each sentence nullified by a pardon from the Governor.

In 1924, Magee had the satisfaction of campaigning against Leahy and winning. In 1925, while Magee was sitting in the lounge of the Meadows Hotel at Las Vegas, Leahy came up from behind and assaulted him. After knocking Magee sense-less ex-Judge Leahy continued to kick him. When, some time later, Magee recovered consciousness, he fired his re-volver at Leahy but killed a friend who was coming to the rescue. He was tried for murder and acquitted.

So much for one fighting editor. Now consider another type.

Fred G. Bonfils and H. H. Tammen, owners of the *Denver Post,* having heard about the Magee charges, published one sensational story. Then Tammen went to see Harry Sinclair. On November 5, 1922, the *Denver Post's* rival, the *Rocky Mountain News,* published a long story with the headline:

"TEAPOT DOME SCANDAL NICELY HUSHED

"Fulsome praise in place of vitriolic attacks [said the *News*] will be the lot hereafter of Harry Sinclair, oil magnate, in the *Denver Post,* for, in the vernacular of the street, the *Post* owners have 'got theirs' in the Teapot Dome deal in oil lands in Wyoming. There are reports current that the tempest in the Teapot has been stilled by dollars. . . . Stack immediately charged that in plain language he had been 'double crossed' in the deal. His contention was that Blackmer, Doheny and Sinclair had conspired together to beat him out of his contract. . . . he refused (to withdraw his complaint) asserting that the Teapot Dome lease, known as the Stack lease, as it had been obtained in his name, was worth $100,000,-000. . . . Now is where F. G. Bonfils and H. H. Tammen, owners of the *Denver Post,* come in on the play. Stack, realizing that he had a hard fight on his hands and was opposed by many millions of dollars, looked around for backing and also publicity. His deal with Bonfils was that he was to receive the first $100,000 paid and the rest over his $100,000 was to be divided 50-50 with Bonfils. . . . Bonfils played true to form. The columns of the *Denver Post* opened the first week in June last its vitriolic attacks upon Sinclair, Secretary of the Interior Fall and even President Harding. . . ."

In the Senate Investigating Committee's report it is stated that Sinclair settled the suit by paying a quarter of a million dollars, agreeing to pay seven hundred and fifty thousand dollars more when the newspaper stopped its attacks.

Among the newspapers which exposed the blackmail plot of Tammen and Bonfils were the *St. Louis Post-Dispatch,* the *St. Louis Globe-Democrat,* the *Kansas City Star* and the *South Carolina Columbia State.*

The American Newspaper Editors' Society committee on ethics investigated Bonfils and Tammen, reported gross violation of the code of ethics but also the fact that the blackmailing was done in 1922, a year before the committee on ethics had been formed! It refused to act. Bonfils resigned. The Associated Press heard the blackmail discussed but within a year and despite the facts, issued one of its invaluable franchises to the two gentlemen.

According to Frank Vanderlip a period of twenty-two months elapsed between the date of the signature of the Elks Hills oil leases and the first mention of the oil scandal in the general press of the country. It is also to be noted that Senator La Follette made the most direct accusations, and that his name was rarely if ever mentioned as the instigator of the Senate investigation. La Follette until his death remained on the "son-of-a-bitch list" of a great number of papers.

It is also interesting to see how the Associated Press treated the matter of the Elks Hills reserve lease to Doheny. The night wire of December 14, 1922, began:

"A huge fuel supply for the Pacific Fleet will be built up, an extensive tract of country developed and facilities for handling oil increased, and the government will get immediate benefit of royalties from Naval Reserve No. 1 in California as a result of the extension today of a contract between the government and the Pan-American

Petroleum & Transport Co., it was said after the announcement of the changes made by Secretary Denby."

On page 1631 of the Walsh committee report the entire eight-hundred-word A. P. dispatch may be found, cheering the transaction and allaying the doubts which might have arisen over the La Follette exposure made in May, 1922, the month following the date on the first leases. More than one thousand papers received the A. P. story. The *Los Angeles Times* ran a headline:

OIL ASSURED FOR FLEET

It was loyalty or ignorance, perhaps both, which motivated President Harding. Certain newspapers did publish the attacks of Kendrick and Walsh; the liberal weeklies and his own magazine printed the charges by La Follette; a few newspapers hostile to the Republican administration were picking up Magee's suspicions. At his regular press conference President Harding was asked about attacks on Daugherty; he replied, they are being made by "political blackmailers"; he cautioned the American press to "put on the brakes" in dealing with the oil scandal.

Senator Caraway denounced Fall and Ned McLean of the *Washington Post*. The *New York Times* called Caraway a Bombastes Furioso. On February 10, 1924, the owner of this great newspaper, commenting on Lewis Gannett's exposure in the *Nation* of the corruption of the French press by Tsarist gold, said, "Fortunately American newspapers, with whatever faults and defects they may have been charged, are not open to the accusation of venality." On February ninth Bonfils had confessed in Washington that he had obtained two hundred and fifty thousand dollars from Sinclair upon promise to stop his exposure. Senator Dill used the word blackmail for the Denver proceedings. March thirty-first the *Times* said editorially:

"A few Senators at Washington have borne themselves like men who at heart are enemies of lawful and orderly government. They profess to be engaged in the laudable effort to uncover corruption. . . . But they make it seem that their real purpose is to paralyze the Administration, to terrorize members of the cabinet, to break down the efficiency of the government." It called the investigators "scandalmongers and assassins of character." On the twelfth of April when Andrew Mellon was mentioned in the hearings, the *Times* said this was "one more step in the movement which will have the effect, if not the design, of throwing the government into disorder and demoralizing those charged with the duty of conducting the public business."

Doheny some time later realized that public opinion on the Elks Hills and Teapot Dome cases was decidedly against him. He sent word "indirectly," says the *Nation,* to the *Times.* The *Times* sent a man to the west coast to see and stay with Doheny for a while. The great paper which thought the Washington disclosures unimportant gave thirteen full-length columns to Mr. Doheny's thoughts and meditations. One learned that Mr. Doheny had developed the Elks Hills field out of pure patriotism. Gone was the thought, which he once let slip on the witness-stand, that he might make one hundred million dollars out of the lease; and utterly missing from the story— at his lawyer's behest—was the little black satchel in which he sent one hundred thousand dollars to his old pal, Albert Fall. The entire Cabinet, he said, had sanctioned the leases— as to that either Mr. Doheny is in error or Messrs. Hughes and Coolidge fibbed. Naval officers begged him to get out the oil and save America. War threatened, and we were in a parlous state. As the *World* promptly noted, the Washington-conference treaties were signed before the leases, and the brashest naval officer could no longer breathe fire. The whole story is simply tosh—the most interesting thing about it is the enthusiasm of the *Times* to give Mr. Doheny thirteen columns of free advertising."

What was the purpose of all these editorials in the most powerful newspaper in America? The *Times* is nominally a Democratic newspaper, but not a member of that part of the political press which uses all weapons to fight the opposition.

No one would dream of connecting the *Times* with any person or institution involved in the Fall case. But the Fall case had become more than a financial scandal, it was now the equal of the scandal which involved the French press, the French Government and the Russian Government. In other words, it was an attack on government itself. It was an exposure of the corruption of not only certain newspapers but our whole political business system.

A *Brooklyn Daily Eagle* reporter interviewed Mr. Ochs and published this statement: "I know that here on the *Times* we are very careful of the accuracy of our news. . . . We had early information concerning the oil scandals, but we would not print one word about them until the reports were confirmed at Washington. I could mention numerous instances to you. The point I am making is that a responsible newspaper is always very careful to see that the news it publishes is true."

To which Silas Bent, journalist, admirer of the *Times* and critic of the press, comments: "This 'responsible' newspaper, however, not only betrayed its public by refusing to investigate this public scandal; after a Senate 'smelling' committee had fortuitously discovered the facts, and had forced them into the light, the *Times* attempted to howl down the investigation with derision and denials."

The epitaph to oil is written by Paul Y. Anderson, who has been and remains my ideal of a Washington correspondent. In discussing the propaganda in the press against Congress and congressmen, he notes that it began against the Senate simultaneously

> "with the oil investigations conducted by Senator Walsh and the investigation of the Department of Justice conducted by Senator Wheeler. In the light of what has occurred since, I dare say few editors will relish being remembered as defenders of Fall, Sinclair, Doheny, Daugherty, Jess Smith, and 'the little Green House on K Street.' Nevertheless, it was the *New York Times* which described Walsh and Wheeler as 'the Montana mud gunners' when they undertook to expose the unspeakable frauds which had been perpetrated against the nation and

the unutterable rottenness which existed at the very heart of the government. And the language employed by the *Times* was temperate and fair beside that which appeared in the *Washington Post, Philadelphia Public Ledger,* and other large molders of public opinion.

"The oil thieves and the Ohio Gang have long ceased to be objects of editorial solicitude, but the campaign of calumny launched in their behalf against the Senate has never faltered since Senator La Follette's proposal to investigate the Teapot Dome lease was denounced as 'a fishing expedition,' and Wheeler's motion to examine the official conduct of Harry Daugherty was solemnly condemned as 'an attempt to embarrass President Coolidge' and to 'desecrate a shroud.' Always the tender-hearted editors have been able to discover some new subject to be defended against senatorial 'outrage.' In turn the tariff lobbyists, the post office promoters, the armorplate manufacturers, the recipients of large tax refunds, the radio buccaneers, the 'yellow dog' contractors and the power pirates have inherited the fountains of editorial pity and protection which originally gushed for Fall and Daugherty."

—and for the *status quo,* big business, and men in power.

CHAPTER VI

BIG BUSINESS AND THE PRESS

THERE would be no reason for this chapter if the newspapers of the world admitted, as William Allen White of the *Emporia Gazette* recently did, that journalism was once a profession, "a noble calling; now it is an 8 per cent investment and an industry."

Not even the seven corrupt newspapers of my Pittsburgh years, however, would admit they were purely business propositions. My own *Leader* was the People's Friend; the *Press* was the clarion of the masses, the conservative papers owned by Banker Given and Senator Oliver and Colonel Rook proclaimed their public service every day, and without exception they published the news as the Pittsburgh bankers, coal, iron and steel interests and politicians affiliated with these interests, dictated.

If these seven newspapers had not pretended to be newspapers, observing a code of ethics, maintaining the honesty and integrity which belonging to a profession connotes—if they had published, as house organs do, an announcement that they represented the Union Trust Company (Mellon) interests, or Farmers National Bank (Given) interests, or the Pennsylvania Railroad and the U. S. Steel Corporation, affiliated with these banks—there could be no reason for criticism.

But there are still many other angles for viewing this problem of the commercialization of the press, the interrelationship between publishing and stockholding, the multimillionaire publisher who may not own stock in any corporation but his own, and the economic system of which he is a part and which he is pledged to preserve.

The present economic trends, the merger of commercial interests, when they include newspapers, according to William

Allen White, can be summed up in the word "bad." In the last thirty years, he says, newspapers

> "have veered from their traditional position as leaders of public opinion into mere peddlers and purveyors of news. . . . The newspapers have become commercial enterprises and hence fall into the current which is merging commercial enterprises along mercantile lines.
>
> "As the newspaper's interest has become a mercantile or industrial proposition, the dangers of commercial corruption of the press become greater and greater. The power trust of course is buying the newspapers in order to control the old vestige of leadership, the remaining fragment of professional status that still remains in the newspaper business.
>
> "As a commercial enterprise the newspaper is yielding good returns for investment.
>
> "But as a political weapon it is worth to self-seeking service corporations hundreds of dollars in under-cover influence where it is worth dollars in direct returns. If this country turns from a democracy into a Hamiltonian plutocracy, it will be because the moral sense, moral intelligence, and moral courage of the American people are sapped at the roots by insidiously corrupt plutocratic influence undermining the sources of courage and intelligence which has been so ably represented by the American press in other generations. Unless democracy is indignant at the encroachments of plutocracy, democracy cannot fight. When plutocracy destroys the sources of information which should make indignation, plutocracy has paralyzed democracy. But it is no sudden thing. It is a part of the tendency of the times. I do not know the answer."

Without giving a definite answer, let us continue the documentation of the influence of big business on the press which we have already seen in department-store advertising, food and drug activities, oil interests, and the utility propaganda system. The railroads, the packers, the coal and steel corporations and the bankers have left behind them a trail just as interesting if not as open.

When Lee M. Russell was elected governor of Mississippi
it was on the inevitable Democratic platform; never has he
been accused of being a liberal, let alone a radical. ₄Here is
what Governor Russell during his incumbency wrote on the
subject of this chapter heading:

"I have noticed throughout the nation for many years
the unmistakable signs that the money power of this
government was controlling the policy of the press. It is
rare indeed to see a journal with any circulation and with
any standing that would dare to speak out in behalf of
the great masses of the people. From the first along to
the last there is unmistakable evidence that these papers
are subsidized. They speak the language of their masters,
the predatory interests.

"In our own State we haven't a daily paper that would
dare to champion the cause of the common people upon
any question, and they follow the wishes of the 'big interests' always. . . .

"The fight in this State now and in the years to come
is against this sort of octopus and others of this kind,
and if we had an honest and fearless press we would
run these criminals out of the State at once, but unfortunately we have but few editors that will take up the
fight against this common enemy. The small country
paper has come under the same criminal influence of these
predatory interests as have the larger papers, until now
our State has only a very small percentage of honest-to-
goodness newspapers. These are making a valiant fight,
but the common enemy is continually closing in on them,
and unless a revolution takes place it will not be long
before they are all silenced—I pray this revolution may
come soon."

How much does big business pay and how many papers
does it influence? In the case of the government versus the
New Haven railroad, Attorney (now Supreme Court Justice)
Louis D. Brandeis insisted that the investigation include the
publicity department whose pay vouchers he demanded be

seized and made public. The New Haven president, Mr. Mellen, testified as follows (Court Record, page 1350) :

"Mr. Folk.—Was not something paid practically to every newspaper in New England?
Mr. Mellen.—I do not know as to that.
Mr. Folk.—The records show that more than 1,000 newspapers got something.
Mr. Mellen.—Well, I have no doubt that is correct."

Then there is the testimony regarding amounts. (Court Record, page 1363) :

"Mr. Folk.—The New York, New Haven & Hartford Railroad paid about $400,000 a year, it appears from this document, for publicity purposes. For instance, to the *Boston Republic* you paid about $3,000 a year, it seems. . . . Why did you pay so much to that paper?
Mr. Byrnes.—Well, because I thought it was worth it.
Mr. Folk.—Why did you think it was worth it?
Mr. Byrnes.—Do you mean the *Boston Republic?*
Mr. Folk.—Yes.
Mr. Byrnes.—Well, that is Mayor Fitzgerald's paper."

In the hearings of the New Haven the fact was established that the four hundred thousand dollars a year was "relatively less than was paid by any other large railroad in the country."

In the Mulhall investigation in the Senate it was shown that the National Association of Manufacturers and the Merchant Marine League were using enormous sums to influence newspapers. By spending two million dollars a year various marine corporations were able to drum up opposition to La Follette's seamen's law.

In the insurance companies' scandals, many newspapers paid by the corporations' publicity bureau for favorable articles were named.

These are matters of record. They happened not so long ago. And they show the same method of big-business procedure which the public utilities employed later.

Here is the testimony of Senator George W. Norris, of Nebraska, in 1921, regarding another big-business enterprise, the packers. He calls it "one of the most remarkable attempts to control the public sentiment through the instrumentality of the public press"; he writes that

"the packers are not the only corporations engaged in this great undertaking. There are many other great corporations that are equally guilty. It is a nation-wide campaign to build up a reactionary sentiment in favor of the great corporations of the country. But in this article we are dealing only with the packers and I confine myself in my comments to the part which they have taken in this colossal undertaking. I do not want to be understood as claiming that all of this advertising was unnecessary or subject to criticism. Neither do I argue that because a newspaper accepts advertising it is necessarily controlled in its editorial policy. The assertion is made, however, that the advertising of the packers is far beyond any legitimate, fair, or even liberal allowance for that purpose, and neither can there be any doubt but that some newspapers are controlled in their editorial policy by the advertising end of the business. Many others remain silent in their editorial columns when they would otherwise condemn, if it were not for the oiling of the business machinery through advertising.

"There can be no doubt, but that one of the objects of this campaign was to mold public sentiment, and to close up the criticism that their acts would otherwise receive at the hands of newspapers. There was evidence developed upon the investigation to show that this was the real intent and purpose of a large portion of the advertising. The packers carry large page and half-page advertisements in all the newspapers of the United States. No country paper was too small to be taken into consideration by them. Large display advertisements appeared in newspapers that had only two or three hundred subscribers. Moreover, the greatest of this advertising took place at a time when there was a shortage of production, when they were positively unable to supply the hungry with the food desired. . . ."

To illustrate his charges Senator Norris tells the story of what happened in Fort Worth, Texas, where both Armour and Swift have packing plants. Both loaned money to a man named Armstrong to buy up an unfriendly paper and convert it into a packer's paper. Three packers, Swift, Armour and the Stock Yards Company lent five thousand dollars to Armstrong's rival, Senator Norris adds, thus controlling public opinion in the town.

When big business in the form of coal comes up for discussion there are documents made public by the Senate Committee on Manufacturers which was considering a fuel control bill. Senator La Follette, writing in 1923, said it was an "amazing indictment of certain of the newspapers of the United States." The transcript of the meeting of the National Coal Association "contains indisputable evidence that the coal operators set out . . . to subsidize the press and use it as a medium to create 'shortage' scares, and to induce the people to buy coal at high prices. The object of the National Coal Association was not merely to use the advertising columns of the newspapers but to obtain the publication of inspired news stories and editorials. The record shows that in this object the association was eminently successful."

The evidence made public by the Senate committee showed that the coal corporations assessed themselves one mill a ton, raising between three hundred thousand dollars and four hundred thousand dollars for their "educational campaign . . . safeguarding influence against the enactment of harmful and expensive legislation in coal-mining districts and in the nation at large. . . ." The verbatim transcript of the National Coal Association meeting as published in the hearings of the Senate Committee on Manufacturers, contains the statement from one coal operator that he obtained the assistance of Melville Stone of the Associated Press who agreed to send between three hundred and four hundred words of coal corporation propaganda daily.

Senator Kenyon read a statement charging the publicity department of the National Coal Association with supplying certain propaganda to the Associated Press: "Over telegraph

wires that night the Associated Press carried a news report of
over 1,000 words to its 3,500 or more newspaper plants, written by its Cleveland manager after consultation with the (coal)
publicity director."

"In other words," commented Senator La Follette,
"at the time the newspapers of the country were publishing the 'shortage' advertisements and news stories
prepared by the National Coal Association (and while
receiving hundreds of thousands of dollars from the
Association in advertising contracts) the actual facts as
to coal were entirely at variance with the information
'fed' to the people through the press.
"A coal operator appearing before the Calder committee admitted that the extortionate prices charged the
American people for coal in 1920 may have reached
$600,000,000 in excessive profits.
"This is an operator's estimate of what the 'educational campaign' of the National Coal Association in
1920—conducted through the columns of the daily press—
cost the people of the United States."

Something more recent and perhaps more important? Here
is an item of December 14, 1934. It concerns the House of
Morgan.
If the reader is curious enough to look up the sayings and
writings of certain persons opposed to the entry of the United
States in the World War—and they range all the way from
William Randolph Hearst to Eugene V. Debs—he will find
that they alone among other issues raised the cry of commer-
cialism. Money, they said, was taking us to war. Big busi-
ness, they declared, wanted our entry. The international
bankers, especially the fiscal agent of the Allies, John Pierpont
Morgan, wanted us to join the Allies.
Such statements became sedition after April 6, 1917.
In 1919, September fifth to be exact, it was not Eugene
Debs but Woodrow Wilson who confessed that commercial-
ism, money, big business, was responsible for the war. The
President of the United States admitted exactly what the

pacifists said two years earlier. But the President did not name the bankers.

From 1917 on, newspaper men have from time to time heard the report that the American Ambassador to Great Britain cabled to Woodrow Wilson to come into the war to save the Morgan investment. The Germans were the original authors of this charge. They supplied no evidence.

Very recently part of the text of Ambassador Page's cable to President Wilson was being reported by many persons, notably Father Coughlin in one of his radio speeches in 1933. Father Coughlin told millions of Americans this was the absolute proof we entered the war to save the House of Morgan.

On December 14, 1934, the Nye Committee investigating the munitions industry, gave to the world the text of Ambassador Page's cable to President Wilson, the most important paragraphs of which are:

"The pressure of this approaching crisis, I am certain, has gone beyond the ability of the Morgan financial agency for the British and French Governments. . . . It is not improbable that the only way of maintaining our present pre-eminent trade position and averting a panic is by declaring war on Germany.

". . . pressing danger that the Franco-American and Anglo-American exchange will be greatly disturbed; the inevitable consequences will be that orders by all the Allied governments will be reduced to the lowest possible amount, and that transatlantic trade will practically come to an end.

"The result of such a stoppage will be a panic in the United States. . . . We shall soon reach this condition unless we take quick action to prevent it. Great Britain and France must have a credit in the United States which will be large enough to prevent the collapse of world trade and the whole financial structure of Europe.

"If the United States declares war against Germany, the greatest help we could give Great Britain and the Allies would be such a credit. If we should adopt this policy, an excellent plan would be for our Government to make a large investment in a Franco-British loan. Another plan would be to guarantee such a loan. A great advantage would be that all the money would be kept in the United States.

"We could keep on with our trade and increase it, till the war ends, and after the war Europe would purchase food and an enormous supply of materials with which to re-equip her peace industries. We should thus reap the profit of an uninterrupted and perhaps an enlarging trade over a number of years, and we should hold their securities in payment."

Nothing that has come out of all the secret archives of the world is so illuminating as the foregoing appeal. It shows up the political leadership of the world as dealing with investments and profits, not with human suffering and human lives. It incidentally and forever removes the American diplomats from the category of naïve children, where Europeans usually place them, and puts them first in realism, in *Realpolitik*.

This appeal to arms was dated March 5, 1917; the United States declared war on April 6, 1917. The Morgan millions were saved.

The Nye Committee has been clever in its publicity campaign. Knowing as it did that there would be opposition from certain War, Navy and State Department officials, from all the corrupt businesses in the nation, from all the merchants of death and from the press controlled by all the interests opposed to international peace, Senators Nye and Vandenberg timed some of their sensations to make the headlines of the morning and evening press. But events ran away from them. There were not merely two daily sensations, there was a torrent of them.

Certainly by every rule or custom in the newspaper game the publication of one of the most guarded documents of the World War was a news item. But what happened to it? A member of the staff of the *New Republic* immediately made an investigation, and this is his report:

"The full text of this [the Page] cablegram was released to the public by the Nye Committee on December

14, 1934. The United Press put the text of the cable into its munitions story of that day. So far as we can learn the Associated Press, International News Service and Universal Service did not. We have examined some twenty leading papers of the country, both in New York City and elsewhere, and find the following interesting facts: Only four of these papers carried the text of the cable. The *New York Post,* the *New York World-Telegram,* the *Louisville Courier-Journal* and the *Pittsburgh Press* did so. The *Cleveland Plain Dealer* carried the U. P. munitions story, but, in the edition that we examined, cut out all mention of the Page message. The *New York Tribune* printed a denial that the Nye Committee would investigate the cable but did not print the cable itself. A number of other papers printed a denial of an investigation of Morgan's, but were careful, even in the denial, not to mention the existence of the cable. Is this the freedom of the press about which the publishers have lately been so solicitous?"

At my request the writer of the foregoing editorial, Lawrence Brown, has supplied additional information. He talked to the Associated Press but received an evasive answer, and finally a statement that the committee had not given out the text at all; he then asked the telegraph editor of the *Herald Tribune* who said he had received the United Press story and telegraphed his Washington bureau about it, but the correspondent had apparently not been interested. The *Times* does not receive the United Press service.

The *New York Post* not only printed the cable, but reprinted it the night of December seventeenth with the editorial suggestion that fifty thousand doughboys died to make the world safe for profits. "The same newspapers which ignored or buried the Page revelations," continued the *Post,* "will spread propaganda for our entrance into the [next] war because our entrance into the war will safeguard those investments and those profits."

From a world war and the Morgans to California and the state brewers is a far leap, but it reaches another angle of the same subject. Again, as with almost every example which

is mentioned here, the thanks of the reader are due to the one
or two papers which always refuse to go along with the rest.
Testimony is from Stephen F. O'Donnell, publisher of the
Huntington Park Signal, who alleges:

"The California Newspaper Publishers' Association
accepted money from the California Brewers' Association
to pay for the authorship, printing and preparation of
matrices, of articles ostensibly designed to encourage the
citizens to vote, and actually designed to encourage them
to vote Republican [meaning, of course, against Sinclair]. . . .

"I think all honest newspaper men will agree with me
that it is not a proper function for an agency such as
the California Newspaper Publishers' Association to circulate brewers' propaganda by means of such a flimsy
device as the re-christening of the brewers by some such
flossy title as 'Steadfast Californians, Associated.'

"Anyone familiar with the current campaign in California can see that these editorials were conceived by some
one interested in the preservation of the *status quo* and
hostile to both the New Deal and to Upton Sinclair's
EPIC program. Regardless of the merit of the political
theories advocated in these articles, the fact remains that
many people and even some newspaper publishers are not
in favor of them. Thus the effort to get propaganda of
the type contained in the 'Stand Fast—America' series
into the columns of all member publishers of the California Newspaper Publishers' Association in California,
at a very nominal fee, intended only to defray mechanical
costs, has every mark of an effort to give away the support of the country press in this state to one party. . . ."

Editor O'Donnell wrote to the publishers' association that
the eight matrices they sent the newspapers to arouse Americans to the fact "their liberty and peace" were being "attacked
on all sides by strong outside forces" was "unmitigated
bilge"; to which John B. Long, general manager, replied that
the "publicity campaign, which I have read clear through, is
non-political and is based upon the anti-communism campaign

of the Elks, Junior Chambers of Commerce and the American Legion," which should make it holy in California.

Of California journalism and big business there is much more to be said. According to Guy Emery Shipler, editor of the *Churchman*, the *Los Angeles Times* is not only reactionary but a social menace. He contrasts two trends, the way it dealt with the electrocution of Sacco and Vanzetti, and its relation to big-business interests of the city. Regarding the former he quotes from "The Lancer" column signed by Harry Carr, as follows:

"Executions of murderers usually hold a melancholy but negative value for the public. The execution of Sacco and Vanzetti has been of sad but positive value. It has brought into the revealing light an amazing number of vicious fools who have been, until now, secret enemies of the United States. As usual, the outcry over this murder case comes from three classes of people—parlor socialists of the Greenwich Village variety, who are seeking cheap excitement; dangerous Reds, who are against everybody on the general principles of a mad dog; and small-bore writers. All of these vermin would be making trouble about something else if Sacco and Vanzetti had never existed."

But while radicals are mad dogs, public utilities are sacred cows. Writes Mr. Shipler:

"During the same period the *Times* has continued its campaign of vilification and misrepresentation against the Bureau of Power and Light of the city of Los Angeles, representing one of the most successful public ownership enterprises in America. The explanation lies in the fact that the ownership of the *Times* is heavily interested financially in the Southern California Edison Company, the private competitor of the Bureau of Power and Light. The municipal group has no newspaper through which to reach the taxpayers in order to offset the campaign of the *Times*, and is forced to resort to circularization by mail."

Every newspaper man can add to these examples of big business editing or making the news. There are even newspaper owners who admit it. Lord Northcliffe, for example. He is the author of a pamphlet, *Newspapers and their Millionaires,* in which he says, "Some of the provincial papers, like some of the London newspapers, are maintained by wealthy men for the purpose of political and social advancement. There is nothing wrong in that. . . . The *Westminster Gazette* . . . was always a 'kept' paper. For years it passed from one millonaire to another." Sir Robert Donald, editor of the *Daily Chronicle,* said to the Institute of Journalists that "during the last twenty years the press has been commercialized. Under syndicate ownership the main concern of shareholders was their dividend, and dividends must be earned even if principle had to suffer." Sir Willmott Lewis, of the London *Times,* deplored the fact that "in my country by reason of national circulations and the passing of control of newspapers to men who are primarily millionaires and not journalists, we have the immediate and pressing danger of the view that the press should make its will prevail."

In America the same thought was expressed by Dean Ackerman, of Columbia, who holds "the great basic fault of the press is its ownership. The press cannot be an impartial and true advocate of public service as long as its owners are engaged or involved in other businesses." Professor E. A. Ross, of the department of political economy, University of Wisconsin, who believes that the aspiration of the press has been upward, that venality has waned, makes "the one deadly, damning count against the daily newspaper as it is coming to be, namely, *It doesn't give the news."* This apostasy of the daily press, Professor Ross believes, is due to three economic developments in our time: the capitalist-owner instead of editor-owner; advertisers censoring the news; and the newspaper organ becoming an organ of special interest.

The majority of sacred cows are the big-business corporations. The packers, the medicine men, the coal companies, the railroads, the public-service corporations, the traction companies have always been sacred cows in a great many newspapers. If one may "point with pride" to the fact that the street-car companies, the railroads and the packers no longer bribe newspapers, one may in turn "view with alarm" the activities of the medicine men and the public utilities.

In all these specific instances there have been outright conspiracies, propaganda—or enlightenment campaigns for those who prefer milder and more euphemistic terms—by organized big business. In all these specific instances they were caught and brought before the humbugged public by congressional investigations.

Yet every intelligent reader of the newspapers knows that there are stronger but unseen ties which make a great number of the most powerful organs of public opinion part of the big-business set up. Take for example the case of Whitelaw Reid and his widow, Mrs. Elizabeth Mills Reid. They owned the old *New York Tribune*. May 26, 1934, the will of the late Mrs. Reid showed the estate held securities valued at $16,210,809. Among them were:

2093	shares	American and Foreign Power.
2000	"	American Car and Foundry.
1200	"	American Smelting and Refining.
1780	"	Bethlehem Steel 7% prf.
2120	"	Commonwealth Edison.
1000	"	Consolidated Gas prf.
7000	"	Standard Oil of N. J.
10,761	"	International Paper & Power.

and so on through the list of railroads, mines, public utilities worth three or four million dollars, Mexican and Cuban stocks and bonds, etc.

Every move the American Government made toward intervention in Cuba and Mexico affected Whitelaw Reid's and Mrs. Reid's Mexican and Cuban investments. Every adverse policy of the public utility commissions or President F. D. Roosevelt is a blow to the utility portfolio of the Reid estate.

A Republican *Herald Tribune* would naturally attack a Democratic administration, and poke editorial fun at Demo-

crats, as well as Republicans aligned with them, who would
have the state and nation control the utilities, as for example:

"What is a reforming Administration without a whipping boy? The bankers served Mr. Roosevelt admirably
in this capacity from inauguration day, when he lashed
them out of the temple, to the late love feast in Washington. Mr. Walsh's report is just one more sign that the
wicked utility companies are to be promoted from relative
obscurity to this new and important post as the Administration's principal devil."

And here is a cavalry charge against the committee which
is providing the nation with sensational disclosures of the
war traffic *(Herald Tribune,* lead editorial, December 15,
1934):

"A BLUNDERBUSS ATTACK

"The Nye Committee started out to investigate the
munitions traffic. It has already reached the point of publishing lists of all who made a million dollars or more
during the war, regardless of whether their income had
the slightest connection with munitions or not. . . . Many
of those whose names are thus being mentioned feel, not
unreasonably, that this is going pretty far afield and that
they are being unjustly pilloried as munitions makers and
profiteers of death when they were nothing of the kind.
Their resentment is warranted, for the Nye Committee
has manifested a cheerful carelessness about letting its
inferences fall where they may.
". . . . the 'munitions maker' is largely a myth. Or, to
put it a little differently, he is all of us . . . the war wealth
did not go merely to manufacturers of powder or shell
casings; it went to everybody; farmers, shipyard mechanics, workers in mines and every kind of factory . . .
every sort of business industry."

One more illustration of the relations of big business and
the press: the Montana copper companies, according to Mr.
Villard, owned outright the following newspapers:

Montana Standard of Butte
Daily Post of Butte
Anaconda Standard
Helena Independent
Record-Herald of Helena
Missoulian
Sentinal of Missoula
Billings Gazette
Livingston Enterprise

The press of the state of Montana was heavily subsidized by the copper industry and many papers were run at a loss. The biggest and most powerful daily, the *Tribune* in Great Falls, was published by friends of the owners of the Anaconda Copper Company. In 1928 W. A. Clark, Jr., son of the copper Senator, established the fearless independent *Montana Free Press* at Butte. A whispering campaign and an advertisers' boycott caused the loss of thirty thousand dollars a month, and eventually the paper was sold to the *Anaconda*. Villard believes it would have succeeded if young Clark had held out a little longer. But even if it had paid for itself it is doubtful if it could have broken the monopoly of public information which the copper interests maintained. Of course the fact that Montana makes it a habit to elect enemies of copper to Congress is one of the many proofs that big business although controlling a large part of the press sometimes drives the electorate, grown suspicious of the newspapers, to defeat both the corporations and their political manikins.

The establishment of a lone paper in a journalistically corporation-owned state is not the answer to the problem, nor do I feel that I could solve it when Mr. White, one of the notable leaders of the free press, refrains from trying. But we do know this, that when a president appoints certain important officials they dispose of their commercial bonds, literally and figuratively. This may not solve the problem but it helps. Mr. Mellon of course remained a business man although he sold his holdings. The law already requires newspapers to file a statement of all bondholders. We know that the position of editors and publishers of important newspapers is, to say the least, the equivalent of a place in the Senate, if not in the White House. Unless we can assure ourselves that all the editors and publishers of our powerful newspapers are not bound to big business by millions of dollars in stocks and bonds, in mortgages on their plants, in common business enterprises, or in directorates in outside corporations, we cannot be sure that their protestations of serving the reader, published daily, have any meaning.

Perhaps the best solution of the problem of business and the press would be to let real newspaper men run the newspapers. But that is a subject for a later chapter.

Chapter VII

PROPAGANDA MARCHES ON

> Why is propaganda so much more successful when it stirs up hatred than when it tries to stir up friendly feeling? The reason is, clearly, that the human heart, as modern civilization has made it, is more prone to hatred than to friendship, and it is prone to hatred because it is dissatisfied, because it feels deeply, perhaps even unconsciously, that it has somehow missed the meaning of life, that perhaps others, but not we ourselves, have secured the good things which nature offers for man's enjoyment.—Bertrand Russell.
>
> All propaganda must be so popular and on such an intellectual level, that even the most stupid of those toward whom it is directed, will understand it. Therefore, the intellectual level of the propaganda must be the lower, the larger the number of people who are to be influenced by it. (Page 197.) Propaganda must not serve the truth. (Page 260.) Through clever and constant application of propaganda, people can be made to see paradise as hell, and also the other way round. (Page 376.)— (14th edition, *Mein Kampf.)—*Adolf Hitler.

THERE are many definitions of propaganda. "Effort directed systematically toward the gaining of support for an opinion or course of action," says the *Standard Dictionary.* During the war we threw millions of postcards over the German lines promising starved soldiers white bread; that was considered our best propaganda. But the best illustration I know of oc-

127

curred when the Detroit soldiers were fighting the Bolsheviki at Archangel.

One day the Americans saw a Russian with a white flag wave a request to approach. They signaled agreement. The Bolshevik entered the American line.

"Comrades," he asked, "why are you fighting us?"

The doughboys were speechless for once. To answer back "to make the world safe for democracy" would have sounded ridiculous out there in the Arctic, with the World War over. It had never entered their khaki-clad minds to ask why they were fighting.

"Comrades," continued the Bolshevik soldier, "we don't know why you are fighting us. We don't want to fight you. We want to go home. Why don't you go home? You want to go home, too, don't you? Well, why are you here—why are you fighting us?"

The Red soldier departed. The American soldiers watched him go. Everyone spoke at once. Why were they fighting? None knew. They would ask their officers. The officers knew everything in this man's war.

"Colonel," the soldiers asked, "why are we out here fighting?"

Colonel Steward, commanding the 339 Infantry Regiment, Michigan troops, mostly Detroiters, could not tell the men why they were fighting. Jay Hayden, soldier, newspaper man, and historian of this episode, recounts that the commanding officer thought a while, and then made this brilliant reply:

"We are fighting," said Colonel Stewart, "because we will be annihilated if we don't. That's reason enough for me."

But it wasn't for the men. They had talked to a Bolo soldier and they knew the Bolos had no reason or intention to murder them, that the Bolos wanted to go home. The men told the Colonel that. So the Colonel telegraphed to Washington, asking, what are we out here in the Arctic fighting for? But the War Department apparently did not know; at least it did not reply. So Hayden cabled to President Wilson, Colonel House, General Bliss and all the others who were busy at the moment making peace in Paris. But he got no answer.

The Red Army soldiers from just across the way continued to propound the question. "What are you fighting for? Why don't you go home? We want to go home. We don't want to kill you. Why do you shoot at us?" The doughboys repeated the questions to the officers.

One day they were told to load supplies on trucks going to the front. They refused. Instead they began marching from Shenkursk to the vessels docked at Archangel which would take them out of this white hell back to sane America where perhaps their questions might be answered.

The British troops had mutinied. The French troops had mutinied. The White Russians, who were supposed to do the fighting, had malingered and finally mutinied. And the British military censor, who had suppressed all mention of the three mutinies, now flashed the world the news that American troops had mutinied.

The American troops, however, were merely going home because they could not answer Bolshevik propaganda.

One could draw many morals from this true story. I quote it here because it seems to me to illustrate the fact that propaganda is a double-edged sword, a weapon that may drive us into war one day and drive us into peace another day. The Russian soldier who asked the question was a propaganda agent, no less a propagandist than scores of newspapers and newspaper men who invented stories about Bolshevik atrocities, the nationalization of women, mass slaughter, assassinations and the reign of terror in Russia in 1919 and the whole decade that followed. Propaganda had carried the youth of Michigan to the ice-fields of Archangel, and propaganda restored them to their peaceful homes. Neither voyage, with attendant suffering and bloodshed, would have been necessary had it been possible to tell the truth—the common every-day fallible human truth—which the men who made the war knew but which the press of the world had failed to publish.

Nor is the situation much different, today, in time of peace. In time of peace prepare for war. To prepare for war the mind of the mass must be influenced by positive and negative propaganda: the truth about commercial rivalry as a cause of war, for instance, must be censored, while the danger of Japanese jingoism or the Bolshevik menace must be emphasized, luridly colored, distorted if need be, and invented when all else fails.

The American press reeks with Japanese scares. The Japanese press reeks with American scares. Both are largely propaganda. The statements of commanders of the American Legion, the articles signed by officers of the National Security League, the entire press work of the Navy League of America, the addresses before the Daughters and Sons of the American Revolution—who forget that their ancestors were revolutionists, "reds" in the eyes of their rulers—are full of propaganda. Every reader of ninety per cent of the world press, whether he knows it or not, is the victim of purposeful propaganda. Fortunate indeed is he who can detect or withstand it.

Patriotism is the sugar coating of a great part of the propaganda which appears in the newspapers of the United States. There are two sorts of patriotism in the world, and of one brand the man most honored in America said: "Beware of the impostures of patriotism." These words of George Washington are never quoted by those patriotic societies which are subsidized by gentlemen who have munitions to sell and who make money out of wars.

To be effective the patriotic societies of both sorts have to reach the public. As with the utility corporations they use all avenues of approach, women's clubs, boy scouts, meetings, advertising; but like the utilities they know that the main avenue is the press. Here are some facts about the most important organization which stood out for years as the embodiment of all that was noble in American patriotism and which for a number of years filled the press of the country with its propaganda. I am referring to the National Security League.

As the leading exponent of preparedness for the war with Germany the League led the successful armament propaganda campaign and the propaganda attacks on newspapers, political leaders, pacifists and others who disagreed with its patriotism. The press played its game. Its clip books showed millions of columns of propaganda published by patriotic editors.

In 1919, thanks to the National Security League's over-confidence in its attack on members of Congress, that body ordered an investigation and found that the League was financially supported by the following patriots: Nicholas F. Brady, H. H. Rogers, William K. Vanderbilt, T. Coleman Du Pont, Henry Clay Frick, George W. Perkins, Simon and Daniel Guggenheim, the American Smelting Company, J. Pierpont Morgan and John D. Rockefeller.

Brady represented power and light, Du Pont munitions, Frick battleship armor and the system of hiring thugs to murder striking workingmen, Morgan the Allied war loans, the Guggenheims copper; the backers of the National Security League were without exception multi-millionaires who profited by the war. The judgment of the Congressional Investigating Committee (House of Representatives, 65th Session, Report No. 1173, page 6) is that "if the curtain were only pulled back, in addition to the interests heretofore enumerated, the hands of Rockefeller, of Vanderbilt, of Morgan, of Remington, of Du Pont, and of Guggenheim, would be seen, suggesting steel, oil, money-bags, Russian bonds, rifles, powder, and railroads." In short the National Security League was proved to be the apogee of commercial patriotism financed by the profits of war.

Completely exposed in 1919, the same organization has hoped to regain public confidence by its propaganda against radicals, pacifists, communists, by pointing to the red flag, by hiding in the folds of the Star Spangled Banner, the final and fittest subterfuge of big business and war profiteers.

Very much chastened, but still engaged in patriotic propaganda, the National Security League functions today with the support of numerous editors and publishers. Let me quote one example. Here is a lurid and sensational article in the Sunday *Springfield Union and Republican* signed by Lieutenant-General Robert Lee Bullard, former commander of the Second Army, A. E. F., a man known to all the war correspondents and honored by them for his military intelligence and personal integrity. General Bullard is now president of the National Security League. That too need cast no shadow on his honor or integrity. I do not doubt his sincerity in his sensational articles in which he finds the American public school and college system being perverted by Moscow through the "youth movement." I do not believe that American youth is being "organized and regimented behind issues identical with those which our openly avowed revolutionists, members of the Communist party, conduct their campaign for the overthrow of our government." This is the usual Red scare propaganda. What does interest me most is the little copyright line at the end of Bullard's article: it has been syndicated to many papers by Hearst's Universal Service, an organ of anti-Japanese jingoism and anti-Red ballyhoo, and it is exactly on the level with the anti-German jingoism and ballyhoo which other syndicates sent out in the years 1914 to 1918.

The question remains: why do newspapers print this sort of tripe?

Sometimes the editors can plead they were ignorant of its origin, that the propagandist was too subtle. Everyone of course knew that Ivy Lee had the reputation of being the most successful propagandist in America, but no one brought up the question which is a corollary: the more success Lee had, the more proof it is that, ignorant or not, newspapers cooperated with him. The propagandist who cannot get into the newspapers is no propagandist.

Our daily press is full of European propaganda. Boast or confession, it was the testimony of Ivy Lee that suggestions for statements of policy by the German Government for guidance in its relations with the American people, were prepared by Lee's publicity bureau in America and submitted to Hitler from time to time through Lee's son and agent in Berlin. The American people listening to Hitler's declaration for peace never suspected that such statements, hypocritical or sincere, might have been mere propaganda inspired by American so-called public relations councilors or international propaganda experts.

Testifying before a congressional committee (May 19, 1934) Mr. Lee said that the heads of the German Dye Trust and other corporations (which Mr. Lee did not admit but which we now know were the financial backers of the Fascist movement) were anxious for him to meet the Fuehrer "just to size him up." Several months later he went to Germany again and reported to von Papen, Goebbels, Neurath and Schmitt his statement that Nazi propaganda in America was unwise. One of the first suggestions affecting international relations offered by the Lee bureau was that Germany make official declarations regarding disarmament and this was accepted. Another, that Joachim von Ribbentrop, former special commissioner for disarmament, visit the United States and explain Nazi Germany to President Roosevelt, the Foreign Policy Association and the Council for Foreign Relations, was not accepted. Mr. Lee, who ridiculed Nazi propaganda, then explained how his propaganda worked.

"I told them repeatedly," he testified, "that the only way for Germany to get understood in the United States was for responsible people in Germany to make authoritative utterances which would receive publicity in the normal way. . . . Everything that savored of Nazi propaganda in this country was a mistake and ought not to be undertaken. Our people would regard it as meddling with American affairs; and it was bad business."

Asked whether the German contract was the only one of this character which Lee ever had, he replied, "I had a relationship some years ago with the Polish government and the Rumanian government."

"Involving their relations with this government or this people?" asked former Senator Hardwick, of Georgia.

"No, sir," replied Mr. Lee.

"Involving dissemination of information favorable to those countries in this country?"

"Only with reference to their finances," was the reply. He denied working for Russia or Italy, "despite the popular impression."

Newspapers readers will remember the excitement in the

press preceding Hitler's special session of the Reichstag, the
speculation about his declaration of policies, the hope of peace
or war in Europe hanging on the words of the new dictator.
And then, the climax: front-page headlines in the morning
and evening papers, editorials, comment, sermons. Hitler
had come out for peace! The world sighed its relief. That
is, the newspaper readers of the world may have sighed. The
war and state departments of the world knew too much about
the orders for scrap iron and airplanes, the doubled shifts in
the gas factories, the expenditure of all the gold in the Reich
for war preparations. Anyone who had any knowledge of
affairs knew that Hitler was, to use understatement, not telling
the truth. And today we know that specialists in national
psychology, seeking to overcome antipathy to Hitler in peace-
loving countries, were the real authors of der Fuehrer's
Machiavellian declarations. Now, as in war time, public
opinion is manipulated by publicity men.

Ivy Ledbetter Lee was known as the foremost press-agent
in the world and some of his clients have paid him more than
the twenty-five thousand dollars a year he got from the German
dye trust. He has represented Charles M. Schwab, who with
tear-filled eyes and a bleeding heart told the Shearer Investigating Committee that he would gladly sink his armament
plant to insure world peace and who made millions out of the
World War and will make more millions out of the next war;
John D. Rockefeller, Sr., who needed vindication after the
massacre of his workmen in Ludlow, Colorado; the Armours
who figured in the beef scandals; the Thompson-Starrett
Company, Portland Cement, the Guggenheims, the Inter-
borough, the Pennsylvania Railroad, Chrysler, the Universities
of Harvard and Princeton, the Red Cross, Poland, Rumania
(the land of corruption, Queen Marie and Magda Lupescu),
the Waldorf-Astoria Hotel and the Cathedral of St. John the
Divine.

To many people he was known as "Poison Ivy."

In the early years of the present century the robber barons
were not only despoiling the country but poisoning the food
and the minds of the people. The beef trust, which had

killed many more soldiers than Spanish bullets, continued to sell rotten beef; the Woolen Trust continued to corrupt the press; the Wall Street speculators continued to fleece the lambs; the proprietary medicine companies put opium in soothing sirup for children, the power trust continued to buy up newspapers, the oil trust stole lands and put independents out of business by corrupt methods—in short, rugged Big Business, untamed and unregimented, ruled the nation. But thanks to a new group of magazine writers many of the worst abuses in our political and financial system were exposed to the public. Will Irwin, Charles Edward Russell, Ida Tarbell, Upton Sinclair, Lincoln Steffens, Tom Lawson, Mark Sullivan, Ray Stannard Baker and many other journalists, by documented exposures, sensational in proportion to the crookedness and corruption dealt with, forced a great reform upon the big-business system.

This reform would have gone deeper and wider were it not for two elements. President Theodore Roosevelt, who had come into office by the accident of assassination, and who threatened to "bust" the trusts, was quickly tamed by them, and replied to the challenge of the fearless journalists by branding them "muckrakers." A typical Roosevelt trick. Unable to answer the challenge of the people to whom he had made promises he was no longer able to carry out, he turned upon the gadflies of the administration with an insult. That part of the press which was on the side of corrupt business, sorely attacked, leaderless and disarmed, picked up the word of salvation. Throughout the country there was an attack upon the muckrakers. Neither Roosevelt nor his supporters would admit, however, that there was plenty of muck.

The second force which stopped the reform wave was propaganda. Big business did not originate the press-agent system; the press-agents had to beg and wheedle for the job, but once the ex-journalists proved their success in changing public opinion from disgust and hatred into tolerance and eventually approval of the "captains of industry" and their methods, the propagandists, under the nice euphemistic title of "public relations counsel," were assured of a golden era. They more than earned their wage.

The late Mr. Lee's leading competitors are Edward L. Bernays who is credited with getting an Edison electric light bulb on a postage stamp, and Carl Byoir who, like Lee, confessed being an agent of Nazi Fascism.

In September, 1933, the firm of Carl Byoir & Associates was hired, according to testimony before the McCormack-Dickstein Committee, to present the Hitler viewpoint in America. It sent its junior partner, Carl D. Dickey, and a wartime German-American propagandist, George Sylvester Viereck, to interview Hitler, Goering, Goebbels, Frick and Schacht in Berlin for the purpose of preparing a series of "unbiased and unprejudiced" articles for American readers. The contract called for six thousand dollars a month and was nominally for the purpose of stimulating travel in Germany by propaganda for the German (Government) railroad system. Defending himself before the investigators, Viereck declared that "there is not the slightest touch of impropriety in the contract between Byoir & Associates and the German railroads nor in my connections with that distinguished firm. . . . If it is right for the Russians to hire Mr. Ivy Lee, why is it wrong for the German railroads to employ Mr. Carl Byoir and Mr. Carl Dickey? It was specifically understood that the work involved no propaganda and no anti-Jewish activities. . . . I always regarded it almost a consecration to interpret the land of my fathers to the land of my children. . . ."

The investigating committee, however, learned from Mr. Dickey that in 1933 his agency received four thousand dollars from the German Consul General in New York, Herr Kiep, to "explain" Hitler's attack on the Jews in well-written publicity releases.

Let us look into the history of Carl Byoir. He is of course a newspaper man. During the war he served the American propaganda machine (the committee on "misinformation" as it was generally called by journalists) presided over by George Creel, and after the war he moved to Cuba where he became publisher of the *Havana Post* and the *Havana Telegram*.

For several years Pew in his *Editor & Publisher* warned the editors and publishers of the American press that bloody tyranny ruled in Cuba and that the Machado administration handed out "gobs of free stuff, inspired by Carl Byoir and others." A few newspaper men refused to accept the "hand-outs" of the government or the invitations for an interview with the tyrant, "but in general," wrote Pew, "Machado had his way with newspapers and newspaper men" and propaganda "was the strongest entrenchment he [Machado] was able to throw up in defense of his sinister regime."

What was the result? Cuban patriots, once hopeful of American sympathy, grew suspicious, then bitter, and finally believed that the American press "was an accessory before the fact in the tragic crime" of the recent Cuban revolution. "The wall of faked propaganda that had long sustained him [Machado] fell at last," commented Pew. . . .

"Press agentry, dirty as it is known in the world, played a leading role in the Cuban tragedy. It was cruel, bold, reckless, venal. The people of Cuba were betrayed by propaganda, cooked up to suit the Dictator, and so were the people of the United States. A few newspaper men wrote honest news, but not until William G. Shepherd, for *Collier's,* took the lid off a few months ago did anyone seem disposed to make a searching inquiry into the politico-business conspiracy. Too many fed at the crib of the great Presidente; too few looked down city alleys and in squalid provinces. The press-agent game was conducted successfully along primitive lines. The visiting correspondent was met at the dock and escorted to Sloppy Joe's or some other bacchanalian funny-place, and thereafter did not want for amusement and four sumptuous meals per day, under the shade of the palms. He learned much about the sacredness of sugar plantation investments, but nothing about gaunt poverty. It was a system, gay and festive. And the 'pay-off' came when the correspondent was informed that the press-agent out of the goodness of his heart, had arranged for an exclusive interview with his Excellency, the venerable President of Cuba, at the glittering palace. . . . An authority who has recently investigated the Cuban situa-

tion, makes the statement that the Machado Government
spent at least $4,000,000 on propaganda, agent fees, en-
tertainment of correspondents and influential visitors. . . ."

And here is Mr. Pew's concluding verdict on the Cuban
tragedy:

"The cover which hung like a thick veil over the bloody
Machado regime was propaganda, vicious, venal, cun-
ningly executed by sharpers. Cuba's plight could have
been exposed and readjusted by honest-minded men years
ago if the whole people had known the simple facts.
Rarely has there been a clearer exposition of the evil
portent of political control of the press. Some responsible
body, such as the American Society of Newspaper Editors, ought to investigate and expose the dirty thing in
public to safeguard reader rights in the future. And
also to conspicuously mark the American publicity 'expert'
for what he is—a menace."

The *Havana Post* was wrecked by the revolutionists.

All in all, the Hitler propaganda machine (whose internal
function, its most important work, I have not mentioned) is,
like most of Hitler's ideas, programs and acts, an intensified,
improved, faster and concentrated Mussolini propaganda
machine. Almost everything that has happened in Germany,
from the suppression of the press and human liberty, to the
blood purge, is the compression in a year of Italian Fascism's
history of four or ten years.

I first wrote about Italian propaganda in 1925, before and
after my expulsion. Hiram Motherwell, of the *Chicago Daily
News,* Bolitho, of the *World,* and one or two other journalists also exposed the Fascist plan to bunco the American people
for the purpose of floating the twelve billion lire loans which
"balanced" the budgets annually and gave Italy the appearance of a prosperous country. But we were always completely
submerged by the flood of buncombe from the Rome bureau,
the New York international bankers' bureaus, the tourist propaganda of such men as Congressman Sol Bloom, Harold

MacGrath, Senator Reed, of Pennsylvania, Ambassador Richard Washburn Child, Colonel S. S. McClure and similar leaders of American thought.

In 1925 I pointed out the fact that hundreds of Italian newspapers in foreign countries, and numerous American dailies were being bribed by Mussolini through the present of five thousand words free cable tolls. Can anything be more corrupt than that? Imagine the scandal in the United States or England if it were suddenly disclosed that numerous newspapers had been subsidized by free telegraph tolls by another dictatorship, the Communist, at the same time? But American newspapers continued to take this bribe, and it was not until September 24, 1932, that the *Editor & Publisher* announced that "we hear that none of the British or American news agencies will any longer carry the five thousand word free cable handout that Mussolini offered to all correspondents a few years ago as a subsidy inducement."

I have in the past ten years said so much about Fascist propaganda in America that I am afraid it may be boring to readers, but it is obvious in this case that exposing the corruption does not correct the situation. It is obvious that many people and many newspapers, furiously on the defensive against propaganda from sources they hate, accept lovingly propaganda from movements and nations which they respect and approve. But I must again corroborate my standpoint by quoting the authority whom the newspaper editors of America respect and trust. Says Marlen Pew:

"I doubt if there was ever, in history, more dubious foreign propaganda issued to the people of this country than that which Mussolini poured into our eyes and ears when Italian bond issues were being floated. It took a foreign bond expert to fully appreciate the boldness of it. The impression was generally created back as far as 1926 that Italy was one of the most able and genuinely prosperous countries in the world and therefore about as good a risk as any investor would want. But we know now that in 1926 a heavy economic recession took place in that country, which by 1927 became black. There were temporary recoveries, but the Italian depression of this day cannot be concealed.

"Hard times have worked many amazing transformations, but nothing more bizarre than the debunking of the Fascist boast of superior economics. Those foolish Americans who fell for the loud noise and surface glitter of the Duce pretty well comprehend now that the world economic crash hit Italy long before it hit us and that not only the general reading public, but some astute bankers were badly taken in by Mussolini's juggling of figures to conceal growing deficits in the Italian budget. Mussolini obtained a balance by borrowing and loading debts on the provinces and municipalities. Recent official figures show that between 1925 and 1928 the debts of the municipalities and provinces increased nearly 70 per cent. Treasury revenues for 1928-29 fell far below expenditures, and the public debt of Italy increased from 86 billion lire to 91 billion in a single year. From 1926 to date every official figure shows increases in public debt and bankruptcies, and also immense declines in trade and governmental revenues. Unemployment has been intense in Italy for years, but was covered up. Beggars were kept off the streets, but millions suffered want and privation.

"There is a story in Europe that even back in his Milano newspaper days Mussolini was not averse to taking French money for editorial favors. After the fashion of the reptile press of the Continent. Maybe such a common European practice as this does not bring much stigma to the Duce, but if true it is a character tip-off for American newspapermen."

Recently (in 1934) in addition to the Stefani agency and the Duce's own press bureau, the most comprehensive press and propaganda agency of any nation was opened in Rome under the direction of Count Galeazzo Ciano, Mussolini's son-in-law. It is housed in the Balestra Palace in the Via Veneto and it is so powerful that it has been likened to a new ministry with part of the functions of the department of state. Its three departments are: domestic press, foreign press and propaganda. When not at work influencing journalists from foreign lands and preparing the news and views of Italian writers, the new bureau watches the press of the world, newspaper, magazine, pamphlet and book. Not a printed word of criticism or praise is missed and all the air waves of the world are translated by a corps of stenographers. From this vast material a summary is made for the Duce daily, together with a scrapbook of complete news items, thus making it possible for Mussolini to learn at a glance the international reaction to every declaration, every pose, promise, threat, rattle of the sword and gesture of peace.

New Year's Day, 1933, the Japanese propaganda bureau attached to the delegation at the League of Nations reported that two bombs had been thrown by Chinese soldiers against a Japanese outpost at Shanhaikwan, the junction of the Great Wall with the Peiping-Mukden railway; this propaganda never did say whether the bomb exploded, whether anyone was killed or injured, whether any property was destroyed. It merely reported a bombing, which later was denied officially by the Chinese, but immediately it justified the march of the Japanese Army into China. The Japanese dropped bombs on soldiers and civilians alike, captured Shanhaikwan, opened the road for the control of Jehol, entered the Great Wall, and prepared, as rumor then had it, to name Pu-yi, their puppet, Emperor of Manchuria, which they had already renamed Manchukuo. The bombing story was for Japan the equivalent of the Sarajevo assassinations. In Sarajevo, however, there was an assassination, while in Shanhaikwan there was simply a cloud of propaganda to hide a marching army. It was equally effective.

Official estimate of what the nations spend on propaganda was given in the supplement to the French Foreign Office budget of the spring of 1933 when Foreign Minister Joseph Paul-Boncour, who asked for and received an additional thirty-three million francs for French propaganda abroad, defended his claim by citing the following sums (in francs) spent by rivals:

Germany	256,000,000
Italy	119,000,000
France	71,000,000
Britain	69,000,000
Poland	26,000,000
Hungary	23,000,000
Czechoslovakia	18,000,000
Jugoslavia	13,000,000
Rumania	7,000,000

The German sum, equivalent to some seventeen million dollars, was the annual expenditure of the German Republic; under Hitler the amount has been multiplied, and some figure it as high as eighty million dollars. Monsieur Paul-Boncour's demand for an increase was for the purpose of propaganda in America: to combat anti-French sentiment, to study the Hearst newspapers and "permit prompt reply to anti-French attacks" in them, and to subsidize pro-French articles in newspapers and magazines by prominent authors.

"The American people [wrote the Foreign Minister] go to no trouble to inform themselves. We must place under their eyes some simple truths. . . . An American may honestly ruin his best friend just to prove he is the stronger, then offer him his hand and help him to arise. Friendship has nothing to do with business. . . . The American people are ignorant of their own history. They must not be expected to know French history. . . .

"The American feminine element has an important viewpoint; we must address ourselves particularly to it. . . . It is vital that young, good-looking and active speakers be sent to the United States instead of unhealthy, decrepit, tired, feverish, worn-out, coughing and trembling ancients bound into frock coats. These have to be put to bed upon their arrival with hot water bottles at their feet, have to be awakened just in time for a conference, and when rushed to a station thousands of precautions have to be taken. That is why France is pictured as a tired, worn-out country."

Concluding his study of propaganda, the Foreign Minister stated that "these inquiries have allowed us to establish a general basic plan to be undertaken in the near future . . . by collaboration with the Associated Press and the Havas news agency. . . . The Quai d'Orsay assures the technical and financial control of this news service."

The denial of the Associated Press was hardly necessary. Every newspaper knows that it is impossible for the American organization to make any such arrangement. What is obvious, however, is that the French official, knowing that his national agency, Havas, can be controlled financially and politically, took it for granted that correspondents of Havas, of which the Associated Press is one, can be influenced in a like manner. So long as the A. P. is a colleague of such agencies as Havas it will naturally be subject to accusations which rightly apply to its partners.

Sometimes propaganda hits its owner. One of the finest bits of propaganda, which helped turn world opinion toward the Germans after the war, was the newspaper story of Black Troops on the Rhine. The French were accused of using negro regiments and the soldiers were accused of many indignities and crimes. The French replied they were using Moroccans, not negroes. Lewis Gannett, of the *Nation,* found that black troops were present and that their behavior was better than that of the whites, but the controversy continued.

The best proof that America had forgiven the Germans was the protest mass meeting in New York. "The usual crimes against women" were euphemistically reported, but later investigations proved there was no greater proportion of rape than in the British, French (white) or American zones of occupation. However, aroused American opinion made itself felt.

But there was an unlooked for result: thousands of tourists who had intended taking in the Rhine, stayed away. The Rhineland shopkeepers and hotel owners were hard hit financially. So they sent out protests: there was no "black horror" in the Rhineland; in fact there were no cases of rape at all. The Germans swore to that.

We all know that Washington is the home of hundreds of lobbies and propaganda bureaus. We all know that there are lobbies which work for peace and lobbies which work for the munitions corporations. Every Washington correspondent receives many thousands of words of propaganda per day from scores of groups. When these lobby and propaganda groups overstep the line of honesty or good sense there are usually investigations, notably of the National Security League, the Navy League of America, the Shearer and the mail subsidy case.

The ocean mail contract propaganda fund and its newspaper ramifications are among the more recent ones. On October 2, 1933, R. J. Baker, secretary-treasurer of the American Steamship Owners' Association, testified as to its activities. It was shown that large şums were paid to obtain favorable public opinion for merchant marine subsidies. Between 1928 and 1931 a fund of $292,670 was used for financing propaganda. Thomas R. Shipp, publicity agent who received $1,000 a week for his work, explained it as being the education of Washington correspondents on the merchant marine problem.

This propagandist, like Lee and other notables, realizing that pure propaganda rarely gets into the newspapers but that the editors will fall for the same stuff, if signed with a big name, used the new method: he prepared speeches for a general in the army, a former Assistant Secretary of Commerce, and others.

Mr. Shipp's record of twenty-eight instances in which he obtained favorable press notices was read into the investigation's record. One of them relates to the *New York Times*. See report in the *Times*, October 2, 1933.

Another Shipp item reported that the *Washington Star* and the *Washington Post* had published editorials supporting the ocean mail contracts after the situation had been explained to them. It continued:

"Arranged with chief of Washington Bureau of Associated Press for them to carry a statement interpreting mail contract situation in Congress. Wrote such interpretation and took it to Second Assistant Postmaster General Glover, who revised it slightly and approved it. Glover's statement was carried by the Associated Press."

Lenin and Trotsky, in the early days of the Soviets, when with almost no exception the world press attacked them and their system, were bitter. Trotsky was brutal and Lenin cynical and humorous as usual when asked their opinion of foreign newspapers. Stalin is the only Russian dictator who has openly discussed Bolshevik propaganda.

No newspaper, declared Trotsky in 1922, publishes the truth about Russia, but propaganda and lies are spread throughout the world. He said, further, that there were two categories of lies, one, "fake pictures assembled from individual true elements;" to the other "belong the products of a malicious and self-seeking imagination: stories of Soviet dignitaries at banquets, of leaders mutually arresting each other, of artillerymen nationalizing the bourgeois women, etc. etc. These lies are full of self-contradictions, are monotonous and stupid. Only the most backward wives of footmen and lackeys and a few ministers of state believe them."

Lenin, asked what American newspapers he read, replied: "I read the *New York Times,* the *Chicago American* and the *Los Angeles Times* regularly. Through the *New York Times* I keep track of the atrocities, the assassinations, and the new revolutions in Russia. Otherwise I could not know where to find them." Of the editor of the *Los Angeles Times* he commented: "I find Mr. Chandler very refreshing. He writes that I am the bloodiest assassin the world has ever known. Now, I wonder, when this mess is all cleaned up and I visit Los Angeles on a trip I want to take around the world, I wonder if you could arrange a luncheon for me with Mr. Chandler? And could you invite Charlie Chaplin? I've always wanted to meet Charlie Chaplin. Doesn't he too live in Los Angeles?"

Stalin's only declaration on the value of propaganda, so far as I can find, was made to Walter Duranty in the first of the two illuminating interviews granted this noted correspondent. They were through with a discussion of the Russo-American debt settlement, when the interview continued as follows:

"STALIN (puzzled, thoughtful) : It is not debts that matter—there is something else.

"DURANTY (boldly) : You mean 'Bolshevist propaganda' or the 'arming-the-burglar theory,' and that, as many Americans say, 'Why help build up a country whose avowed aim is to overthrow our Constitution and upset everything which we believe made the greatness of the United States?'

"STALIN (refusing to be drawn out, sharply) : They provide equipment and technical help, don't they? And we pay them, don't we, for everything—pay top prices, too, as you and they know. You might as well say we are arming Americans and helping to maintain their capitalist system against ours. No, that is nonsense. That isn't the point at all. All this talk of propaganda is ridiculous. Propaganda doesn't do *anything*. Constitutions and systems are changed by natural causes, not by talk and books.

"In the old days the Czars blamed the French and German socialists for importing socialism into Russia, forgetting that the conditions of life and not socialist propaganda determine the course of events. Now I suppose they are making the same mistake in the United States when they say we are re-exporting socialism to Europe.

"DURANTY (interrupting) : The re-exportation of a finished product, perfected by your experience and scientifically adapted to modern needs?

"STALIN (impatiently) : Not a bit of it! Of course we Bolsheviki studied carefully enough the French, American and German revolutions in the past, especially their most radical revolutionary wings, and learned from experience how to overthrow the old regime. That was their real export of revolutionary methods.

"If you want to say we are sending back to the West its merchandise by re-exporting the practical experience of creating a Socialist society, then you are right, and I take it as a compliment. And how do we do it? We show visiting foreigners and the whole world that Socialist production is possible and is growing and will succeed.

"Whether they like it or not, Socialist economics will

develop and exist for them in turn to study. That is propaganda, too—but there is nothing to be done about it."

The most serious treatment of the whole subject of propaganda as far as I know, is Professor Frederick E. Lumley's *The Propaganda Menace*. Rightly Professor Lumley regards propaganda as the opposite of education. Analyzing all definitions he adds his own, describing propaganda as information veiled "as to (1) its origin or sources, (2) the interests involved, (3) the methods employed, (4) the content spread and (5) the results accruing to the victims." He offers a suggestion for the cure of the evil: "Probably man's only lasting protection from propaganda is in learning to think straight."

That is all very well as far as general propaganda is concerned. The subject discussed here is the relationship of the press to propaganda. The press announces itself the guardian of public mental health. The press itself is only rarely misled by propaganda. Every newspaper in America which published the propaganda of the public utility corporations after saying it would do so "if with advertising" or "if paid for" knew exactly what it was doing when it poisoned our mental health.

We cannot expect the press to suspect that a Hitler peace statement was actually written by an Ivy Lee, but we can suggest that it beware of a duplication of the Byoir Cuban episodes, and the Byoir Nazi episodes, and we must insist it refrain from employing pro-Fascists in Italy. Not until the press quits publishing propaganda knowingly will there be any hope of killing this "hydra-headed menace."

CHAPTER VIII

1929: CRASH, PANIC AND PRESS

ON OCTOBER 19, 1929, five million shares were traded in New York; the drop was five to forty points; the loss was three billion dollars; the press, quoting the leaders of Wall Street, said it was "a technical correction."

Five days later thirteen million shares were sold despite the statement that "the technical position of the market had been sufficiently corrected." Mr. Lamont said the crash was due to "technical conditions of offers and no bids"; some newspapers blamed it on "tardiness of the ticker"; Colonel Ayres spoke of "paper losses," a security panic "with no economic basis"; Professor Irving Fisher thought the market would recover because stocks were down to ten times earnings; Mr. Raskob said fifteen times earnings was a good price for General Motors; Teagle, Robert Dollar, Swift, Montgomery-Ward directors and treasury and Federal Reserve Bank officials agreed that a recovery was due and on the twenty-sixth President Hoover "on the advice of economic advisers" declared: "The fundamental business of the country . . . that is, the production and distribution of commodities . . . is on a sound and prosperous basis." History has proved this statement fundamentally untrue.

The stock market replied to it on the twenty-ninth when sixteen million shares were traded. It was a black day in American history.

In *The Years of the Locust* Gilbert Seldes analyzes the so-called depression. He says:

"Much later it became clear that some of our most effective leaders not only offered us false economic doctrines, but preferred to believe them and were attempting to conduct the business of the country as if the lies were

148

great economic truths. In that effort they came close to wrecking the mind and spirit of America. . . .

". . . we were not permitted for many months to confront the reality of our situation. . . . [there was a] psychological effort . . . to lull people to sleep in the hope that by the time they awoke the conditions of September 1929 would have returned. . . . The reality was this:

"The crash which came in 1929 was a natural outcome of the American system of industry, finance, politics, and social life;

"It was not inevitable;

"It was predictable, it was predicted, and slight efforts were belatedly made to head it off;

"It required an immediate and summary change in the American way of living if its results were not to be disastrous."

The press, instead of furnishing America with sound economic truth, furnished the lies and buncombe of the merchants of securities, which termed an economic debacle a technical situation, which called it the shaking out of bullish speculators, which blamed everything on lack of confidence. The press accepted the declarations of the President of the United States, a famous engineer, and also the economic viewpoint of the economically illiterate ex-President Coolidge who blamed 1929 on "too much speculation" and 1930 on "dumping from Russia" and 1931 on "the economic condition of Austria and Germany" breaking down. "It will be observed," said that patriot-economist, "that all these causes of depression, with the exception of the early speculation, had their origin outside of the United States."

With even greater indignation a writer named Lothrop Stoddard pointed to the congress of the Third Internationale in 1928, when Moscow predicted that the capitalist world would enter a prolonged depression, a crisis lasting several years, reaching its maximum intensity in 1932 or 1933. Trotsky in 1928 from exile also wrote a complete forecast of 1929 and following events in America, and he too, being a Communist, was not accepted as an economist. When the French

Government, business men and speculators, early in 1929 withdrew gold, sold stocks and bonds, they too were accused of causing the panic instead of getting out from a position their economists well understood.

There were also American economists who proved that in the boom years there was no national prosperity, that there were two million unemployed; that the farmers were bankrupt, that thirty million of them were suffering; that seventy-one per cent of the population was living on a scale hardly above the margin of necessities. But such economists were considered traitorous radicals in 1928 and 1929. They found a small public through the magazines; the newspapers would not touch their anti-American ideas or facts.

Meanwhile the booming industry of advertising kept intimidating the public into more instalment buying, kept inculcating the theory of more waste more prosperity, fostered the idea of living-beyond-income and kept up the "new standards of living" by high pressure salesmanship. The nation's press was party to this achievement of the advertising profession.

Every New Year's morning of the depression and panic years the one hundred and twenty million American population could open its newspapers and reassure itself that nothing had happened, that good times were in sight again, that prosperity was just around the corner, that we had scraped bottom, that we were on the road to recovery. Here is a sample full page, the *Boston Herald* of January 1, 1930, from left to right under an 8-column line:

CONFIDENCE IS KEYNOTE OF NEW YEAR

LEADER OF INVESTMENT BANKERS HAS NO FEARS FOR NORMAL PROSPERITY.

PRESIDENT FARRELL OF U. S. STEEL EXPECTS EARLY SUBSTANTIAL GAINS.

NEW ENGLAND'S BUSINESS NEVER MORE HEALTHY.

SECRETARY LAMONT SAYS GENERAL BUSINESS ON SOUND AND STABLE BASIS.

BONDS RETURN TO FAVOR AS STOCKS
BREAK.
GENERAL ELECTRIC HEAD PREDICTS GOOD
YEAR WITH STEADY EMPLOYMENT.

Of the few dissenting voices which greeted Mr. Hoover's
announcement of the moratorium for foreign debtors in June,
1931, the only important one was Mr. Hearst's.   According
to Gilbert Seldes, Hearst made "the one important point, that
the moratorium favored the bankers and the large investors
over the people as a whole, since it gave precedence to private
debts and postponed, and, as he suspected, made it simple to
cancel public ones."   The stock market rose.

From 1930 on, the public was advised by leaders and press
to buy again "for investment," "for the long pull" or "for
dividends."   In concluding his investigation Mr. Seldes says
that throughout the years the nation went along "on the assumption nothing serious had happened"; this assumption was
colored by our desires; when radical measures were suggested
by economists, the reply was that "the healing process of time"
would cure the nation and the world.   Mr. Seldes reports ques-
tioning many economists and "not one believed in the healing
process of time."   The press did.

It is held by many people that the failure of our newspapers
to inform us honestly and accurately about the economic situation from 1927 to 1929, and the wish-fulfillment policy from
1929 on, constituted its greatest failure in modern times.   The
defense of the editors and publishers is simply this:

1. We knew no more than the public;
2. When we learned the truth, we believed we were
doing a noble action in preventing panic by giving only
the cheerful, optimistic news.

Whether or not these excuses are valid the reader may decide.   I have always been in favor of the facts, the whole
truth within the bounds of the canons of journalism or the
code of ethics of the Newspaper Guild.   As the great Dana of

the *Sun* said, "What the good Lord lets happen I am not ashamed to print in my paper."

As for the defense of ignorance, the answer in law is that ignorance is no excuse. Intelligence could have been bought at a small price. The press might have investigated the reports from Moscow, found out if these were merely Communist wish-fulfillment predictions or economic reasoning, but it chose denunciation instead. The press could have looked for more than anti-American ravings in the European journals which began warning investors in 1928. The press, which spends millions of dollars on a Snyder-Grey or a Hauptmann case, could have hired for a few hundred dollars the best unbiased economic brains in America; it could have investigated unemployment instead of publishing the figures of interested parties; it could have investigated the reports of living conditions, of discontent among farmers, of the unrest of labor.

Obviously there was no desire or intention to do so. Obviously just as stores and corporations are the sacred cows of certain smaller newspapers, so Big Business is the great Sacred Golden Bull of the entire press.

On January 5, 1933—two months before a new President closed the banks of the nation—Senator Carter Glass made a statement on the floor of the Senate that the banks of the country were in a bad way due to depositors' money having been lent for two years on worthless and doubtful securities; that the Comptroller of Currency had winked at the violation of banking laws; that the situation was dangerous for the country.

Not a single newspaper in New York City and not a paper in the United States, so far as a search in the public library could reveal, printed Senator Glass's allegation that a high government official was breaking the law. Whidden Graham, who made this search, wrote five New York newspapers, asking them if the charge was true, but none printed his letter and one, the *Wall Street Journal,* wrote Mr. Graham it did not regard it "advisable" to discuss the matter.

On February 21, 22 and 23, 1933, during the sensational disclosures regarding the National City Bank and Charles E.

Mitchell, not a single New York City newspaper made editorial comment on the matter. Heywood Broun of the *World-Telegram,* however, pointed out that he not only criticized Mitchell but wound up his column by saying "in addition to reform we should have resignation." The *Nation* replied to Mr. Broun that his experiences with the *World* should have taught him that his column cannot be considered as an editorial department. However it did learn from the Staats-Herold Corporation that the *New Yorker Staats-Zeitung* on February twenty-fourth published a vigorous editorial comment on the National City scandal. The *Staats-Zeitung* is a German language paper.

The first editorial comment appeared February twenty-fifth in the tabloid *News.* Finally, when Mr. Mitchell resigned, the conservative morning newspapers ran their first editorials, and when James H. Perkins became president of the National City he issued his first statement: "The primary business of the bank is to serve the domestic and foreign commerce and industry of the United States in the field of commercial banking . . . along the same lines as in the past." In the *Times* editorial this last phrase appeared as "along the well-marked lines of commercial banking."

It is Mr. Graham's opinion that "the greatest obstacle to a public understanding of the real causes of our industrial and business troubles is the attitude of our ignorant, cowardly or venal newspaper editors, who suppress so far as possible all discussion of the fundamentals of our economic system that make inevitable such conditions as now obtain." It is the opinion of the *Nation* that the daily press is unable "to see, hear, or know any evil in advance of catastrophic events which implicate the mighty."

There was a similar though less acute state of affairs when the war began; on the position of the press, Charles Edward Russell then said:

"If there is anything about which people might be supposed to have a right to know it is the condition of business—particularly in a 'business nation,' you know. But

in seven years scarcely one newspaper in the United States
has reported accurately the state of business in or out of
Wall Street whenever such a report would show any considerable depression. In all important offices the necessity
of maintaining a fictitious cheerfulness about the business
situation is now so well recognized that such doctored
reports are no longer regarded as faking; they are as much
a part of the day's work as putting the paper to press. . . ."

These are opinions from the "left"; before giving the view
of Editor Pew, there is another smaller angle to be noted. In
April, 1932, Mr. Pew published a sensational story from
Washington giving the details of Representative La Guardia's
statement before the Senate Committee on Banking and Currency. The New York Congressman said that Wall Street
pools paid $286,279 to financial writers to ballyhoo stocks
while they rigged the market. La Guardia produced nineteen
checks endorsed by writers as follows:

"Check for $50 dated July 24, 1924, made to J. F.
Lowther, then of the *New York Herald Tribune,* but now
with a stock firm; one for $140.50, dated July 11, 1924,
to W. J. Gomber, then with *Financial America;* another
to Lowther for $50, dated July 15, 1924; check $184,
dated December 5, 1924, and endorsed by Charles T.
Murphy. . . .
". . . one endorsed by William J. Gomber, for $209,
and dated December 18, 1924; one for $200 dated De-
cember 20, 1924; and endorsed by W. F. Wamsley, then
of the *New York Times;* three checks totalling $1,800
dated in January, 1925, which La Guardia said would be
identified by the 'pay off' man, whom he expects the
committee to summon; $468 check endorsed by Richard
Edmondson, then of the *Wall Street Journal,* dated January 20, 1925; a $100 check endorsed by Lowther; one
for $184 endorsed by William White, formerly of the
New York Evening Post; another check, date and
amount not given, endorsed by Murphy; $284 check to
Gomber."

After the introduction of evidence the following testimony was taken:

Chairman Norbeck (referring to Gomber check): "Isn't he the same gentleman who is writing in the *Wall Street Journal* panning this investigation?"

Mr. La Guardia: "I wouldn't be surprised. . . ."

Mr. Pew, admitting that in the years preceding 1929 "financial pages were fairly loaded with 'inspired' news, press-agent written," believes this "constituted as wicked an exploitation of the reading public as our press has ever been guilty of." He himself had no difficulty whatever in spotting the bulk of the material in the conservative metropolitan newspapers "obviously contributed by agents paid by persons written about." A few editors protested, but "the rank and file accepted it as a system beyond control . . . why kick against a stone wall?" Can any radical or liberal critic be more damning than the *Editor & Publisher?*

Two New York editors, Mr. Pew also reports, put their financial staffs on the carpet, cleaned house thoroughly, as a result of the La Guardia exposure. "One writer," adds Mr. Pew, "resigned recently in a huff because his office complained that he had failed to expose press graft in Wall Street. His answer was that he wrote the story months ago and it was spiked." As regards the banks, Mr. Pew points out the fact every newspaper man knows, that nothing is more sacred, more taboo, than "Madame First National," whatever the city. A true but unfavorable news item might start a run, and a run would ruin depositors. Therefore the press is silent. Mr. Pew is probably the first editor to favor removing the immunity of banks and bankers.

It is no exaggeration to say, as one Washington correspondent who reported the Pecora cross-examination of Messrs. Mitchell, Kahn, Lamont and others said, that the financial writers of the New York newspapers fawned upon the great bankers of America and wrote "reverential drool" about them.

Again, as during the Teapot Dome investigation, powerful forces attempted to sabotage the Pecora investigation; again certain conservative newspapers accused the investigators of

demagoguery and inveighed against all such inquiries into the
methods of big business. Later on, in the Nye investigation
the same methods were continued. Nye too was hurting business—the business of profits in death.

But above and beyond these facts there is a great question,
the part the press plays or should play in keeping the public
informed on the economic status of the nation. Should it
devote itself to maintaining morale as it did so effectively in
war time in all nations, should it remain silent when times are
bad, hoping by this silence to prevent a panic which publication
of the truth might cause, or should it tell the truth and let
economic inevitability take its course?

In March, 1933, for instance, the *Times* mentioned the fact
that the record of the great banks of New York even in the
years before the crash of 1929 was "humiliating and even
shameful." Would it have been possible for the *Times,* in the
position of constructive critic in the years before 1929, to
point to some of these shameful and humiliating tactics and
thereby prevent them from increasing and making the collapse
all the more dangerous?

Even as late as March 2, 1933, the *Herald Tribune* placed
on page nineteen the story of the moratoria in Alabama,
Louisiana, California, Oklahoma, Kentucky and Tennessee.
The *American* on page twenty-three referred to a "financial
muddle" and the *Times* on page eight spoke of "Banks pro-
tected [sic] in five more states." On the night before the
"holiday" the *Post* alone gave space on its front page to an
inkling of the truth when it disclosed that thirty states had
limited bank operations. "The next day, astonished New
Yorkers," comments the *New Yorker,* "saw across the very
front pages of their papers that Hell had broken loose even
in their own dear state. The policy of pussyfooting, hitherto
unexcelled as a national tonic, had collapsed." What good,
then, did it do the press, which undoubtedly meant well, to
keep the truth from the public?

At the end of the black year 1931 all intelligent men knew
that it was not a depression. It was not a panic. It was an
economic crisis for the whole world. It would require the

best brains of the world and tremendous sacrifices on the part of wealth to bring us out safely, and when that happy day arrived there would still be millions unemployable because the machine age had dispensed with them forever.

In this period of crisis Mr. Pew asked the editors of America—these few hundred leaders who mold public opinion—what their own opinions were. In the condensed replies which follow I have tried to retain the most interesting and important points:

Frank E. Gannett, president of the Gannett newspapers: "Fear and unenlightened selfishness are probably the maladies from which the world is most suffering. . . . I am not ready to admit that the world is yet ready to abandon the profit motive. It has been a tremendous incentive to advancement, to progress. . . . We must also, of course, have a more equitable distribution of the profits of industry, without resorting to socialism."

Alexander Dana Noyes, financial editor, *New York Times:* "To a very great extent, our recent trying experiences must be ascribed to our own extravagance in 1929. . . .

"The world will emerge from this period of violent economic readjustment as it has emerged from many other and equally trying episodes of the kind. It will do so through adjusting itself to the new conditions, reestablishing normal relations between supply and demand, and developing the new groundwork of prosperity along conservative lines. But the world will have to shake off its present hysteria first."

Lawrence Todd, in charge of Washington Bureau, Federated Press: ". . . Congress can and should promptly take over the manufacturing, mining, extraction, transportation and distribution industries. It should organize a nation-wide system of economical distribution of consumers' goods to the people, such distribution being devised primarily to furnish to all the people a comfortable standard of living. Employment should meanwhile be rationalized on a basis of shorter working hours, which should be progressively reduced as improvements in mechanization and method may be developed. Private property rights which enable individuals to profit by the toll or ingenuity of others should be eliminated through confiscatory rates of taxation on estates and incomes."

Robert R. McCormick, Editor, *Chicago Tribune:* "The devastation has its cause in the grafting of socialistic and communistic parasitical growths on political institutions which they kill. The Farm Board is one for instance.

"The results have been (1) paralysis of the private initiative which is not intended to coexist with the Socialist state and which could not, even if it were not to be exterminated by·edict; (2) the strangulation of the use of private property by excessive taxation designed to throw activity under bureaucratic control, to furnish public works of a magnitude not needed by public service and to make punitive levies on productive wealth and absorb it into political action."

Charles G. Ross, chief of the *Post-Dispatch* Washington Bureau in the *St. Louis Post-Dispatch:* ". . . the capitalistic system of government is on trial. To deal intelligently with the depression the naked facts must be known to the people. . . ."

Frank Knox, publisher, *Chicago Daily News:* "My own philosophy, for which I make no great claims, is that elemental economic forces are at work beyond the power of any human effort to control."

Fred Fuller Shedd, editor, *Philadelphia Evening Bulletin* and President American Society of Newspaper Editors: "The way out. Reapportion the available supply of work. Five-day weeks or six-hour work days would spread the chance to work, wage-earning power, buying power to much greater number; would help to take up the surplus in labor market. . . ."

Charles K. McClatchy, editor, *Sacramento Bee:* ". . . First—To collect from the welching Allies the billions they owe. . . . Second—To abolish prohibition and let the citizenry have legalized light wines and beers."

John D. Raridan, executive editor, Brush-Moore Newspapers, Inc.: ". . . The times call for a great sweep of concentrated good advertising on the part of all manufacturers and merchants. . . ."

J. S. Parks, president, *Fort Smith* (Ark.) *Times Record* and *Southwest American:* ". . . Place an embargo on the use of all stock tickers. Old-fashioned castor oil is potent."

Charles P. Manship, publisher, *Baton Rouge State-Times Morning Advocate:* "One of the best ways to meet the present depression is to work more and talk less about hard times."

Bernarr Macfadden, Macfadden Publications: ". . . Find jobs for the jobless. . . . I have maintained again and again that men who cannot find work in the city should go to the country. . . ."

Ralph W. Trueblood, managing editor, *Los Angeles Times:* "It seems to the *Times* that the root of our economic difficulties lies in the drying up or semiparalysis of normal consumption and buying power, and that this condition is largely the result of cumulative and self-perpetuating fear. . . . The main thing is to restore something approaching to normal consumption which, at present greatly reduced prices for everything, can be paid for with much less money than at any time since 1913."

William T. Ellis, the Ellis Service, Swarthmore, Pa.: "Aren't we all making the basic blunder of treating what is really a spiritual phenomenon as merely an economic emergency?"

George Fort Milton, editor of the *Chattanooga News:* ". . . Intelligent forward planning is indispensable if our American civilization is to endure."

An analysis of these typical ideas for dealing with the crisis shows many things: it shows for instance that we have several publishers and reporters who are extremely intelligent men who know what they are talking about; it shows that we have many idealists too, but it also shows that we have molders of public opinion who belong in the most prejudiced and narrow-minded and ignorant stratum of society, men who can be justly called either knaves or economic illiterates.

President Roosevelt gave to the nation his New Deal, a plan for regaining our economic feet. Radical economists, silent for a little while, now arise to call it an ineffectual palliative. It is certainly open to discussion. But the heaviest attack upon the new deal comes not from the "left" which has other economic plans, but from the "right" which has nothing but the anger of big business to offer.

Our economic crisis is a subject that calls for brains, not Republican or Democratic brawls. The press, which failed the public in 1929, can rescue it today. A small amount of money can buy a large amount of brains. There is plenty of intelligence left in America, but what paper will employ it without asking first if it is radical or conservative? Above all we need a willingness on the part of the men who mold public opinion to place the economic problem outside the realm of party politics and business profits. Is that asking too much?

CHAPTER IX

HEADLINES AND TRUTH

> The key is found in the steadfast adherence to principles of Moderation, Decency and Truth; in concentration on all the news and nothing but the news.—
> *New York Times.*

THE word "Truth" is dragged into this investigation because Truth is the announced policy of most newspapers of the world and appears in thousands of mastheads and public declarations by editors and publishers. For myself all I can say is that I have never written a story which I knew to be untrue. Most newspaper men, I am sure, can make the same unqualified statement.

But such statements are not enough. To them must be added the sin of omission. I have already said that as a cub reporter I would bring in the daily report on the Mellon divorce case, or a story involving a department-store owner, or any one of a hundred advertisers, to find the story suppressed not only in mine but in all the other papers of Pittsburgh. In my second year I would take notes which I would write out for the city editor, but when I found they were used to extort advertising, I soon began to overlook all stories which I knew in advance would be suppressed or become an instrument of blackmail.

In Europe I learned that any story derogatory to liberal and radical elements was sure to be published and all stories favorable to them would be played down or left out. It was generally a waste of cable tolls to report any fact favorable to Russia or any Soviet progress. From Mexico I wrote a series of twenty articles, the first of which stated that every angle of the situation, from the oil war to the Catholic war would be mentioned factually, leaving to the reader the formation of an opinion. One of the articles dealt with *The Case for American Intervention,* another with *The Case against Intervention;* one recited the wrongs done the American business men in Mexico, another stated the case of the radical Calles program against the oil exploiters, reciting the wrongs done Mexico. For some reason or another, it may have been due to lack of space, all stories giving the case against the Mexican Government got either front page or prominent place while the charges of Calles, Morones and others against American business interests got little or no space.

When year after year similar experiences occur to a trained newspaper man he usually quits reporting both sides of a controversy. But he still publishes nothing but the truth.

The writer learned something about the difficulty in dealing with that word from Professor Hugo Muensterberg's experiments at Harvard. Muensterberg would stage a brawl in his class room. Two students, acting their rehearsed parts, would engage in it, and the rest of the class would describe what they saw. No two reports were alike. Muensterberg would go further: he would hold up a string and ask his pupils to note its color and length, and the color would be every known one in the spectrum while the length would vary from an inch to a foot.

This test was improved recently at Tulane University when one sudden day a young wild-eyed and disheveled student, carrying a red pump in his hand, burst into a classroom shouting "I'll get you for that quiz." The professor disarmed the youth and drew a pistol from his desk while several lads, believing they had to do with a maniac, made a flying tackle for him.

At this moment the professor ordered quiet. "Everyone will now sit down and write exactly what happened."

The students wrote marvelous stories. One had the intruder wielding an ax, another quoted alarming curses, and a third swore that the professor had actually fired at him.

Professor Edgar James Swift of the psychology department, Washington University, St. Louis, staged an even more effective little drama. He had four students, two men, two girls, break into his classroom, one holding a banana as if it were a pistol. Professor Swift, protesting, fired a small Fourth-of-July torpedo and one of the intruders fell down crying, "I'm shot."

Not only were no two accounts of this thirty second episode alike, but two witnesses said they saw a dog, five heard a pistol shot, eight named students who did not participate in the event, and six could not remember anything but the rush into the room. How in the world, therefore, can you expect the exact truth from reporters who usually get their story second hand from miscellaneous persons who claim they were eyewitnesses?

The best case in my quarter of a century of journalism was brought to me in Vienna in October, 1927. In the Paris edition of the *Chicago Tribune* appeared a tiny item with the slider head:

ACTRESS HANGS HERSELF
IN THEATER DRESSING-ROOM

Herewith follows the paragraph and the facts as related by a person who was present:

The story:	The facts:
BELGRADE, Oct. 27.—A few moments before she should have appeared on the stage at the Lioubliana Theater last night, Mme. Alla Behr, a Slovene actress, was found hanging dead in her dressing-room. The reason for the suicide is unknown.	After the first act. Not at Lioubliana, but Klagenfurt. Her name, Ella Beer. Not Slovene, but Viennese. Not in dressing-room, but hotel. The reason was known.

In type there were exactly six and a half lines, containing exactly seven facts, and of these seven, one, the suicide was correct and all the others were wrong.

Yet there was no malice, no skulduggery, no violation of

the code of newspaper ethics, in this completely mistaken news item.

Now consider for your amusement the relation of headlines to truth in the following ancient episode. These, tradition says, are the reports on the march of Napoleon from Elba to Paris, March 9 to 22, 1815, as shown in contemporary Paris newspapers:

March 9, 1815
The Anthropophagus Has Quitted His Den
March 10
The Corsican Ogre Has Landed at Cape Juan
March 11
The Tiger Has Arrived at Cap
March 12
The Monster Slept at Grenoble
March 13
The Tyrant Has Passed Through Lyons
March 14
The Usurper is Directing His Steps Toward Dijon
March 18
Bonaparte is Only Sixty Leagues from the Capital
He has been fortunate enough to escape his pursuers
March 19
Bonaparte Is Advancing With Rapid Steps, But He Will
Never Enter Paris
March 20
Napoleon Will, Tomorrow, Be under Our Ramparts
March 21
The Emperor Is at Fontainebleau
March 22
His Imperial and Royal Majesty arrived yesterday evening at
the Tuileries, amid the joyful acclamations of his
devoted and faithful subjects

From 1815 to June 11, 1934, is a considerable leap. On that later date "Guy Fawkes," otherwise Robert Benchley, noted dramatic critic of the *New Yorker,* made a study of the headlines in the New York newspapers on a little event affecting the prosperity and politics of same. The American Association of Advertising Agencies had held a convention in Washington. The facts as given in *Editor & Publisher* carried this front page headline:

SIGNALS ARE RED AGAINST ADVERTISING,
D'ARCY WARNS AGENCY CONVENTION;
OTHER SPEAKERS ALSO EMPHASIZE
GROWING DISBELIEF IN COPY
AND NEED FOR REFORM

and the story in part:

"Advertising was distinctly on the defensive this week at the seventeenth annual convention of the American Association of Advertising Agencies. . . .

" 'Quite frankly, advertising as we have been practicing it is losing public confidence,' Chairman D'Arcy told the convention. 'This is evident in every quarter. . . . The tide, gentlemen, has turned against us. The signals show red.'

"Later in the same session the gathering vigorously applauded Miss Alice Edwards, executive secretary of the American Home Economics Association, for an address in which she recited one instance after another of consumer dissatisfaction with advertising."

The *New York Times* headline:

NRA IS HAMPERING,
AD MEN ARE TOLD;
SEES COMMUNISM DANGER

which was followed by a speech by Dr. Paul H. Nystrom saying "higher prices resulting from price-fixing of the NRA codes are retarding business recovery," and Allyn B. McIntire's remarks condemning "professional reformers in government." The *Times'* last paragraph had a few words about D'Arcy but Miss Edwards was left out.

The *New York Herald Tribune* headline:

D'ARCY ASSAILS NEW DEAL
GRIP ON U. S. BUSINESS

with a summary stating a "small amount" of advertising was either exaggeratedly untrue or vulgar. No mention of Miss Edwards.

The *New York American* headline was:

AD MAN SCORES U. S. MEDDLING WITH
BUSINESS

and there was no story mentioning untrue advertising.

Commented Mr. Benchley: "Of course *Editor & Publisher* is written for newspaper men and advertisers, and the daily papers are written for the public. But the public could do a lot worse than to take a look at *Editor & Publisher* once in a while."

Now let us turn the picture around to catch a couple of items in the radical press. The diligent reader, aided by an interpreter, should get a copy of the official organ of the Union of Socialist Soviet Republics, the *Izvestia*, of February 19, 1928, and give himself plenty of time to make the search. He will first of all read all the headlines and find no mention of a certain gentleman who had a little something to do with creating the Union of Socialist Soviet Republics. Let him be more careful. There are several items tucked away in inconspicuous places where no headings are required, and one of them reads:

"L. D. Trotsky, on account of anti-Soviet activity, pursuant to a resolution of the Special Advisory Consulting Committee of the OGPU [the secret police, successor of the Cheka] was exiled from the territory of the Union of the Socialist Soviet Republics. Upon his request he was accompanied by his family."

A tiny paragraph deserving no headline.

On the other hand a milk strike, followed by several demonstrations against the foreclosure of mortgages by the banks in 1932 in the Middle Western States, was headlined in the Soviet press as UPRISING OF THE AMERICAN FARMERS.

The wish is so often father to the headlines.

Finally, there is the case of the *Daily Worker,* the Communist daily published in New York. On the morning following the death of Calvin Coolidge the press of the United States devoted all its seven- and eight-column headlines, most of its front page and from one to three inside pages relating the great career of the president whose reign was marked by the greatest boom in the stock market, the man who had earned a national reputation by his claim that he broke the Boston police strike, and the author of the line "Civilization and profits go hand in hand."

The death of a former president was neither streamer nor page one news to the *Daily Worker.* Nor was it worth columns. On an inside page there were twenty lines, one column wide, with a one-column headline saying:

ENEMY OF LABOR DIES

In nations at war, of course, no one but hundreds of millions of poor deluded ignorant and naïve citizens and subjects expects a word of truth in the newspapers. We now know that Allied propaganda was so effective in neutral countries, including our own, from 1914 to 1917, that the whole world was deceived. Here is Ponsonby's brilliant example of distortion of a war-time fact as it appeared in the newspapers of four war participants:

"When the fall of Antwerp got known the church bells were rung. (i. e., at Cologne). . . ." *Koelnische Zeitung.*

"According to the *Koelnische Zeitung,* the clergy of Antwerp were compelled to ring the church bells when the fortress was taken. . . ." *Le Matin* (Paris).

"According to what *Le Matin* has heard from Cologne, the Belgian priests who refused to ring the church bells when Antwerp was taken, have been driven away from their places. . . ." The *Times* (London).

"According to what the *Times* has heard from Cologne, via Paris, the unfortunate Belgian priests who refused to ring the church bells when Antwerp was taken, have been sentenced to hard labour. . . ." *Corriere della Sera* (Milan).

"According to information to the *Corriere della Sera* from Cologne, via London, it is confirmed that the barbaric conquerors of Antwerp punished the unfortunate Belgian priests for their heroic refusal to ring the church bells by hanging them as living clappers to the bells with their heads down. . . ." *Le Matin* (Paris).

All of which goes to prove what? That there are many kinds of truth? That truth is relative? Perhaps an accident— perhaps an intention? That there is coloring and corruption of headlines and news?

The press of the world, its editors and publishers, shout the challenge Truth. But news is headlined and written, all too frequently, by other elements.

PART THREE

SOURCE AND FORCES

CHAPTER X

A. P.: OUR MAIN SOURCE OF NEWS

To SAY that, as reporter and editor, I considered the Associated Press as honorable as Cæsar's wife is not enough: wives have been known to commit historic adultery. The A. P. to most newspaper men, including many arrivals, was more like their own mothers, the sacred sentimental mothers of Mother's Day, the women about whom most men will not hear criticism.

An A. P. item was sacred. The Associated Press, we were told, was the greatest news gathering organization in the world, co-operative, serving hundreds of newspapers of every shade and prejudice, and doing its job with Olympian detachment and almost godly rectitude. You could print most anything in some newspapers, you could even call a president a name, but you worshiped at the shrine of the Associated Press.

With that "conditioning" I never doubted A. P. reports on strikes in Pittsburgh, nor was I worried by its failure to give space to my testimony before the Steel Trust Investigating Committee, and I did not suspect propaganda in its reports during the World War.

Before I recount other personal experiences with the Associated Press and give a small part of the mass of evidence I have collected in the last fifteen years, I must present a few excerpts from public declarations of important men because they illustrate the problem which faces anyone who attempts to criticize the great organization. Melville Stone, head of the agency, the man who "made" it, after speaking of the "brave, conscientious, patriotic body of journalists," the founders, their responsibility and obligations, declares "their purpose was to tell the truth about the world's happenings—perhaps not the whole truth—but nothing but the truth. The newspaper members it serves as a joint reporter include papers of every sort of affiliation—Republican, Democratic, free trade and protection, capitalist and trade unionist, conservative and radical—and this carries with it a trusteeship. Newspapers have but one common demand upon the organization: that it shall furnish news and not views; that as nearly as possible, considering the frailties of human nature, its service shall be free from bias or deduction or opinion. And the only tie that binds any member newspaper to it is the confidence of the newspaper member in its integrity and impartiality!"

Again, in the service bulletin of December 3, 1919, it is stated that "The spirit of the Associated Press today, as when it was founded, is the spirit of truth, of enterprise and impartiality. It devotes itself to public enlightenment, to the dissemination of facts, to serving those ideals of right and justice and democracy upon which the American Republic was founded." Who could ask for anything more?

But when the first charges against the A. P. had appeared Mr. Adolph S. Ochs issued this imposing manifesto:

"I challenge any man in the world to show that any item of news sent out by the Associated Press was doctored or distorted for personal interests. There may have been errors, maybe news was dishonestly reported to The 'A. P.' but so far as The 'A. P.' is concerned, every news story is carefully scrutinized with the sole view of giving unbiased information to the public."

To Sinclair's fulminations Mr. Frank B. Noyes, president, replied that "we are accustomed through long experience to the railings against our service of the uninformed, the notoriety seeker, and the common or garden liar who charges bias or suppression in the report of the Associated Press. Every newspaper man, every informed person, knows how preposterously untrue these charges are—whoever may make them." But Ernest H. Gruening, editor, author, and now colonial administrator, replied that "it is a public duty of the Associated Press to answer Mr. Sinclair point by point." That, so far as I can discover, was not done.

When Eugene Debs asked the same news agency to retract its damaging report that he had suspended publication of his paper, the A. P. refused to do so. Debs wrote: "Am I to infer from your letter that the Associated Press aims to deal fairly, honestly and justly with all people, to disseminate the truth, and taboo what is false? I happen to know differently by personal experience. If there is in this country a strictly capitalist class institution, it is the Associated Press." Debs went to some length in discussing a report on the Pullman strike, adding that it was "a lie, but I could never get the Associated Press to correct it." Throughout his fighting career Debs had difficulties with the A. P.

The editor of the *Nation,* Oswald Garrison Villard, who for many years was a member of the board of directors of the Associated Press, charged that organization with failure to carry the news that in Florida men, women and children were burned alive in an election riot because some negroes tried to vote, and he is also the author of the strongest statement that has ever been made against the A. P. outside of a soap-box oration. It is: "Again the Associated Press was the medium of wholesale lying and crass misrepresentation in reporting some race troubles in ˉPhillips County, Arkansas, which it portrayed to the American people as a 'negro rebellion . . . of more than local nature possibly planned for the entire south.' "

The Brass Check in 1920 did not arouse the same emotions in journalistic breasts as Will Irwin's articles a decade earlier. Upton Sinclair, not being a journalist, left dozens of Achilles' heels in his presumably ironclad case against the press; not understanding the technique of newspaper making nor the accepted methods of reporting the news, he made numerous errors in judgment and criticism, upon which all the horde of boss-serving boot-lickers and apologists pounced thankfully. Thus among newspaper men at least the main issue which Sinclair raised was obscured by overemphasis on minor or unimportant faults. An old, but very effective trick.

The year of that book's appearance, however, marked my first encounter in the open field with the Associated Press.

The suspicion, shared with the *New York World* and *Manchester Guardian,* that the Berlin Associated Press reports on the so-called "Red Rhineland" were the opposite of what we who were there saw and heard, was increased during the Russo-Polish War. From Warsaw, the Associated Press flooded America with Allied ballyhoo favoring Poland. Pilsudski marched into the Ukraine and the world press applauded. Only a few liberal newspapers mentioned the fact that Pilsudski had invaded Russian territory before the war began and that he had acted against the advice of Lloyd George and military experts. Pilsudski was "the saviour of civilization from the Red Peril."

When, in midsummer, Pilsudski was reeling toward Warsaw, and the Cossacks appeared on the Vistula, Poland asked for an armistice which was answered by Trotsky's order to his generals to cease their advance and make terms. On July twenty-seventh these were rejected by the Allies. Diplomats of the French Foreign Office tricked the Associated Press, which probably needed little tricking as it had been extremely favorable to Pilsudski and Poland for a whole year; the A. P. sent a dispatch on the very day that new armistice terms were under way, saying, "It is asserted in French quarters that a secret code wireless message from Moscow gave instructions to the Soviet commanders to keep pushing their offensive violently."

This report from the French was absolutely untrue. It was not originated by the Associated Press, but it was sent by the Associated Press because some French official thought such a falsehood would serve his end.

How the Associated Press covered the news from Russia, 1917 to 1920, has been exposed in the Lippmann-Merz study of the *Times.* The present writer in 1922 and 1923 found in James P. Howe, Moscow correspondent of the A. P., a journalist of the highest integrity and, exceptional among A. P. men, one who was willing to co-operate with the representatives of his agency's clients. Obviously the A. P. had chosen an unbiased and reliable man for the Russian job to make up for the five years of misleading Polish, French, Finnish, Latvian and Arctic Circle news about Russia.

One of the most important journalistic scandals in our recent history concerns the Associated Press and its Mexican news. Inasmuch as the story has been told only by the liberal weeklies and a few liberal newspapers, I will give it in some detail.

I was sent by the *Tribune* to the Mexican border in 1927. At that time I did not know that certain American interests were preparing for a war with the southern republic, but I sensed that atmosphere in the American Embassy in Mexico City. The oil, copper and hacienda interests with the support of that part of the press which for personal or profit interests was professionally anti-Mexican planned an "intervention" which meant war, victory, annexation or at least paternal control such as existed in Cuba.

What part did the Associated Press play in this big diplomatic game?

In 1924 Elias Plutarco Calles, who promised the people he would carry out the constitution which Carranza wrote in 1917, was elected president and in 1926 he made the legal declaration that the subsoil of the country belonged to the nation and the people. Thus, with one stroke, Calles attempted to right all the wrongs, the graft, the corruption, the thefts and crooked politics and business deals which for decades had despoiled the nation of its vast common wealth.

The United States had just gone through the greatest scandal of the century, Teapot Dome. But Teapot Dome was one drop in the barrel compared to the oil scandals in Mexico. The liberal members of the Senate asked Secretary of State Kellogg if he had any information concerning the Mellon, Doheny and Sinclair holdings in Mexican oil, and the Secretary replied that he knew nothing.

But on November 16, 1926, the Assistant Secretary of State, Mr. Robert E. Olds, resorted to the old red-herring trick, the hackneyed but always effective red scare, under cover of which strikes are smashed and wars are made. Mr. Olds called in the representatives of the Associated Press, United

Press and International News Service and unfolded before their astonished ears a lurid tale of Russia plotting against America, with Mexico as a base, and the Panama Canal in danger of occupation by enemies.

"Gentlemen," said Mr. Olds to the journalists he had previously pledged to secrecy about the source of their news, "we feel that this picture should be presented to the American people. We cannot prove it, but we are morally certain that a warm bond of sympathy, if not an actual understanding, exists between Mexico City and Moscow. . . . I want your advice and co-operation."

"That's easy," replied the representative of the United Press; "let the State Department issue a statement over the signature of the Secretary and every newspaper in America will publish it."

The Assistant Secretary of State was shocked. The Department could not diplomatically accuse a "friendly" country, it had no proofs, it wanted the story published and it did not want responsibility for it.

The United Press refused to touch Mr. Olds' story; the representative of that same Mr. Hearst who had on account of his Mexican holdings always been an ardent interventionist, likewise refused to spread alarming and unauthenticated news. But on the morning of November 18, 1926, the press of the United States flamed with headlines "Bolshevik Plot against America"; "Red Plot to Seize the Panama Canal"; "Communist Plot against U. S. in Mexico." Under these headlines appeared a column of sensations beginning with the following paragraph:

"Washington, Nov. 17 (AP).—The spectre of a Mexico-fostered Bolshevist hegemony intervening between the United States and the Panama Canal, has thrust itself into American-Mexican relations, already strained. . . ."

Continuing, the Associated Press spoke of "the spectre of Bolshevism fostered by Mexico . . . a picture of Bolshevism rampant in Latin America, menacing the safety of the key to

American national defense." No facts were given, no authority, nothing but State Department propaganda, concocted by officials for the purpose of creating hatred and an atmosphere of war.

The A. P. did exactly what the Wolff bureau did in Nazi Germany, or the Stefani does in Fascist Italy: it served a regime, not the public, "with all the loss of independence and integrity which that policy involves," as the *New York World* said editorially.

The *St. Louis Post-Dispatch* was the first to cry fraud. Its correspondent, Paul Y. Anderson, obtained his information from George R. Holmes, chief of the Washington Bureau of the International News Service who had, on his own responsibility, refused to lend the Hearst service to a hoax although that hoax might have been pleasing to the editorial prejudices of his employers. At the conference of the A. P., U. P. and I. N. S. men with Olds it was Holmes who told the Assistant Secretary of State in unflattering terms what he thought of the ethics of "planting" propaganda.

Mr. Anderson's story was immediately taken up by the *Baltimore Sun*, the *New York World*, the Scripps-Howard papers and later by the *Nation*, the *New Republic* and several liberal church weeklies and notably by the *Editor & Publisher*. Thanks to the liberal press, therefore, the scandal was aired. Senator Wheeler introduced a resolution for a Senate investigation but the Committee on Foreign Relations killed it. Senator Willis of Ohio explained to reporters that "Anderson is telling the truth and Kellogg's denial is a diplomatic denial, but we would be foolish to start an investigation."

But the A. P., which had misinformed thirty million readers, replied that the information "came to the Associated Press . . . from sources which it has a right to expect are well informed and correctly represent the views of the government." (Two years later President Noyes of the A. P. still defended the organization although it had circulated the story.)

In January, 1927, Secretary Kellogg took occasion to deny that his department "or any of its officers" gave the Associated Press its information. "Either Mr. Kellogg is making a goat of the Associated Press," commented the *World,* "in which case we hope that the Associated Press will tell him so, or Mr. Kellogg is right, and the Associated Press obtained its information from sources outside the State Department. In this case it would be interesting to know what those sources were." The Washington manager of the A. P., Mr. L. C. Probert, stated that "we got the story in the usual course of news and we had no reason to doubt its accuracy," and the conclusion of the episode is the report of the Committee on Integrity of the American Society of Newspaper Editors: "Your committee believes that an attack on the integrity of the press is launched every time a public official attempts to feed colored news to a newspaper or news service . . . every editor knows that the national government, every state and every local government, contains officials the chief end of whose waking and sleeping hours is to use the press for individual or party advantages. . . . Are we not a little too complacent in the face of this evil?"

In December, 1926, and in the spring of 1927 anti-Mexican propaganda continued to flow from the State Department, and the Associated Press, taking care now that the "dope" was credited to someone, continued to send it out. Secretary Kellogg, for instance, issued a blast entitled *Bolshevist Aims in Mexico and Latin America.* The news agency sent out Kellogg's propaganda in all its gory detail, apparently pursuant to a policy of kowtowing to authority and not to question the divinity of a government official. "Kellog has falsified the record," an anti-interventionist paper commented.

Two years later it was revealed in Congress that at the time of the Olds-Associated Press episode and during the Kellogg broadsides there was also a plot by oil interests, mining concessions, bankers, certain newspapers and other powerful persons and organizations to intervene in Mexico, to annex Mexico at the price of a war. The first warlike act was the concentration of the largest air force in our history at Texan forts in 1927.

That the war was averted was no fault of the big interventionist press nor the propaganda which the Associated

Press had retailed from the sacred State Department. It was a victory for liberalism, for the liberal minority press, for organized labor, a handful of independent congressmen and other elements; it was achieved because the public was not in a mood for war hysteria and refused to eat the red herrings of the red-baiting press bureaus and newspapers. In 1927 at least it seemed that the 1918-1920 Bolshevik myth had finally been exploded.

In 1925 again I had an important encounter with the A. P. Damascus had been bombarded by the French. I take no credit for this world scoop. It is one of those accidents which occurs once in a lifetime to every reporter. It so happened that I was there and was able to get most of the story through the censor. It so happened that I took the only photographs. The captions beneath may tell you that the ungodly French shot down a mosque. I know my photograph shows only a mosque-like bath house. But the Associated Press, which had no correspondent in Damascus, telegraphed a series of tall tales from terrified travelers, with date lines of Haifa, Jerusalem, Cairo, recounting "days and nights of unforgettable horror . . . hundreds (of dead or wounded) lying in the streets . . . at least 2,000 buried in the debris." I had reported first a hundred, then a possible two hundred dead. The official figure later given the League of Nations was one hundred and thirty-five. What the Associated Press had done was send the statements of Arabs or Syrian Nationalists and the Pan-Islamic propaganda bureau in Jerusalem. But no foreign correspondent would think of accusing it of doing so because of prejudices, as in the Russo-Polish conflict; here it was merely another illustration of the A. P.'s refusal to accept defeat. It may be recalled that Peary had an exclusive agreement with the *New York Times* preventing the press bureaus from reporting his discovery of the North Pole, and this may explain why Captain Cook got such a fine deal from the A. P. and the papers which were not able to get the Peary story.

Again, in July, 1927, the Associated Press was beaten badly on the Vienna revolution by the *Times* man and myself who rode to Czechoslovakia in an automobile and telephoned our story to Berlin, Prague and Paris. Now in the Melville Stone days the Associated Press would have made the best of the few reliable bulletins obtained from reliable co-operating bureaus, but under the new dispensation the A. P., like its commercial rivals, cannot accept a setback. As in Damascus and elsewhere, the A. P., unable to obtain reliable reports, proceeded to make the best of rumors, exaggerations, half-truths and distortions, being careful however to specify in each case the sources of false news.

The simple facts were that a spontaneous demonstration occurred one morning following a vicious decision freeing several Fascist murderers who had fired into a workingmen's parade. Now fifty thousand paraded. The moment was chosen by several Communists to turn peaceful protest into revolutionary agitation and the result was the firing of the Palace of Justice. Neither labor nor Communists indulged in other violence. But the "best police force in the world," without warning, without firing blanks, but descending on horses like a brown tidal wave, killed a hundred men, women and children.

The A. P. correspondent, after filing his morning bulletins, faced the general strike. He was incommunicado. But the A. P. delivered to its American clients sensations of this sort:

"London, July 15 (A. P.) An untimed dispatch from the Vienna correspondent of the *Daily Express* said the fighting this evening was assuming revolutionary character and was unabated.

"London, July 15 (A. P.) A Turin dispatch to the *Daily Mail* filed at 10.30 P. M. said it was reported from Vienna that a "red dictatorship" had been proclaimed in Austria.

"Paris, July 16 (A. P.) A Havas dispatch from Belgrade says it was reported there today that Chancellor Seipel has resigned and that a Socialist government has been formed. . . .

"London, July 16 (A. P.). . . . Reuter's Budapest correspondent . . . estimates the total death in the Vienna disorders at 200.

"Vienna, Austria July 16 (A. P.) . . . The number of killed is estimated tonight at 250. . . . The general post-office, the palace of justice and the editorial offices of several conservative newspapers present a scene of wreckage. . . ."

None of these stories is quite true.

They are on a par with the Associated Press dispatches on Russia for a period of years which emanated from far-away cities. Again, as in Damascus, the issue in Vienna was not intentional perversion of news, but sensationalism. The old standards of reliability seemingly were abandoned in the rivalry for hot news.

Let us now look at the record of the Associated Press in handling American labor disputes. Upton Sinclair makes the charge that the A. P. does not cover strikes unless there is violence; I do not think this charge is valid. So long as newspapers are printed for the purpose of recording events they publish only a few words about a strike where there is no violence: there is no news in the fact that the sun rises in the east and sets in the west and there is no more than a line or two necessary to report a strike in which absolutely nothing happens. Under our present system there is no news when nothing happens and big news when there is violence.

On the other hand, Sinclair is absolutely right when he charges the A. P. with obtaining its news from newspapers friendly to the manufacturers, enemies of labor. It is this fact which validates the official allegations of the labor unions against the A. P. and creates for that organization its most serious problem which, in my opinion, it has apparently failed to meet entirely at any time.

Newspaper men who cover strikes for fair newspapers and all liberal-minded copyreaders who have handled Associated Press "flimsy" usually get the impression that the great A. P. is certainly never prejudiced in favor of labor. However, they do not demand that; all that is necessary is objective reporting, regardless of the fact the vast majority of readers come under the term labor and the vast majority of newspaper

owners come under the term capital. Allowing for error due
to human shortcomings, it is still possible to cover a strike,
demonstration, or a labor "war" fairly, provided such is the
intention of the reporter and, more important, the sincere
desire—as distinguished from formal instructions—of the
head of the bureau.

The whole history of American labor's struggles with organized employers is filled with accusations against the press
and notably the Associated Press, but it is not until recently
that there is a record of the American Federation of Labor
making any charge against the A. P. On October 9, 1933,
however, Frank B. Powers, of the Commercial Telegraphers'
Union of North America, told the A. F. of L. convention that
President Noyes "has taken a position that the Associated
Press does not come under the provisions of the National
Industrial Recovery Act, thereby showing his unwillingness
to cooperate with the President of the United States to the
fullest extent in his efforts to bring about a reduction in the
number of working hours as a means to increase employment
without reducing purchasing power on the part of the employes of the Associated Press."

The American Federation of Labor adopted a resolution
declaring that the United Press, the International News
Service and the Universal Service have for over twenty-five
years maintained "satisfactory shop relations" with the Commercial Telegraphers Union "and have grown and prospered
thereunder. . . . Despite these efforts and in the face of efforts
of the Chief Executive and the National Recovery Administration to promote harmonious relations between labor and
management, the Associated Press persists in its attitude of
aloofness from the provisions of the National Industrial Recovery Act, and actual hostility towards organized labor with
respect to its own employes. . . . The Federation . . . vigorously
condemns the anti-labor policy of the Associated Press" and
asks the state and central labor unions to "bring this resolution to the attention of publisher members of the Associated
Press, all of whom are now under the Blue Eagle, and many

of whom have shown by editorials or wage agreements that they are friendly to organized labor."

("This statement is wholly untrue, both in respect to me and in respect to the Associated Press," Mr. Noyes answered over the A. P. wires. "As a matter of fact, the Associated Press has been endeavoring to conform both to the spirit and the letter of the NRA.")

The telegraphers' union, which had already organized the U. P. and the two Hearst services, then attempted to work among A. P. men. The result was described by Arthur Markel, deputy international president: "When we started an organizing campaign among Associated Press operators some months ago we received reports of attempted intimidation of men desiring to affiliate with our organization. Both Mr. Noyes and Mr. Kent Cooper, general manager of the Associated Press, have refused to answer the specific question of whether or not the Associated Press officially countenances such terrorization of its employees."

The "anti-labor policy of the Associated Press" has been a common topic in labor, liberal and radical circles; just before the war there was an opportunity for all the evidence on both sides to come before the general public, but the A. P. thought it wiser not to have this test made. It was during the West Virginia strike. Mrs. Fremont Older had made the statement: "The provost marshal was not only the ruling officer of Paint Creek Junction; he was the Associated Press correspondent. He had the divine gift of creating darkness." In the *Masses* (June, 1913) there appeared a cartoon by Art Young showing a gentleman labeled "Associated Press" pouring the contents of a bottle, labeled "Poison" into a reservoir labeled "Public Opinion."

As a result of this cartoon both Art Young and Max Eastman, the editor, were indicted on November 26, 1913, for criminal libel.

On December twenty-ninth a second indictment was brought against Eastman.

According to Upton Sinclair, the indictment repeated the following from an editorial in the *Masses:*

". . . one trust that I find it impossible to encourage is this Truth Trust, the Associated Press. So long as the substance of current history continues to be held in cold storage, adulterated, colored with poisonous intentions, and sold to the highest bidder to suit his private purposes, there is small hope that even the free and the intelligent will take the side of justice in the struggle that is before us. . . .

"The representative of the Associated Press was an officer in that military tribunal that hounded the Paint Creek miners into the penitentiary, in violation of their constitutional liberties; and this fact is even more significant and more serious than the abrogation of those liberties. It shows that the one thing which all tribes and nations in time have held sacred—the body of Truth—is for sale to organized capital in the United States."

An investigation by Upton Sinclair showed that the official A. P. correspondent was Cal Young, of Charleston, and that his friend, John C. Bond, provost marshal of militia and correspondent for several newspapers, had agreed with him to telephone back news from the strike field, which Young wrote for the A. P. and for Bond's papers. The source of the news was a militiaman, but the man who sent the story was not.

Many a man has been hanged on a smaller technicality. The Associated Press certainly had a case. In the *New York Evening Post* it stated its position, thus:

"The Associated Press is not prosecuting the case in any vengeful spirit, but is fighting for a public vindication. For several years the association has sat silent under accusations of this kind, reflecting upon the integrity of the service and the personal honor of its responsible officers, because the charges were made either on the floor of Congress, where no redress is possible, or by persons who were careful or lucky in avoiding the legal limitations of civil or criminal libel. In several cases the persons making the charges retracted them absolutely. At last they have a case involving libel per se, and they purpose to avail themselves of the opportunity to present to the public the facts regarding the service."

Then in 1914 came the Colorado Fuel and Iron Company strike. Sinclair, convinced that he had legal evidence proving suppression of news, printed a repetition of the *Masses* editorial, and added:

> "I now, over my own signature and as a deliberate challenge, charge that the Associated Press has poisoned the news of the Colorado situation at its source. Will the owners and managers of the Associated Press take up this challenge and make an attempt to send me to prison? I am waiting, gentlemen, for your answer."

He is still waiting. The Associated Press, so far as I can discover, did not try to have him arrested. Both indictments on the *Masses* count were dismissed by the court on November 30, 1915, apparently with the acquiescence of the District Attorney.

In every notable instance where impartial fact-finding bodies or impartial newspaper men have made a study of the press and labor, considerable evidence has been alleged reflecting on the fairness of the Associated Press. When Charles Edward Russell investigated the Calumet strike he filled seven magazine pages with damning parallel columns, the first headed "Associated Press," the second "The Facts." Although the A. P. was charged with publishing "a string of subtle and knavish falsehoods" I fail to find that it either apologized or sued for libel.

A strike is labor's weapon against tyranny: it is a continuation in a small way of the strike of the first American patriots against a misguided British king. Strikers as a rule do not start violence. Every honest newspaper man knows that the hired thugs, the *agents provocateurs,* the coal and iron police, the armed forces of the city or state or federal government, are responsible for most of the provocation and the violence.

But strikes, as Russell points out, are won by public opinion, and public opinion is made by the newspapers, and the newspapers usually blame violence, disorderly conduct and lawlessness on the workingmen instead of the armed forces. This was true in San Francisco only a few months ago; it was true in the great Pittsburgh steel strike just after the war, and it was true at Calumet. Every impartial investigation has proved this fact.

The greatest force in American public opinion is the Associated Press. Russell says in introducing his case against the organization in the now defunct *Pearson's Magazine* (April, 1914),

> "Here is the most tremendous engine for Power that ever existed in this world. If you can conceive all the Power ever wielded by the great autocrats of history, by the Alexanders, Cæsars, Tamburlaines, Ghengis Khans and Napoleons, to be massed together into one vast unit of Power, even this would be less than the Power now wielded by the Associated Press.
>
> "Because thought is the ultimate force in the world, and here you have an engine that causes 30,000,000 minds to have the same thought at the same moment, and nothing on earth can equal the force thus generated.
>
> "Well-informed men know that the great Controlling Interests have secured most of the other sources and engines of Power. They own or control most of the newspapers, most of the magazines, most of the pulpits, all of the politicians and most of the public men.
>
> "We are asked to believe that they do not own or control the Associated Press, by far the most desirable and potent of these engines. We are asked to believe that the character and wording of the dispatches upon which depends so much public opinion is never influenced in behalf of the Controlling Interests. We are asked to believe that Interests that have absorbed all other such agencies for their benefit have overlooked this, the most useful and valuable of all. We are even asked to believe that, although the Associated Press is a mutual concern, owned by the newspapers, and although these newspapers that own it are in turn owned by the Controlling Interests, the Controlling Interests do not own, control or influence

the Associated Press, which goes its immaculate way, furnishing impartial and unbiased news to the partial and biased journals that own it.

"That is to say that when you buy a house you do not buy its foundations."

The president of the Chicago Federation of Labor adds to the evidence in the following telegram to the A. P.:

"The Associated Press reports of the packers' arbitration at Chicago are running true to form. You are suppressing the avalanche of hideous facts which show the injustice practiced against the workers and blazon forth as truths the lies and evasions of the packers.

"You are garbling and distorting your accounts to serve the selfish interest of the packers and to help keep a hundred thousand suffering and struggling humans in a condition of abject slavery which means starvation and death for men, women and children.

"The local papers accounts are exposing your conduct. We want you to know the people of Chicago appreciate what you are doing.

"Mr. Frank P. Walsh is counsel for the laborers and can verify my statements.
(Signed)   "John Fitzpatrick."

This communication, taken from the confidential service bulletin of the A. P., is followed by an explanation. There are many more similar complaints in these bulletins and the usual answer given is that the news was sent out fairly and fully, so the A. P. is not to blame for the failure of the editors of America to print the news they receive.

But the same old typical Associated Press strike story was repeated in 1931 and 1932 in Kentucky when the local editors and publishers, most of them financially linked with the mine owners, raised the same old red menace bugaboo when workmen who were starving went on strike. In the accompanying disorders the Associated Press had the distinction of having its representative a leader of a mob which assaulted and deported delegations of writers and investigators from other states.

Theodore Dreiser, Waldo Frank, Malcolm Cowley, Edmund Wilson and thirteen other writers sent a letter to Kent Cooper, general manager of the A. P., protesting a "policy of misrepresentation of facts by local representatives of the Associated Press in the Kentucky coal area and a deliberate misuse of them by the Associated Press facilities."

Herndon Evans, editor of the *Pineville* (Ky.) *Sun,* head of the local Red Cross and local correspondent of the A. P., was further accused in the letter of saying to Allen Taub, who with Frank had been beaten up by night riders, "Well, Taub, why don't you make us another speech on constitutional rights? This is the last chance you will have to make such a speech in Kentucky!" Mr. Evans, the writers said in their protest, then wired the A. P. that Frank and Taub had received their injuries in fighting each other!

The Associated Press, attacked by liberal and other fairminded publications throughout the country, replied:

"The only interest the Associated Press has in the Kentucky situation and the New York group of writers is in obtaining and presenting accurately and fairly the news of both sides.

"When the situation first developed, a policy of assigning staff men to cover developments, whenever it was possible to do so, was determined upon and this has been followed. The record copy of stories handled by the Associated Press on the visits of the New York group of writers to Kentucky shows that we carried both versions of the alleged beating of Mr. Frank and Mr. Taub. Complete coverage on all other phases in the Kentucky situation has been given both sides. An earnest effort has been made to be fair and accurate.

"Mr. Evans is a local newspaperman in Pineville, Ky. He is not a staff correspondent of the Associated Press and the Associated Press is not responsible for his personal conduct."

Thanks to Marlen Pew, editor of *Editor & Publisher,* we have a little more light on the foregoing statement which denies Evans as "a staff correspondent of the Associated Press." Mr. Pew, unable to satisfy himself in New York as to the correspondent's status, wired to Kentucky and received Mr. Evans' illuminating answer:

"There has been so much misrepresentation in the press about my connection with Taub and Frank affair that I am glad to advise you about it. As correspondent of the Associated Press and representing several metropolitan dailies, I went to scene of deportation of the New York writers. . . .

". . . Any statement that I saw the fight or was a participant in the plan is utterly false, though from the hell the Reds have raised here in the past six months I don't blame the people for taking them to the state line."

In other words Evans, by his own statement, *was* a correspondent of the A. P. and red-baiter. For several years he had sent this brand of "news" about an important strike, which the A. P. disseminated throughout America. Not until noted writers brought this scandalous situation to national attention did the Associated Press act.

In March, 1932, the situation became a bit too thick for even the A. P. It announced that it had discontinued the services of the editor of the *Pineville Sun* as "string correspondent." Mr. Jackson Elliott wrote Dreiser that since Evans "has been so prominently projected on the other side of the controversy the Associated Press feels it would be unwise to accept further dispatches from him. . . . Herndon Evans is the only newspaper man in Pineville and as such has acted as a 'string' correspondent, filing dispatches not only to the Associated Press but to others. He is not a staff correspondent of the Associated Press, and the Associated Press is not responsible for his personal actions. It is certainly our responsibility, however, to keep our reports unbiased and accurate."

Examples of the Associated Press treatment of officially organized labor, and of all dissenting unions which it usually

terms "reds," and of the victims of mobs and legal injustice
can be continued indefinitely by every reporter who ever covered a labor dispute.   God is on the side of the biggest bat-
talions, Napoleon cynically announced, and the Associated
Press is on the side of God.   In 1934 labor troubles spread
throughout America.   With the apparent first successful results of the recovery program and the establishment of Blue
Eagle codes, labor began asking for a better share of this
world's goods and satisfactions.   In many instances the
strikers demanded what the official codes promised but the
employers refused to grant.

In San Francisco, in Minneapolis, in Ambridge, in Kohler,
along the Pacific Coast and in many places violence and bloodshed marked the uprisings of the workingmen.   In almost
every case, as in the long history of labor wars, the violence
was provoked by the forces of law and order, the police, the
militia, the Black Cossacks, the national guard, the private
armies of the manufacturers.   If the Associated Press said
otherwise, or failed to mention this little point, the United
Press frequently did mention it, and frequently the sound
newsreels gave indisputable proof that the armed forces shot
down unarmed men unnecessarily.

But the Associated Press, which claims it is fair to labor,
which denies it ever issues propaganda, and which claims it
never writes editorials into its news, had this to say in 1934:

"Washington, Aug. 4—America's 'soldiers of the sov-
ereign states' have been marching on the double-quick
from the relative obscurity of armory drills and summer
camps into big places in the national spotlight.
"These national guardsmen, preservers of peace and
protectors of the public, have been called on to maintain
order during the menace of industrial warfare in Pacific
Coast cities and in Minneapolis, in the governorship battle
in North Dakota, in labor troubles in Alabama and sundry other disturbances throughout the country."

The Associated Press, in short, seems always on the side of
authority; it appears to make no difference to this great or-

ganization whether authority is a great president or a crooked secretary of the interior, a bloodthirsty dictator or a mild constitutional ruler, a city policeman or a steel company's hired thug. If the Associated Press had reported the Boston Tea Party it would probably have been an indignant story of Reds defying authority and destroying private property.

There are many reasons for the A. P. being what it is. According to Roy Howard (chairman of the board of the Scripps-Howard newspapers, the A. P.'s No. 1 enemy, who has bought eight of the highly prized and priced franchises and thrown them out of the window), the monopolistic rules of the organization are "archaic" and "immoral"; as for being a mutual co-operative society, he points out that its original founders hold one hundred and fifty thousand dollars' worth of bonds, each priced at twenty-five dollars, each entitled to a vote, thus giving a small handful of rich and powerful publishers six thousand votes against the twelve or thirteen hundred co-operating editors and publishers.

This was the group which Will Irwin in 1914 called the "ring of old, Tory, forty-one-vote papers in control" of the Associated Press. Despite the Cooper regime with its jazzy news, its millions of words of slobbering sentimentality in instances like the Harding funeral, its entry into the photographic field and other signs of modernization, control of the A. P. remains not only conservative, but Tory in the extreme. Naturally, says Irwin, a journalist gathers around him men who look at life and events as he does, and the A. P. is no exception. The subordinates

"have drifted inevitably toward the point of view held by their masters. Sharp, efficient news-gatherers, with the devotion to their organization characteristic of the American reporter, they doubtless believe that they are giving all the important news all the time and giving it unbiased. . . . A movement in stocks is to him news—big news. Widespread industrial misery in a mining camp is scarcely news at all. The flare and action of a strike in Paterson is news. The weight of vested power crushing down the union after the strike is not news. A Califor-

nia hop-pickers' riot with murder on the side is news.
The trial which follows, with its illumination on the methods of Tory interest when they have their own way, is not
news. . . .

". . . The agents of this dominant bureau, owing to
their point of view, select from the events of the day
such news as squares with their conservative picture of
our world; and their organization hinders or prevents
the rise of publishers who might present the other side.
And, including though it does a few newspapers of most
radical tendencies, the Associated Press is in bulk a powerful force of reaction."

In the opinion of Mr. Villard, one of the reasons the A. P.
fails to be what it claims is its failure to discipline members
which break the code of ethics; he once called upon the A. P.
which had won a suit from Hearst in which it alleged its news
was being stolen, to expel all the Hearst papers.   But nothing
was done.   In the case of a smaller paper, the *North American* for example, a fine of three hundred dollars was levied for
a statement that a certain A. P. cablegram was in all probability "written in New York or Washington, and never was near
an ocean cable."

This right to fine a paper for criticism, I would like to add,
is another of the chief faults of the A. P.   To most journals
the franchise is their most valuable asset; in New York it may
be worth a million dollars.   But it may be cancelled if the
organization is offended by the critical attitude of the franchise
holder.   I know of several instances where mildly liberal
editors have written protests to the Associated Press, alleging
that the news of the recent textile strike, the San Francisco
general strike and other labor troubles was unfair to labor.
So long as these protests remain confidential letters, the A. P.
need not worry; but if the papers published them the A. P.
might be forced from its reactionary position.   In the mean-
time the editors would lose their membership.   So they refrain from publishing criticism.

As regards worship of authority Mr. Villard believes it is

"in no small measure due to the personal attitude of Messrs. Noyes and Ochs."

But the fairest criticism is caused by the A. P. structure itself: its source of news is its membership.   Not one, but thirteen hundred little and big fountains.   The *Pittsburgh Leader,* for example, was one of these medium-sized fountains daily gushing forth its filth and poison into the world stream of information.   If the Associated Press had its little dam against our noisy little brook, it, on the other hand, welcomed the Tory flow from Senator Oliver's dignified reactionary newspapers,

CHAPTER XI

THE NEW YORK TIMES: ALL THE NEWS THAT'S FIT TO PRINT?

> I believe we are safe in saying that there is no other newspaper in the world whose columns are as free and open for expression of diverse hearing to those with whom we differ. And we have proved beyond all doubt there is a demand for news itself— that news is a legïtimate commodity which can be honestly purveyed so that the process may be remunerative.—ADOLPH S. OCHS.

THROUGHOUT the nation, years ago, the paper which reporters who could afford a nickel read daily was the *New York Sun*. It was "the newspaper man's newspaper," and no higher praise could be spoken. No one questioned Dana's integrity or the reactionary editorial policy: journalists then were interested chiefly in news presentation. Then some time before the war and almost unanimously afterward, they acknowledged the *New York Times* their favorite. Even Mr. Villard called it the greatest newspaper in the world.

In the biography of this institution, which Elmer Davis wrote, the *Times* policy and ideals are clearly stated:

"The paper has never had much confidence in efforts to remove all human evils overnight by magic formula. It has distrusted patented and proprietary remedies for political and economic ills. In both minor and major matters it has usually managed to awaken the fiery hostility of the long-haired. It has not believed and does not believe in Socialism, Fourieristic, Marxian or Leninist, in Greenbackism, Free Silver, or the political-economic system of the Non-Partisan League; in putting the Government

194

into business; in the medical sociology of anti-vivisection or the artistic philosophies of dadaism. . . . Conservatism, in its literal meaning, implies an inclination to preserve the good that has come down from the past, and a reluctance to discard institutions that have worked at least well enough to survive until there is strong reason to believe that substitutes would be more satisfactory."

No one doubts that Mr. Ochs believed he was liberal in his conservative policy. He no doubt believed he was publishing all the news that's fit to print. And no one should ask that the *Times* be the leader as well as the reporter of public opinion, that it engage in crusades for public betterment as it did before Mr. Ochs arrived, or that it support labor in its fight for better living conditions, or the progressive members in Congress in exposing corruption in oil leases or public utility propaganda, or that it take the side of the consumer against the makers of bad medicine or bad food. All that one can ask of the *Times* is that it give all the news, that it report both sides of controversies with equal fairness. If it has no space for those who differ with its policies, it should at least publish corrections or retractions when it errs, but does not err enough to warrant a libel suit.

Journalists throughout the world measure newspapers by the *Manchester Guardian.* The *Guardian* today compared to the *Times* is a much more important journalistic, social and political force because a spirit of truth-seeking and tolerance (as well as a liberal political policy) animates it and places its integrity beyond the suspicion of readers. Before Hitler, the *Frankfurter Zeitung*, which had many of the characteristics of the *Times*, was equally honored.

Papers like the *Frankfurter* and the *Guardian* require rich independent publishers who can afford integrity at any price. Mr. Ochs was such a one. So far as we know he was not tied by mortgages, banks loans, stock ownership in munitions or public utility plants, interest in patent-medicine companies; he was a multi-millionaire, whose gross takings were many million dollars a year from the *Times;* he was therefore so independent of all outside influences that he could afford the luxury of producing the world's greatest newspaper.

Merely to believe that his paper was independent, that "it tolerates no tampering with the news, no coloring, no deception," is not enough, nor is the fact that it has achieved the highest reputation in America "for the fullness, trustworthiness and impartiality of its news service." Says Mr. Ochs' sternest critic, Mr. Villard:

"It would be pleasant to be able to agree with him, but the truth lies elsewhere. The *Times* is no more independent than it is swayed by a desire to be just. It is a class paper, pure and simple, as much so as the *Call,* or any labor journal. Its news can pass only the quantitative and no qualitative test. No journal has exceeded it in disseminating falsehoods, misrepresentations, and half truths during the unparalleled era of wholesale lying in which the whole world has lived since 1914. Just how shameless, for instance, it has been in its treatment of Russian news has been repeatedly set forth both by the *Nation* and the *New Republic* without any refutation. To excuse it, as some try to do, by placing the responsibility upon the Associated Press is ridiculous. In the first place many of the worst fabrications have come from special correspondents; in the second place no newspaper is compelled to print the Associated Press news it receives; in the third place Mr. Ochs is, with one exception, probably the most influential director in the Associated Press. . . .

". . . Endless are the letters of correction and reproof which go to the *Times,* never to appear in print for lack of space doubtless, but justice is denied again and again. Certainly the protestant has no standing in the *Times's* court whatever, unless he is of the elect and the powerful and on the popular side. Before the god of wealth the *Times* ever bows down. . . ."

Villard's strictures were made shortly after the Lippmann-Merz investigation of the *Times* correspondence on Russia. Before I report on a similar but less thorough investigation of the *Times* news from Italy, I would like to give a very short summary of "A Test of the News." The *Times* was selected because it was the most important newspaper in America, not because Messrs. Lippmann and Merz had a grudge against it, and Russia was the topic "because of its intrinsic importance and because it has aroused the kind of passion which tests most seriously the objectivity of reporting." It was a penalty for greatness.

In the two years following the Bolshevik Revolution the *Times* reported that the Soviets were tottering to their fall exactly ninety-one times and Petrograd itself fell six times, was on the verge of capture another three times and was additionally burned twice and in a state of panic another two times. It also revolted against its own Bolshevik rulers six times. As for the victories of the White generals, all the investigators had to do was compile *Times* figures of casualties and captures in guns and men to achieve a total many times larger than the armies and the materials that had ever existed in Russia.

The test appeared first in the *New Republic,* August 4, 1920, and the reader is urged to read the full text. The *Times* the next morning ran a cable which is given in contrast to another dated November fifteenth.

(From Walter Duranty)
"Paris, August 4. — Wrangel at least is the first of the anti-Bolshevist Russian leaders who has shown a genuine liberalism in his administration. . . ."

(From Walter Duranty)
"Paris, November 15.— The causes of Wrangel's disaster are the same as in the case of Denikin, Kolchak and Yudenich—graft, incompetence, jealousy and reaction. . . . The widespread rumor that Grand Duke Michael would be chosen Czar struck the knell of doom six weeks ago. . . ."

But a few days before the November fifteenth report, when Wrangel's center had been broken and his wings crushed, the *Times* headline had been

WRANGEL'S RETREAT CALLED STRATEGIC

and when the Soviet troops had driven Wrangel into the Black Sea peninsula whence he started, and the defeated General was planning his escape to Constantinople, the *Times* headline (November seventh) read:

WRANGEL LETS REDS RUSH INTO HIS TRAP

Such were the reports in a conservative newspaper not given to sensationalism but pledged to the objective truth. The out-and-out red-baiting newspapers contained out-and-out lies, but these did not concern Messrs. Lippmann and Merz. What did concern the investigators was the motive behind these years of unfair reporting about Russia. "The news as a whole," they concluded, "is dominated by the hopes of the men who composed the news organization. . . . In the large, the news about Russia is a case of seeing not what was, but what men wished to see.

"This deduction is more important, in the opinion of the authors, than any other. The chief censor and the chief propagandist were hope and fear in the minds of reporters and editors. They wanted to win the war; they wanted to ward off Bolshevism. These subjective obstacles to the free pursuit of facts account for the tame submission of enterprising men to the objective censorship and propaganda under which they did their work. For subjective reasons they accepted and believed most of what they were told by the State Department, the so-called Russian Embassy in Washington, the Russian Information Bureau in New York, the Russian Committee in Paris, and the agents and adherents of the old regime all over Europe. For the same reason they endured the attention of officials at crucial points like Helsingfors, Omsk, Vladivostok, Stockholm, Copenhagen, London and Paris. For the same reason they accepted reports of governmentally controlled news services abroad, and of correspondents who were unduly intimate with the various secret services and with members of the old Russian nobility.

"From the point of view of professional journalism the reporting of the Russian Revolution is nothing short of a disaster. On the essential questions the net effect was almost always misleading, and misleading news is worse than none at all. . . .

"In devoting so long a study to the work of a single newspaper the authors have proceeded without animus against the *Times,* and with much admiration for its many excellent qualities. They trust that the readers of this report, among them the proprietors and editors of the *Times* will not regard it as an 'exposure' of the *Times,* but as a piece of inductive evidence on the problem of the news. The authors do not wish to imply, because honestly they do not believe, that the less conservative press is necessarily more reliable. . . . Something much greater is at issue, for the reliability of the news is the premise on which democracy proceeds. A great newspaper is a public service institution. It occupies a position in public life fully as important as the school system or the church or the organs of government. It is entitled to criticism, and subject to criticism, as they are. The value of such criticism is directly proportionate to the steadiness with which the ultimate end of a better news system is clearly and dispassionately kept in mind. . . ."

The case of the *Times* is complicated by the history of its noted Moscow correspondent, Walter Duranty, who had been assistant Paris correspondent and whose dispatches were used frequently by Lippmann and Merz as revealing examples. The *Times* sent Duranty to Moscow when the Hoover relief opened the railroad, and from that time on there was a decided change in the character of the news. In fact, I have heard many *Times* foreign correspondents and staff men in New York complain that Duranty leans to the side of the Soviets. I do not think that is so.

In 1927, for instance, the *Times* published a sensational story about bloodshed on the Rumanian frontier. It was followed a few days later by a cable from Moscow in which Duranty gave the lie to this *Times* scoop. The reader of both dispatches was forced to make an emotional choice: he could believe what he wanted to believe.

But this is what happened. In 1927 the Vienna correspondents rushed to Bucharest for the burial of the King. The Rumanian foreign office tried to exploit the occasion for a tricky attack on the favorite enemy, Russia. It offered all of us the blood-and-thunder story about war on the Bessarabian border and none but Navarre Atkinson of the *Times* fell.

After one day's joy in his scoop Atkinson received a cablegram informing him that inasmuch as he had described the fighting, he had better proceed to the front as a war correspondent! At this moment Duranty exposed the story as a fraud.

In November, 1930, Duranty again had occasion to disprove the *Times* reports from outside Russia about a revolt within Moscow. "There is not the faintest evidence of the preposterous alarms that have surpassed all the records of inventiveness for Riga or Berlin 'news sources' and of the credulity of the foreign press and public," he cabled, and he was right again. He points out that nowadays it is possible to telephone to Moscow or for a nation to ask for the facts from its ambassador. "It is possible to dismiss foreign reporters as nincompoops or cringing under the censor's knout, but nobody can question the word of the ambassadors of Britain, France, Germany, Italy and Japan."

On a visit to America in 1932 Duranty said, "I have been, and still am, as anti-Bolshevik as anyone could wish. This is not unusual since I was with the French, Lettish and White Russian armies when they were fighting the Reds in 1920. But when I began covering the news of Soviet Russia, everyone round me seemed so prejudiced about it, I decided to try and be fair. It wasn't any desire to be unusual that led me to this attitude. It seemed to me that the Soviet story as much as any other, deserved to be handled with an open mind. . . ."

The Duranty case is therefore an object lesson in journalism. I am convinced that we would have nothing but objective and reliable news if all the editors in America (1) chose correspondents of the Duranty caliber and (2) insured their economic security even when the news received completely denied the editorial policies or the less reliable reports of the same newspapers.

It is my contention that the *Times* (and the Associated Press too) are just as wrong today in their presentation of news out of Italy as they were a decade ago in their news out of Russia.

To prove this contention I could do one or two things: I could write a pamphlet the size of the Lippmann-Merz inquiry into the *Times* on Russia, say fifty thousand words, giving the deadly parallels or I could make one statement which might be enough to convince some readers.

That statement would be: The *Times* employs a man in Rome who may be a gentleman, a scholar and a good judge of *chianti,* but who by birth and politics is an Italian and a pro-Fascist. The press law of Italy makes it a penal offense for an Italian journalist to do anything but serve the Fascist regime. Arnaldo Cortesi is an Italian journalist. He must serve the Fascist regime. The *Times* situation in Rome could be paralleled in Moscow by the employment of say Karl Radek as its Soviet correspondent. Mr. Radek is the most brilliant journalist in Russia. If, however, he deviated from Communism in his writings he would go to jail, whether or not a party member, and so would Mr. Cortesi if he wrote things about Fascism which displeased Mussolini.

In Italy there are no wars and no rebellions outside of occasional uprisings in factories and villages, no new bloody purges. The Cortesi system in dealing with daily events is that of all true friends of Fascism: little or nothing is ever written which is unpleasant to the bayonets in power; apologies are always in order; bad news is usually omitted entirely; the Fascist official viewpoint is always given.

For example, the 1924 and 1934 plebiscites: Mr. Cortesi reported truthfully enough of the latter that "the result of this so-called election is a foregone conclusion"; the voters "may vote either 'Yes' or 'No' or return a blank ballot. No list of candidates in opposition to the Fascist state has been presented by any other party, this being forbidden by law." But you will never read in a Cortesi report anything about the terrorism that brought out the vote. The *Chicago Daily News* and the *New York World* reported the blackjacking of those who voted "No" in the 1924 election but not the *New York Times*. Nor did the *Times* reveal, as the weekly *Time* did in 1934, that "in Italy . . . the envelope in which plebiscite ballots are cast is so thin that it reveals how each man votes." Mussolini announces the elections are free. Cortesi cables that. Other papers report terrorism of the voters. Mr. Cortesi sees none, does not believe others, and cables nothing.

As any student of dictatorial affairs knows, few if any rulers permit any other man to grow strong. In Italy it has been especially noticeable. In my time Farinacci and Federzoni were members of the ruling triumvirate and both are now powerless. They were followed by Dino Grandi and Italo Balbo.

In July, 1932, Grandi made world headlines by talk and actions in Geneva. Immediately he was dismissed. Mr. Cortesi reported that the change "had been announced as imminent" but was postponed "because it was feared it might give a wrong impression." The *Chicago Tribune* reported that the *Gazetta del Popolo* said the change was "in accordance with the principle of rotation." Mr. Cortesi said, "The changes are explained as being simply due to the application of the system of 'rotation.'" The *Chicago Tribune* said the generally accepted version in Rome was that the dismissal was due to "reversals of Fascist diplomacy" which had been "dictated by Mussolini." Mr. Cortesi said nothing about this. The *Tribune's* Rome correspondent is an American.

Then came Balbo. America made him a hero. Every newspaper published his biography but none mentioned his career as a gangster or his trial for the murder of Dom Minzoni, the heroic priest of Argenta. Where Grandi had been kicked upstairs to the London Embassy, Balbo was kicked into Africa. The press of the world outside Italy and the *New York Times* so reported. Compare:

New York Times
"BALBO MADE GOV-
ERNOR OF LIBYA
"By Arnaldo Cortesi
"Rome, Nov. 6.—The uni-
fication of the ministeries
of War, the Navy and Avia-
tion, which has been among
Premier Mussolini's intentions since he took over the
Ministry of War last July,
became to all intents an accomplished fact today. . . .
"One of the difficul-
ties . . . was the necessity
of finding a new post for
Marshal Balbo, it being desired to avoid any act
which might give the im-
pression that he had fallen
into disgrace."

New York World Telegram
"BALBO SHELVED BY
MUSSOLINI
"By the United Press
"Rome, Nov. 6.—Premier
Benito Mussolini today ef-
fected his long planned
reorganization of the Cab-
inet. . . . Balbo . . . was
relegated to the colonies as
Governor of Libia, on the
north coast of Africa."
"By the Associated Press
"Rome, Nov. 6.—Air of-
ficers today described Gen-
eral Balbo as dejected. . . ."

This contrast between A. P. and U. P. on one hand and the illustrious *Times* on the other was noted by a neutral commentator, Benchley, of the *New Yorker,* who sums up the Cortesi situation as follows:

"Whatever foreign correspondents are thrown out of Germany and Italy for the dissemination of stories 'contrary to the good of the State,' the *Times* can rest assured that its Rome correspondent, Mr. Arnaldo Cortesi, will never incur the displeasure of Il Duce. His dispatches couldn't be more favorable to the good of the State if Mussolini had written them himself."

Another 1934 example, again the Associated Press versus the *Times* report:

(New York Times)
"MUSSOLINI WARNS YUGOSLAVIA TO END INSULTS TO ITALY
"By Arnaldo Cortesi
"Rome, Oct. 6.—A virtual ultimatum to Yugoslavia . . . (etc. for a column). After making a few brief remarks about Italy's relations with Switzerland . . . (the Duce) turned his attention to France.

" 'Our relations with France,' he said, 'have very greatly improved in recent times.'

"This remark was greeted with a loud outburst of applause, which moved Premier Mussolini to remark:

" 'Your reactions to this speech of mine are so intelligent they prove to me that while it is true that diplomatic action must be secret it is possible to speak freely on foreign politics to a great people.' "

(Springfield Union & Republican)
"500,000 ITALIANS LAUGH AT 'JOKE' ABOUT FRANCE
"(By the Associated Press)
"Milan, Oct. 6. Half a million Italian mouths opened in uproarious laughter today at a declaration of Premier Mussolini that relations with neighboring France in the last year had been notably better.

"Whether or not the laughter was inspired by a wink of Mussolini's eye as he finished the phrase, it was probably the most dramatic interruption ever accorded a public address. Five hundred thousand . . . roared at what seemed to them a huge joke. . . .

"Then he (Mussolini) said: 'Your attitude toward this exposition (of foreign policy) is so finely intelligent it demonstrates . . . I can well talk to the people directly. . . .' "

One of Mussolini's great achievements has been the destruction of the Mafia. The *Times* news columns and the *Times* editorials have said so. Professor Salvemini, ex-Premier Nitti, Professor Gilbert Murray, the late William Bolitho, claim that the bulk of the Mafia gangsters were incorporated and are now active in the Fascist militia, but that is another story. In 1926 the *Times* shouted the Duce's victory over the Mafia.

In 1931 it did so again. In May, 1932, it repeated the

story. And in June, 1934, "About 400 persons have been arrested in a determined effort by the government to stamp out a mainland Mafia organization. . . ." This is an A. P. dispatch. The *Times* evidently recognizing the position in which Mr. Cortesi has placed it, runs a light-fingered editorial *A Solved Problem Returns.* To the *Times* "the new bandit trial comes as a surprise."

The great achievement of Mussolini is the Corporate State. According to Mr. John Strachey there is no such thing. According to the *Times* the corporate state was announced, was functioning, in 1926, 1928, 1930, etc. In 1934 the *Times* announces it is again "created by Mussolini."

When the budget is balanced Mr. Cortesi cables "Fascist victory"; when there is a deficit, Mr. Cortesi reports "Italian deficit." When Nobile flew over the North Pole it was a Fascist achievement. When Nobile was wrecked, it was an Italian tragedy. Every banker who praises Mussolini gets a cable out of Cortesi, and when Fascists crack the skull of an American consul, Cortesi and the *Times* are silent. And so it has gone for thirteen years.

Is objective correspondence at all possible from an Italian who is more Fascist than many members of the official party? Every item that Cortesi touches is tinged with his nationalistic patriotism and his political faith. It cannot be otherwise. The Duce tells a woman representative of the *Times* that the climate on the islands of exile for political opponents "is the same as that of Capri, is healthy" and Cortesi cables a column about a lawyer, "released after three years, calls life on Lipari and Ponza not unpleasant—prisoners virtually free. . . ." The *World* once called the islands waterless hell-holes. Greenwall of the *London Express,* the only journalist who ever visited them unannounced, reported them as hell on earth. Hitler denies murder in his concentration camps. Stalin denies the horror of Solovetsky. The press of the world believes neither Hitler nor Stalin. The Duce, Mr. Cortesi and the *Times,* however, unite in praising the delights of Lipari, the penal island.

Among other Cortesi gems are:

RADICALS NOW LAUD FASCIST LABOR RULE

ANTI-FASCISTI FAIL TO STIR ITALIANS

ITALIANS HEARTENED BY RECOVERY SIGNS

In fact, not a week goes by without the *New York Times* publishing items favorable to Fascism.

The labor bureau of the League of Nations has for many years published statistics on the national standards of living. These objectively gathered and presented statistics show that the standard of living in Italy, never too high, has gone down year after year from about 1925. Under Fascism the standard of living has gone so far down that it can hardly go further. Some thirty-seven nations are listed by the League and Italy is last but one. This is part of the statistical truth about Italy. The *Times* need not prove its integrity by permitting anti-Fascists such as Professor Salvemini and John Strachey to answer its pro-Fascist propaganda—it can, if it wishes, obtain from its Geneva correspondent the truth about the economic, social and spiritual decay which Fascism has produced.

Frequently the *Times'* publication of reports in praise of Fascism has been followed by letters from intelligent persons asking for corrections. The American Friends of Italian Freedom report that "we are continually being nettled by misrepresentations in the *New York Times*. . . . The *Times* stubbornly refused to print this correction of its mistakes." E. C. Lindeman in 1930 protested a Cortesi item which amounted to an editorial calling upon France to bar anti-Fascist refugees. "And this, it seems," he wrote in the *Nation,* "is a sorry role for an American to play. Mr. Cortesi is half-American by blood, wholly Italian by citizenship. If this particular correspondent wishes to place himself at the service of Mussolini, this is, of course, his affair, but when he attempts to influence American citizens in the same direction he performs a public function, and this is not wholly his affair. How much more consistent would it be if American correspondents abroad attempted to interpret the news of Europe in the light of the essential American tradition."

In January, 1935, the *Times* boat reporter interviewed John Strachey and Eddie Cantor. Mr. Strachey spoke on the menace of Fascism. Mr. Cantor lyrically described Mussolini as a great man. "Everything in Italy is done for the people." The *Times* gave a line or two to Strachey's arrival but it gave a column to Cantor, possibly because the comedian's social and political lucubrations are better fit to print.

Now for a few examples of fair and honest presentation of news when the will to such presentation is present. Here are two headlines of October tenth, following the assassination of the King of Yugoslavia:

KING IS EXTOLLED
AS A STATESMAN
Legation official asserts the people regarded Alexander as their Counselor
By Captain Gordon-Smith, acting military attaché Legation of Yugoslavia.

KING WAS A TYRANT,
LOUIS ADAMIC
HOLDS
Author, native of Yugoslavia, asserts Alexander reduced the people to slavery

From 1917 and 1922 to this very day the avenues of similar reporting on Bolshevism and Fascism have been open to the *Times*. All that has been necessary was a word from Mr. Ochs to present both sides of the case. It was done in 1934 with Yugoslavia, and in 1921 with Russia, but never with Fascism.

As for Hitlerism, that is another story. I do not for a moment believe that Mr. Ochs' non-Nordic blood had anything to do with the case. What happened was that Mr. Birchall, having resigned his managing-editorship, was spending a journalistic vacation in Germany and he reported what he saw. None but Nazis have found fault with a single word or line in the Birchall dispatches.

Moreover, it is reported that Birchall's story of the mistreatment of tourists at the German frontier hurt German business more than all the reports of bloodshed and tyranny, and that the immediate result was the threat by the Nazified

German steamship lines which had begun extensive full-page advertising coincident with the attacks on the Jews, to withdraw this advertising from the *Times*. Mr. Ochs, the story goes, told the advertisers to go to hell. Mr. Birchall continued his cables. He is an Englishman. He has a British passport. He represents the most important newspaper in America. These facts probably explain why he has not shared exile with Dorothy Thompson and Mowrer of the *Chicago Daily News*.

Here are some miscellaneous *Times* items over a range of years.

Will Rogers, answering a critic, said concerning the fact his contributions sometimes miss publication: "The *New York Times* left out some of my articles because they were not in favor of the Democrats, and the *San Francisco Chronicle* got letters of kicks about all that was against the Republicans, so I must have not been so bias after all." Twice Rogers was left out in 1932. On September thirteenth he had intended to print something critical of newspaper ethics; he wrote that a man cannot commit suicide nowadays without the gentlemen of the press interfering, that they dig up the corpse and ask impertinent questions such as, "What's the big idea killing yourself around here and not notifying the press?" "Who did you love, and when, and why?" Moreover, Rogers opined, the press would have the corpse get up and pose for the photographers and promise to behave in the future. The *Times* skipped these items.

In the "full-dress riot" in the Empire Room of the Waldorf-Astoria when certain writers spoke out in favor of the striking waiters, the *Times,* according to Benchley, concocted a whimsical story "combining fiction with fact" in the tabloid manner. "The *Times* man became so wrapped up in his social satire that he went so far as to make up the name of someone who was not even there, and let himself go in his humorous treatment to the extent of making a whole new story out of it."

In December, 1934, when the Senate munitions investigation was making sensational exposures which the liberal press of the world applauded, the leading *Times* editorial one day was headlined *More Munitions Gossip*.

That same month the President of the United States declared himself unequivocally in favor of the ratification of the child labor amendment to the Constitution. It was in the form of a letter to the National Child Labor Committee and said: "It is my desire that the advances attained through the NRA be made permanent. In the child-labor field the obvious method of maintaining the present gains is through ratification of the child-labor amendment. I hope this may be achieved."

The release of this letter is news. How important it is, is not for me to say, as every editor and make-up man has his own point of view. Ask your friend the reporter. But it is also a fact that the first or second largest employer of child labor in America is the Publishers' Association, and it is also a fact that the greatest enemy of the abolition of child labor is the Publishers' Association of America, and although it may not be a fact, it is a belief of many, that no legislation which offends publishers is ever enacted.

Whether or not any of these facts have anything to do with the following fact the reader may decide for himself. The President released his endorsement of the child-labor amendment. The story instead of appearing on the front page, as with practically all presidential stories, appeared on page seven of the *Herald Tribune* and page twenty-six of the *Times* "alongside its announcements of Business Records and Arrival of Buyers"; in fact, no one whom I have asked has ever heard of it.

On September 19, 1934, the *Reformer* of Brattleboro, Vermont, where the present writer was then arranging the notes on this chapter, carried the following front-page item:

"BAYER CO. ORDERED TO CEASE TACTICS

"Federal Trade Commission calls for dropping of unfair advertising practices.

"Washington, Sept. 19.—The Bayer Aspirin Co., Inc., of New York was ordered by the federal trade commission to cease 'unfair competitive practices' in the sale of

aspirin. . . . it is prohibited from stating or implying that
the word 'aspirin' is the company's trade-mark and from
asserting without proper qualifications that the product
has 'no harmful after effects,' 'does not depress the heart'
and the like."

Is this news or a business operation report? Ask your neighbor. Numerous New Yorkers living in Brattleboro made
wagers on whether the New York newspapers, which carry
large Bayer advertising, would print the government findings.
The next morning the New York newspapers were searched.
Everyone reported there was no mention in the *Times*. But
these persons were mistaken. On page forty-one, which is
devoted to business news, following a tin plate report, appears
a small item with a one column head:

"BAYER BOWS TO AD ORDER

"Company consents to Federal Ban on 'only Genuine
Aspirin' Claim

"Washington, Sept. 19.—The Federal Trade Commission announced today that Bayer Company Inc. of New
York City had consented to the issuance of a cease and de-
sist order issued against certain alleged unfair competitive
practices in the sale of the company's aspirin. . . . The
commission, the announcement said 'makes it clear that
its order is not to be construed as preventing the Bayer
company from making proper therapeutic claims or recommendations based on reputable medical opinion or recognized medical or pharmaceutical literature.' "

The writer knows several *Times* and many other New York
newspaper men. Each of these reporters and journalists replied:
1.   that he had not seen the item in the *Times*.
2.   that it was a news item, not a page-forty item.
But that is not all. An important fact is the government
decision which the *Brattleboro Reformer* prints, that aspirin,
any aspirin, can have harmful after effects and does depress
the heart. In Brattleboro the order against the Bayer Com-

pany to delete opposite claims is published but not in the *Times*.

Editor & Publisher quotes the government charge as containing the following sentence: "Relying upon medical opinion the commission says there are persons by whom Bayer tablets may not safely be taken even in small or moderate doses, as well as persons who may not safely take them into their systems in amounts in excess of the prescribed dose, while to some persons excessive use of aspirin is highly dangerous and may be fatal."

Doctors know this. But when the government acts it is nevertheless news.

Knowing nothing at all about Wall Street, I take from *Harper's Magazine* some excerpts from an article by John T. Flynn. He speaks of Pecora exposing bad practices and dishonest promotions of bankers, investment houses, corporation executives, "ranging from the legerdemain of Mr. Insull in Chicago to the holding-company and affiliate banking adventures of Cleveland, Detroit and New York" and here, with millions of other Americans I know that Mr. Flynn is reporting realities. The exposures, continues Flynn, were answered by "the voice of that cold and lofty being who affects an immense and overpowering intellectual superiority, a solemn pretension to calm philosophical detachment, unmoved by the small hatreds and partisanships of lesser men. Such a voice was supplied by the *New York Times*. It lost not an opportunity to play the game of the horde of parasites who prey upon the nation one day and hurry to its pages for the dope the following morning. It was shocked and saddened by the messy and immature methods of Mr. Pecora. It preferred the unprejudiced and selfless lucubrations of Mr. Richard Whitney. . . ."

And again I turn to Mr. Flynn, this time to the *New Republic*, where he reports the New York Stock Exchange asking its members throughout the country:

"Are your newspapers willing to take specific articles giving the facts?"

"Oh, yes indeed," answers Mr. Flynn. "Our newspapers (New York City) are most cordial. In fact, I think that on the whole you need not fret about them. One or two give you an occasional dig in their editorial columns, but the news columns are just dandy. I particularly recommend the *Times*. It carries a splendid department every week by a Mr. Lokey. It is printed double column and in type twice as big as the rest of the paper. Really, you could not possibly do so well if you hired Mr. Lokey yourselves. The *Times* has thus provided you with a publicity agent at its own expense."

At this point I find that I have written thousands of words about the *New York Times* and I must stop. There are still many questions to be answered. Why did the *New Republic* feel it was its stern duty "to take the *Times* to task for its suppressions and distortions of the news from the Soviets"? Why does Mr. Flynn grow bitterly ironic in speaking of the *Times'* financial news, and why does Mr. Villard, who believes it to be America's foremost newspaper, speak of the *Times'* "falsehoods, misrepresenations, and half-truths"? Why does Mr. Benchley join with the foes of Fascism in pointing out that the *Times'* Rome correspondence is ultra-Fascist, and why are news stories harmful to medicine and public utilities corporations buried in the *Times?*

The fact that the *Times* is chosen for all this criticism and fault-finding should, of course, be a source of gratification to its owners because it is the left-handed admission that it is the foremost newspaper in the country. One reason so many friends of a free press watch the *Times* so closely springs from the hope that the *Times* will realize its power, its position and the duty which such power and importance imply, and therefore make good its lapses. It did send Duranty to Moscow when challenged, and it did print Duranty's cables. More recently it has been accused of unfairness to Sinclair in the 1934 California campaign and unfairness to labor in its reports on the San Francisco strike. And an important executive of the *Times* has admitted to the writer that the Cortesi correspondence has been Fascist. Perhaps, many hope, the same *volte face* that was made about Russia will be made about labor, Fascism, the public utilities. . . .

Can one really expect this of the *Times?* In April, 1935, when Adolph Ochs died there was a sixteen-column editorial which extolled his many sterling qualities. ". . . the editorial page," said the editorial page, "was a reflection of Mr. Ochs' personality. Naturally he did not bring to the *Times* editorial writers who were not in sympathy with its general principles; . . . the *Times* editorial staff under Mr. Ochs's direction had room not only for the full freedom of the individual writer's conscience, but for a considerable variety of temperament and opinion. On points not involving his fundamental principles Mr. Ochs was always ready to listen to argument; in fact, he enjoyed the clash of opinions. On certain issues which he felt keenly he did not yield, but even then no man ever had to write against his own convictions. . . ."

In my view this is an indictment against the press. This is the liberty of the press which Hearst editorial writers enjoy. It is also the system which obtains in newspapers owned by banks and munitions companies.

In his will Mr. Ochs said he trusted "the editorial pages may continue to reflect the best informed thought of the country, honest in every line, more than fair and courteous to those who may sincerely differ with its views."

Often those who sincerely differed with the *Times* on really important matters did not receive fair and courteous treatment from the *Times* under Mr. Ochs. La Follette, the elder Lindbergh, Upton Sinclair, Eugene Debs, for examples. Nor have the friends of Italian freedom been permitted to reply to the Fascist viewpoint presented almost daily. Against these cases is the fact that Russia is being better reported, probably, than in any other American newspaper, though a cynic may point out that the new policy was adopted only after the Lippmann-Merz analysis.

The *Times* will continue to take in a million or two a month and will probably remain rich enough to afford the luxury of upholding the publishers' code of ethics even if it should cost something in lost advertising. It may even dare the enmity of big business of Wall Street at times, but will it ever be classed with the pre-Hitler *Frankfurter Zeitung,* the present *Manchester Guardian,* the *Post-Dispatch,* the *Baltimore Sun* papers? It will remain America's greatest newspaper because it is rich enough to employ men who write well, rich enough to operate the largest foreign news service, to print documents in full, to give the public a far greater quantity of news than any other paper. Its greatness is to some extent a greatness of quantity.

The *Times* in America is the organ of the men of the *status quo,* the friend of those in power, the conservative spokesman of a system which dreads change and which fears every reform or radical plan because every change is an attack on the established profit-making order. Friends of the *Times* declare that the corrupting influence of big business is never felt in the *Times* office. It is never felt because the *Times* is a part of the big business system itself.

Nevertheless, a wonderful opportunity presents itself to Messrs. Arthur Hays Sulzberger and Julius Ochs Adler whose names now grace the masthead of the *Times:* if they have the character and courage and an enlightened intelligence they can easily surpass their predecessor. They must not, as so many *Times* men do, merely worship at the shrine of Adolph Ochs. Ochs did many things to make the *Times* the most important paper in America, and that is no mean accomplishment; but there are still vast improvements to be made, not so much in quality of news but under the headings of the Canons of Journalism: Sincerity, Truthfulness, Impartiality, Fair Play. I hope to see the *Times* some day as great as it is important.

Already a change is visible. In June, 1935, the *Times* in an editorial "Baldwin and Mussolini" brilliantly and fearlessly criticized the Duce, attacked dictatorship and implied that the Italian people were in chains, and that they might even overthrow the tyrant. Mussolini banned the *Times* from Italy. (Mr. Cortesi painfully reported the event.) Although the paper did not reply editorially, we may take it as one of the new Signs of the *Times.*

Chapter XII

HEARST, OR THE HUMAN FACTOR

AMONG the fifty-nine men who rule America, in the table made by former Ambassador Gerard, appear the names of five newspaper publishers and most important among them, in my opinion, is William Randolph Hearst.

The *Times* is the most influential newspaper in America but its owner, Mr. Ochs, was a conservative gentleman not given to whims or a desire to arouse mob hysteria; Messrs. McCormick and Patterson of the *Chicago Tribune* and *New York Daily News* permit their hopes or prejudices considerable play but no complete domination of the news; Roy Howard and the twenty-four papers he directs have a known program of mild liberalism. But William Randolph Hearst, now in his seventies, remains the unpredictable playboy of American journalism. He is a collection of egotisms, ideals, whims and prejudices, which are translated daily into news read by some ten million people.

Above everything else, Hearst proves for our time the fact that news is largely a matter of what one man wants the people to know and feel and think. With Hearst, as with Northcliffe, news is a means to an end, the end being whatever ideal, idea or *idée fixe* may arise at the breakfast table or in a dream or nightmare. Reputed masters of mass psychology, men of this type endeavor to become dictatorial leaders without putting in a public appearance; they stir nations, send millions marching, influence history, and unseen and unheard, gloat over their victories in their private chambers, far from the crowd they have maddened. They have Napoleonic complexes. They rejoice in being secret, intramural Napoleons.

This is what power does to people. Most every man, from the reporter to the owner, feels he has some power over the mob, the collection of readers; in Europe the editors go out into the streets or mount the barricades, but in America they sit in their quiet, air-conditioned offices feasting on their secret satisfactions.

Nevertheless they are the human element in the making of the news. The greater the personality of the proprietor, the greater its influence upon the minds of the reading public. The leading personality of our time is not Ochs' successor, or McCormick or Howard or Patterson, or General Otis' successor in Los Angeles, or Bennett's and Greeley's inheritor in New York, but William Randolph Hearst.

This publisher of chain newspapers has not one but many reputations. He is generally credited with making the phrase and actually inventing the "new journalism," although the elder Bennett and the late Joseph Pulitzer and Hearst's associate, Arthur Brisbane, have their supporters for this honor, as they also have for the doubtful one of originating yellow journalism. Mr. Hearst, his employees say, pays higher wages than his rivals, thereby raising pay for the profession generally, but the Washington Newspaper Guild's investigation showed some very low rates in the capital. The pro-Hearstites also point to many achievements. First of all, his opposition to our entry into the World War. Whether it was his inherited Irish hatred of Britain, or sincere idealistic pacifism, or merely some personal whim that actuated this step at a time the majority of newspapers were propagandizing for our entry on the side of the Allies, we cannot know. Very likely it was only Mr. Hearst listening to the voice of the Middle West.

The Hearst papers are credited with smashing the ice trust in New York City, saving citizens half their money; they smeared McKinley and Senator Hanna; they once attacked and curbed the arrogance of the great robber barons who were plundering the nation; they once appeared frequently on the side of the disinherited and the dispossessed; they helped unite the public against accepting the iniquitous Versailles Treaty; a quarter of a century ago they exposed the corruption of politicians and publishers by making public the Archbold letters; they consistently refused to accept the bribe money of power and light advertising and until 1935 they fought for

public ownership of public utilities.   But all these achievements are dated.

Many newspaper men, pro- or anti-Hearst, believe that in
his time he has been powerful enough to drive the country into
wars, to delay such action, to stir up war hysteria, and to
counteract it when other papers have raised it.

James Creelman, one of the great reporters of modern days,
was one of the star Hearst men who covered the Cuban War.
Mr. Creelman in his memoirs published as true the following
exchanged telegrams between his boss, Mr. Hearst, and the
artist, Frederick Remington, who had preceded the war correspondents to Cuba:

W. R. HEARST, NEW YORK JOURNAL, N. Y.
EVERYTHING IS QUIET. THERE IS NO TROUBLE
HERE. THERE WILL BE NO WAR. I WISH TO RE-
TURN.
                                        REMINGTON

REMINGTON, HAVANA
PLEASE REMAIN. YOU FURNISH THE PICTURES
AND I'LL FURNISH THE WAR.
                                        W. R. HEARST

According to one of Hearst's biographers, John K. Winkler,
"Hearst has since privately denied that this telegram was
actually sent . . . but there is no question the words quoted
represented the attitude, the desire and the hope of the owner
of the *New York Journal*. . . . The Spanish-American War
came as close to being a 'one man war' as any conflict in our
history." Mr. Creelman, vouching for the telegram, adds
that in the Cuban War "yellow journalism was blood guilty.
It had broken the peace of the world. Its editors were enemies
of society and its correspondents ministers of passion and disorder. The lying clamors had aroused the credulous mob,
overthrown the dignified voices of government and dishon-
ored international law." But, adds Creelman, when the
results of the war "justified the instrumentalities which produced it," the part played by the newspapers was forgotten,

"and yellow journalism was left to sing its own praises and its voice was long and loud and sometimes tiresome."

Creelman, at the battle of El Caney, saw the Spanish flag flying over the fort. His first thought was it would make a prize for the *Journal*. It was he who suggested a bayonet charge, who led the way until a Mauser bullet brought him down. In delirium he shouted something about getting the story to Hearst, and when he regained his senses somewhat he found Mr. Hearst himself, "a straw hat with a bright ribbon on his head, a revolver at his belt, and a pencil and notebook in his hand. The man who had provoked the war had come to see the result with his own eyes, and, finding one of his correspondents prostrate, was doing the work himself. Slowly he took down my story of the fight. Again and again the tingling of Mauser bullets interrupted. But he seemed unmoved. That battle had to be reported somehow."

"Wasn't it a splendid fight!" cried young Hearst; "we must beat every paper in the world." He mounted a horse and beat it for the seacoast and a cable office.

Creelman not only confirmed, but actually published the letter plotting an action in the Suez Canal by which Hearst planned to prevent the Spanish fleet, rumored on its way to America, from entering the Mediterranean. This letter instructed Creelman to "buy some big English steamer at the eastern end of the Mediterranean and take her to some part of the Suez canal where we can then sink her and obstruct the passage of the Spanish warships." None knew then that the Spanish fleet was worthless, and the press had made a big naval scare. Creelman, devoted to Hearst, applauds all these actions in which the publisher acts the part of a nation, able to declare war and to wage a war and to commit actions involving life and death.

I do not take the "you furnish the pictures and I'll furnish the war" telegram seriously, as do some pacifists, who see in it a confession of the publisher as a war-maker. To me it appears more as the ebullience of a youthful, jingoistic and entirely irresponsible spirit. Much more important is the serious confession of the elder Pulitzer who, according to Walter

Millis, said "he rather liked the idea of war—not a big one— but one that would arouse interest and give him a chance to gauge the reflex in his circulation figures."

Still more serious, I believe, has been the editorial viewpoint and the pointing of news, over a period of several decades, in regard to Mexico. When, before the World War, the revolutionary spirit of the suppressed Mexican nation began to make itself felt against the tyrant, Diaz, the Hearst press went to his defense. Will Irwin then explained that Hearst was the owner of large estates in Chihuahua, a bounty of Diaz to his father.

In May, 1916, Hearst published a signed editorial favoring the occupation of Mexico by American troops. "Our flag," he said, "should wave over Mexico as the symbol of the rehabilitation of that unhappy country and its redemption to humanity and civilization. Our right in Mexico is the right of humanity. If we have no right in Mexico then we have no right in California or Texas, which we redeemed from Mexico."

On the other hand the man who is said to have brought about the Cuban War and tried his best to bring on war with Mexico, fought against our participation in the worst of all possible wars. From the first days he demanded that President Wilson embargo money, food and munitions. He wrote against our "wasting our wealth to continue a carnival of murder, to prolong an era of overwhelming disaster, to encourage the destruction of the white race, to tear down the achievements of civilization. . . ." After the Zimmermann note, which was bound to prove fatal, he wrote, "I believe in war if the people want war," but inasmuch as the people have to do the fighting "they ought to do the deciding. . . . I believe in, first, a referendum of the people; and, second, failing that, a decision by the peoples' representatives in Congress assembled." A month before Wilson declared war he ordered violent cartoons and editorials against Japan with the caption, "Look out, Uncle Sam, your neighbor, Japan, is eagerly waiting an opportunity to strike you in the back." Japan was repre-

sented with knife in hand. On March 4, 1917, he telegraphed
all editors: "Speak highly of Wilson."

Mr. Hearst postponed our entry into the war by many
months, Biographer Winkler believes. Many of his newspapers, however, were merely playing upon the sympathy of
German-Americans and the apathy of the masses. In 1917 and
1918 millions of "patriots" who read pro-Ally propaganda
hated Hearst. With the post-bellum disillusion many said
that if Hearst had succeeded in keeping us out of the war he
would have ranked in our history somewhere in the vicinity
of Abraham Lincoln.

In 1927 Mr. Hearst bought a lot of documents from a non-
descript Mexican-American agent, published them in his
press, then offered them to the Senate. These obvious for-
geries told of a conspiracy between Japan and Mexico against
the United States, of payment of one million two hundred
and fifteen thousand dollars to four senators, of the activities
of certain clergymen and journalists. The two nations involved were Mr. Hearst's pet enemies; the four senators were
the progressives who were always under Hearst attack, and the
clergymen and journalists mentioned in the documents were
also persons whom Hearst did not like. Miraculously the
(forged) documents hit only at the enemies of Mr. Hearst.
After the documents had been printed sensationally throughout the country, experts hired by Mr. Hearst as well as the
Senate's experts proved the documents fraudulent. No attempt, it was shown in the Senate hearings, had been made to
test the documents before publication.

These same documents had been offered to me by Miquel
Avila in Mexico City in April, 1927. A mere glance by fellow journalists who understood Spanish was enough to convince them the work was a forgery. After I made certain
substantiating tests I so informed the *Chicago Tribune* and we
turned Avila down. Other newspapers did likewise.

In the December hearings Senator Norris read into the
record an open letter to Mr. Hearst in which he said, "You
must have known what was common knowledge among the
newspaper men of the United States that many alleged official

documents from Mexico were being offered for sale to all kinds of organizations and to all sorts of publications. . . . Your own newspapers about two years ago exposed the fact that our own State Department had been offered and had accepted forged Mexican documents. . . . Even now, after this discussion, the Hearst papers are undertaking to deceive the people of the United States as to what really was done before the (investigating) committee."

Mr. Hearst's latest phobia is Red. In the spring of 1934, when Hearst was shooting firecrackers at the Roosevelt administration, he also sent up some red Véry lights. Sample:

90 P. C. OF PROFESSORS TEACH COMMUNISM, SAYS FORMER JURIST

Under this sensational headline appeared the statement that "ninety per cent of the professors in the United States are teaching communism to their pupils, former Michigan Supreme Court Justice George N. Clark told . . . the Wayne County Republican Committee," but in the direct quotation of the ex-eminent jurist there is no further explanation except the connotation from the following, "I appeal to you as good Americans to stand by America and true American principles. Don't follow the 'pinks'—those who have a voice in the Government, like the so-called braintrusters—who show red tendencies."

In November numerous collaborators were at work on the Great Hearst Red Scare. Notable among them were Richard Washburn Child and S. Stanwood Menken. This is the same Menken of the National Security League which was thoroughly exposed by a Congressional Investigation Committee after the war. It is also the same Mr. Child who wrote the introduction to Mussolini's autobiography, who was Fascism's first agent in America and who had certain relations with the public utility propaganda campaign. In the Federal Trade Commission's hearings Judge Healy introduced Exhibit No. 872 as follows:

". . . The joint committee has made no expenditures or payments to public men or women for articles or for the use of their names in connection with articles, excepting the payments to Richard Washburn Child for preparation of articles and advice, as shown in the special publicity account. . . .

> "(Stephen Davis [Director Joint Committee of National Utility Associations.])

"Question (by Judge Healy): What was Mr. Richard Washburn Child paid for; what did he do?

Answer (by I. L. Grimshaw of the N. U. A.): $7,500."

On November 15, 1934, the reader will find in Hearst's *American* on page two an article against job insurance by Mr. Child; on page five a pro-Fascist item headed "Praise for schools of Italy"; on page sixteen the editorial slogan Truth, Justice, Public Service; in the first two columns an editorial *Get Rid of the Reds* which concludes with the words, "In fact, throwing Communists out of the colleges and universities ought to be the prelude to throwing Communists out of the country"; two four-column cartoons, one "For Peace with Honor" showing Uncle Sam forging a sword labeled DE-FENSIVE ARMAMENTS, the other showing an overgrown cat labeled BUREAUCRACY lapping up a spilt bottle of milk labeled RELIEF FUNDS; and in the last two columns an editorial headed *America's Answer* giving approval to Swanson's big navy program.

TRUTH, JUSTICE, PUBLIC SERVICE

The Hearst editors in all university towns sent some of their bright young men to school with the instructions to "get the goods on the Red professors." In Syracuse, after the *Journal* had screamed DRIVE ALL RADICAL PROFES-SORS AND STUDENTS FROM UNIVERSITY, its representatives approached Professor John N. Washburne, head of the department of educational psychology, then printed an interview which had the professor admit he was a communist. This was denied. Next day Professor Herman C. Beyle was interviewed; when the indignant professor was asked by Editor Harvey Burrill what shade of red he was, he replied, "What hue of yellow is your journalism?" but this remark was not included. A stenographer was supposed to be present. Professor Beyle said, "I teach no isms"; the *Journal* printed it "I teach isms."   Could it have been merely a typographical error?

Naturally enough, the big Hearst drive was in New York City. The reporters sent by the Hearst press to "bore from within" at Columbia, were spotted, and to their credit, confessed the plan. To Professor George S. Counts one of them said:

"Mr. Hearst is engaged at present in conducting a 'red scare.'

"You realize, of course, that because of my assignment I shall have to select the most sensational statements from the interview in order to make a good case. That is what Mr. Hearst is expecting."

The second "student," spotted by Professor William H. Kilpatrick, also confessed being the representative of the *New York Evening Journal.* "I am in a peculiar position of talking with you as a red-baiter," he said to the professor. "Personally I am not in sympathy with that sort of thing, in fact quite the opposite, but Mr. Hearst wants to get material along this line."

Professor Counts then issued a statement: "If William Randolph Hearst succeeds in his efforts, he will reduce American universities and schools to the ignominious conditions of the German schools and universities under Hitler." He suggested that the Hearst drive might be the beginning of "a nation-wide Fascist campaign to destroy our basic American freedoms." Frank L. Redefer, executive secretary of the Progressive Education Society, demanded an inquiry into the efforts of Hearst publications, munitions makers, utility companies and the United States Chamber of Commerce to "influence teaching in the schools of the United States." A committee of prominent educators asked the McCormick-Dickstein Congressional Committee on Un-American Activities to look into the matter.   A hundred and fifty Methodist ministers sent a similar resolution.

Mr. Hearst then did two things.   He invited thirty-seven college newspaper editors to Washington, where Eleanor Patterson, editor of his *Washington Herald,* entertained at cocktails and notables lectured; Mr. Hearst himself spoke on a national hook-up on the "fearful failure," "assassination and starvation," "bloody despotism," etc. in Russia.

A climax to the latest Hearst war came on January 14, 1935, when fifteen leading college editors signed and published a statement branding Hearst a menace to academic freedom. This statement was published in the *New York Post* and commented on by Broun in the *World-Telegram,* but received only an indifferent line or two in the rest of the metropolitan press. The signatories and the college newspapers represented were:

Charles H. Bernhard, *Wisconsin Daily Cardinal.*
Joseph Carnwath, *University of Pennsylvania Pennsylvanian.*
A. T. Dill, *North Carolina Tar Heel.*
Amos Landman, *Brown University Herald.*
William Landsberg, *Carnegie Tech Tartar.*
Ben Lieberman, *University of Illinois Illini.*
Marcus Purdue, *Indiana University Student.*
John Radosta, *New York University Bulletin.*
Francis Smith, *Princeton University Princetonian.*
Lyman Spitzer, *Yale University News.*
Seymour Sheriff, *City College* (New York) *Campus.*
John Tibby, *University of Pittsburgh News.*
Harriet Tompkins, *Vassar College Miscellany News.*
Marvin C. Wahl, *Syracuse University Orange.*
James A. Wechsler, *Columbia University Spectator.*

These editors, nine of whom were Mr. Hearst's Washington guests (!), pledged to fight attempts to arouse hysteria against "dissenting thought," say in their denunciation that the Hearst campaign "is a deliberate, ruthless attempt to stifle freedom of inquiry and expression and to impose upon American education the terror which characterizes education in

Germany." They might also have added, "and in Italy." Some educators did note that the university part of the red campaign began immediately after Mr. Hearst had interviewed Mr. Hitler.

Meanwhile other papers had taken up the chase. The *Grand Rapids Press,* one of the eight Booth newspapers of Michigan, headlined an editorial *Reds at Ann Arbor.* All the California papers, which had so successfully broken the San Francisco strike and then vilified Upton Sinclair, took a fling at radicalism in California. In Boston the *American,* a Hearst paper, sent James McEnery to ask President Conant and Professor Albert S. Coolidge, lecturer on chemistry, how Communism was getting along under the red banner of John Harvard's school. Mr. McEnery got nowhere. The *Harvard Crimson,* of which Franklin Delano Roosevelt was an editor in his day, then appeared with a daring attack on the Hearst papers which it accused of "pandering to the nation's prejudices" and spoke of the danger in giving "strength and succor to a Fascist movement."

The *Columbia Spectator* then scooped the entire New York press by publishing documents showing ex-Ambassador Child as the personal agent in America of Benito Mussolini, the *Duce* of Fascismo. The documents included a contract between Child and E. Paul Yaselli whereby Child would become selling agent for a movie about the Italian leader. "Child," said the *Spectator* editorially, "one of Hearst's most frenzied writers, author of hysterical statements against the 'red menace' in American colleges, is stripped of 'impartiality.' He stands convicted—without a syllable of defense—of serving Fascism in America. . . . No more startling and conclusive evidence of the purpose of Hearst's 'red scare' could be desired. No more glowing description of his 'Americanism' could be asked." One of the Child letters, quoted regarding a Mussolini film, says, "The time is ripe for the showing of such a picture of the spirit of a nation; the American people would welcome such a picture." In his defense Mr. Child disclosed the fact that President Coolidge had approved his inducing Mussolini to write his autobiography for American publication.

Everywhere the college and university press was aroused by the Hearst campaign. America's undergraduates, whose lack of social conscience has so often been deplored, and America's educational institutions, noted around the world for rockbound conservatism, responded immediately. Over the radio Mr. Hearst said: "Does anybody want the bloody despotism of Communism in free America except a few incurable malcontents, a few sap-headed college boys and a few unbalanced professors? . . ." At the same time Hearst men engaged in operating the new Red scare circulated among the thousand educators attending the convention of the Department of Superintendence of the National Education Association suggesting a rousing vote of confidence in their boss.

At the preliminary session Professor Charles A. Beard, leading American educator and historian, in his moderate, dispassionate manner made a statement about Hearst which lifted the congress to its feet. He said:

"In the course of the past fifty years I have talked with Presidents of the United States, Senators, justices of the Supreme Court, members of the House of Representatives, Governors, Mayors, bankers, editors, college presidents (including that great scholar and thinker, Charles W. Eliot), leading men of science and letters, and I have never found one single person who for talents and character commands the respect of the American people, who has not agreed with me that William Randolph Hearst has pandered to depraved tastes and has been an enemy of everything that is noblest and best in our American tradition. Alfred Smith—a true friend of public education—added to his many deserved laurels when before a cheering multitude in New York City he defied Mr. Hearst. The answer of the people of New York was final and conclusive.

"There is not a cesspool of vice and crime which Hearst has not raked and exploited for money-making purposes. No person with intellectual honesty or moral integrity will touch him with a ten-foot pole for any purpose or to gain any end. Unless those who represent American scholarship, science and the right of a free people to discuss public questions freely stand together against his insidious influences he will assassinate them individually by every method known to yellow journalism—only cowards can be intimidated by Hearst."

The press of New York City with the natural exception of the three Hearst newspapers, published the statement, the *Herald Tribune* which may have feared a libel suit, eliminating two of the best phrases.   No one was surprised when the International News Service carried the item for the private information of editors only, but apparently the great news services also suppressed it.   Heywood Broun, another of the convention's speakers, found that his column referring to Hearst and published in the *Pittsburgh Press* was followed by the explanation: "The speech above referred to by Heywood Broun was not received by the *Press* through its regular telegraph services."   The regular services are the godlike Associated Press and the United Press.

Many newspapers, it appears, were not sent the news, and many which received it suppressed it.   With the usual few honorable exceptions, declares Mr. Broun, "American newspapers either spiked the whole speech as too hot to handle, or decided that Dr. Charles A. Beard, dean of American historians, was fit for their columns only after the most radical sort of censorship.   And this, too, I suppose, is part of 'The Freedom of the Press.' "

As a result of this surprising situation, the Hearst lobbyists who realized that a resolution of support was now impossible, devoted themselves to preventing a vote of censure. However, a resolution saying, "We respectfully request [the Nye-Vandenburg Senate Committee investigating the munitions makers] to investigate any relationship which may exist between the Hearst newspaper, industrial and financial interests and the spurious anti-red campaign now current in the Hearst press," was adopted.

The Napoleon of San Simeon, undaunted by the counterattack from the leaders of American intelligence, ordered a surrounding movement against Moscow.   The world was

raked for anti-Russian matter. Nothing was too old or too
foul. Photographs and stories which for more than a year
had appeared in the Nazi papers in Germany were now served
up with the same text for a still non-Fascist American public.
Several series of articles dealing with an alleged famine—not
the famine of 1921 nor the disputed famine of 1932, but a
famine dated 1934—were published under various names.

It was the 1920 cadaver of the Bolshevik menace dressed in
1935 type; but there was this difference: whereas in the first
Red scare reputable newspapers like the *Times* published their
unreliable news on the authority of French diplomats or Latvian officials, in the Hearst scare no such precautions were
taken.

No sooner had the word gone down from the Olympian
heights in California than editors and certain reporters began
finding Red atrocities everywhere. But an unfortunate slip-up
occurred. Apparently someone had forgotten to advise the
Moscow correspondent of Mr. Hearst's new crusade, and so
it came about that at the very moment the *New York Journal*
was telling of the horrors of death and starvation in the
Ukraine, Mr. Lindsay Parrott of Hearst's Moscow bureau,
returning from the Ukraine, was giving an interview to the
Moscow press in which he said, "Nowhere in any of the towns
or villages on the way did I see any signs or traces of famine
about which the foreign press likes to speak."

At a mass meeting sponsored by the League against War
and Fascism some twenty thousand persons in Madison Square
Garden, New York, joined in denouncing Hearst as the leading Fascist menace in America. The liberal press, daily and
weekly, accused Hearst of Hitlerism. Photographs of Mr.
Hearst surrounded by such leading Nazis as Alfred Rosen-
berg, Karl Romer and Thilo von Trotha, were published, as
well as the fact that the International News Service makes
considerable money selling to the Hitler press. The disclosure
that the leading Hearst writer, Richard Washburn Child, and
Colonel Rogers of the Standard Oil Company were united in
a scheme to spread a Mussolini propaganda film in America
and Mr. Hearst's own statements favorable to Fascism made

during his most recent visit to Germany, were widely reprinted. Certainly no doubt was left that in the liberal and intelligent mind of America the latest Hearst campaign had proved a boomerang.

For decades it had been generally agreed that the Sage of San Simeon "knows more about popular psychology than any man in America." But Mr. Broun believes that Mr. Hearst had made many wrong guesses and many strategic retreats in his time. In his youth he supported many "popular" causes, even created causes and made them popular. In war time he was psychologist enough to attack the war hysteria at a time the majority were indifferent or opposed, then opportunist enough to wave the flag higher than the other patriots when America's entrance was inevitable.

Once Mr. Hearst's big-game hunting was directed against "the entrenched interests." Mr. Hearst, himself a multimillionaire, made his money from his newspapers and his gold mines. But in the past two or three decades he has amassed a fortune which extends into many fields of industry; he has in short become a great industrialist and one of the largest entrenched interests of the country.

He can no longer afford the luxury of crusading against "special privilege" or the public utilities, or the robber barons, or "corrupt wealth" or even to repeat these phrases which he once coined. If ever a man represented the status quo, the big interests, privilege and the profits system today, it is the same Mr. Hearst who so brilliantly attacked them years ago while he piled up his millions. Once upon a time when the New York papers were calling William Jennings Bryan "anarchist, socialist, destroyer and menace," William Randolph Hearst supported him and laughed when he lost a million dollars in advertising. Today Mr. Hearst attacks the Tugwells of the Roosevelt administration who might cost him a few thousand dollars in medicine advertising, and every politician who endangers the profits of big business.

Hearst was for a long time the most acute journalist in America. He is still extremely popular, he has always been ruthless, and he has always exerted his power to please his fancy. He is still the most, notable sample of that considerable body of publishers who do business by prejudice or predelic- tion, by emotion instead of reason, by whim instead of intelli- gence. He is economically illiterate and he has no social conscience. There are hundreds of powerful publishers in this class. This is an important fact which must be considered in weighing the forces and sources of world news.

Chapter XIII

THE PARIS FRONT

THE merger, on December 1, 1934, of the Paris editions of the *New York Herald* and the *Chicago Tribune* ends sixteen years of rivalry for the premier honors in their class.

The *Herald* apparently absorbed the *Tribune*. *De mortuis nil nisi bonum?* All private advice from Paris reports that the merged newspaper has inherited all the leading faults of both. Neither, I think, ever possessed a virtue.

The Army Edition of the *Chicago Tribune* during the war and immediately afterward, under Joe Pierson and Spearman Lewis and Farmer Murphy and Floyd Gibbons was an exciting adventure. It had life; it was bumptious, it made mistakes, it was sometimes ribald, frequently unreliable but always amusing. The *Herald* was just stale.

But when the troops went home the business managers began to arrive from Chicago with orders to make the *Paris Tribune* self-sustaining. That meant getting advertising. And that meant beating the continental European system of advertising which is still in its cancer cure, loan shark and political blackmail stage.

But the American advertising game has—or claims it has—outgrown this stage. But although the European editions go about advertising in a legal manner, it is my belief that what they do is thousands of times worse than bribery and blackmail.

They take money from European governments for governmental advertising with the understanding that they lick the boots daily of those who pay them.

On September 17, 1926, an American consul in Italy gave Jay C. Allen, Paris correspondent of the *Chicago Tribune,* a story which was worth a seven-column streamer in the home edition:

FASCISTI CLUB U. S. CONSUL

The headline beneath was:

AMERICAN LEFT UNCONSCIOUS IN
STREET BY MOB
ATTACKED ON WAY TO SEE
MUSSOLINI

The story concerned Earl Brennan, American Consul in Rome, who had been attacked by Fascists including several positively identified as members of the militia. The Fascists were angry because Brennan had refused passport visas to those who had criminal records. An American consul who gave the story to the press, after it had been suppressed by Mussolini and American Ambassador Henry P. Fletcher in Rome, said that the hatred against Brennan was due largely "to the machinations of the central [Fascist] government."

The story, it will be noted, walked right into the Paris office and was considered big enough to lead the Chicago edition. It was not published in the Paris edition. The business department sent in word to kill it. The business department did not want to lose the Italian Government's tourist advertising.

In like manner the business department regulated the news from Spain, Rumania, Poland and other countries to which it had sold page and half-page advertising space. It would not sell a page to the Bolsheviki.

I have already referred to one of the systems of bribery practiced by dictatorial governments, notably the Italian— the free cables to America conditional on writing pro-Fascist propaganda. Every Italian newspaper in the United States which is pro-Mussolini is entitled to receive this bribe and almost without exception it is accepted. That it is a bribe has been exposed by the *Editor & Publisher* and denounced frequently. I do not know that any American newspaper now receives it, but Italo-American papers still do.

I do know that when I took over the Rome office of the *Tribune* in 1925 I found that my predecessor, De Santo, an ardent Fascist, was using the five-thousand-word free cable gift from the Fascist Government. I informed Colonel McCormick that I could not make use of this bribe. The publisher agreed. In April, 1925, the Paris business office noticed that my cable bill had increased several hundred dollars. I explained. And here is the letter from the business office:

> "If I were you, I would attempt to have reinstated the free telegraph service to America as well as to Paris, because in the first place if the government grants us this privilege now but later decides because of the nature of the news sent by you, to discontinue the service, then and not now would be the time to give the matter consideration and adopt other means of transportation."

In September, 1926, I received from Warsaw, by telephone, a report that Pilsudski planned to dissolve parliament if it refused to accept the existing Cabinet. The Polish Embassy, which was an advertiser in the Paris edition, issued a denial which was published before I was consulted, and later the business office wrote:

> "Of course you are aware that we have an advertising contract with the Polish Government amounting to, as I remember it, about 150,000 francs and desire to continue it; on the other hand, we want to print true news, so that if you will conduct yourself accordingly, I would appreciate it."

In 1927 in the press section of the Rumanian Foreign Office I was upbraided by an official for publishing stories mentioning graft and corruption in the country, Queen Marie, Magda Lupescu and minor scandals. The official said:

"When we arranged a deal with the business representative of the *Tribune* it was with the understanding that the news would be suppressed in Chicago as well as in Paris."

"Have you got it in writing?"

"You can't put things like that in writing. The news is kept out of the Paris edition, why not the Chicago edition?"

"Because,." I replied, "the Chicago edition knows nothing about it."

"But it's the same newspaper," insisted the Rumanian official.

In Belgrade, on December 14, 1927, I noted the following conversation between myself and Mr. X——, traveling representative of the *Paris Tribune* advertising department in the Balkans:

"The different countries, Poland for instance—when they buy the page or half-page ad in the Paris edition, do they think they are buying up the political policy of the home edition also?"

Mr. X——: "Well, the *Paris Tribune* sells these governments advertising on that supposition."

"But they do not buy up the Chicago edition—they buy up only the Paris edition?"

Mr. X——: "Yes, but they don't know that. It's all a blackmail game."

The *Herald* was no better. It kissed Mussolini's toe with even greater slobber than the *Tribune*. Likewise Primo de Rivera's toe. And the toes of all dictators who placed hotel advertising in the *Herald*. I know the majority of *Herald* reporters. They devote much space and time to interviewing tourists, the paper being largely a tourist paper. If the tourist says Russia is terrible, it goes into the paper, but if the tourist says Italy is terrible the item is thrown into the wastebasket. Sample:

"SPAIN IS DELIGHTFUL

". . . nothing but splendid hotels and good food, peace and beauty . . . no evidence whatever of Primo de Rivera's dictatorship being anything but a most satisfactory and benevolent despotism under which the Spanish people were utterly content. This opinion was corroborated by Mr. Cortland Van Clief, a banker of New York. . . ."

(April 8, 1928. Nice reading in 1931.)

And Fascist Italy:

"What Europe needs, and not only Europe, but the entire world, is a few more men with the foresight and ability to organize what is manifest in the work of Benito Mussolini . . . a benefactor of mankind. (Arthur Earley.)

"Practically all the newspapers of the civilized world, including those that most loudly denounced Fascism and the Duce in years gone by, now recognize the magnificent results of a decade of Fascist rule . . . there runs through all of these enthusiastic newspaper accounts a subtle wish that each country had a Mussolini. . . . God bless the Duce and Fascismo. (S. D. Broder.)

"Mussolini . . . has saved Italy, a country of 40,000,000 people, from anarchy, chaos, and social distress. . . . Would that in America we had a man of his brains, heart, disinterestedness and amazing ability! (Grace Upham Bigelow.)"

(Editorial. Oct. 27, 1932)

"FASCISM'S DECADE.

"Today Rome is the scene of jubilant demonstrations. Ten years ago the black-shirted marchers from Naples arrived at the gates of the city and were met by Mussolini, who had preceded them. . . ."

To put it mildly, the last statement is the opposite of the truth, as Mussolini himself testifies.

Finally a big feature article by the Countess Solito de Solis, "an American girl from California."

"Mussolini is extraordinarily young to be the greatest man of the present and the past. . . . Forty-four million Italians pray each day and thank God for having sent them this wonderful man who has saved Italy. He is the only genius the war has produced."

The *Paris Herald* has outdone most of the press of the world in representing nothing but the most reactionary opinion. In 1931 it published a fake picture saying it proved that starving Russia was the scene of bread riots. This picture had appeared in the American press in 1921 and had been proved a fraud. It actually showed a street fight in 1917 during the World War.

The *Herald* was in favor of the electrocution of Sacco and Vanzetti. In 1929 it ran an editorial suggesting that the letters of the two dead men had been "dressed up or perhaps even forged by persons interested in drawing from them either moral or money profit." The Viking Press and editors Marion Denman Frankfurter and Gardner Jackson accused the *Herald* of scurrilous insinuation and blind prejudice when they sued for libel. The *Herald* suppressed mention of the suit, and the *Paris Tribune* did likewise.

In February, 1933, the *Tribune* published headlines saying that Zangara, the man who fired at President-Elect Roosevelt, was a Bolshevik and the *Herald* said he was an anarchist. On the eighteenth the *Tribune* and *Herald* received the same interview with Professor Raymond Moley, economic adviser to the President-Elect. Here are the vital parts of the story:

Paris Chicago Tribune	*Paris New York Herald*
"... Moley ... said, 'this hungry looking, undersized Italian is more intelligent and better educated than he would have the authorities believe. He didn't manifest any interest in political parties but he had a fixed hatred for all heads of governments.'"	"Moley told newspaper men today. . . . 'The man did not manifest any political ideas and gave no evidence of having any interest in Communism. Apparently he has no acquaintance with the theories of anarchism and simply had a fixed idea that he was in opposition to all heads of government.'"

The *Tribune,* it will be noted, suppressed the statement from Moley which would have discounted all its previous reports that Zangara was a Bolshevik agent. Although the *Herald* was as rabid a Russia-baiter, it did, however, publish the news as it was received from New York.

The next day, Sunday, the *Tribune* scooped the *Herald* with a seventy-two-point Gothic streamer *Plot on Roosevelt Revealed,* giving as evidence a letter from Buck Jones, of Newark, that five men were involved. On Monday the *Tribune* buried three sticks under a small head, "Miami plotters only joking they tell U. S. agent." It was a hoax.

The reportorial staff of the *Tribune* was never to blame for its bootlicking and subservience. Almost without exception the reporters cursed the business office which directed editorial policy. The *Tribune* staff was intellectually superior to almost any paper I know. *Transition* was born in the *Tribune* office. Eugene Jolas, Elliot Paul, Whit Burnett, Robert Sage, Wolfe Kaufman, Alex Small, Louis Atlas, Wambly Bald and other writers were *Tribune* men. The *Herald* also had a number of non-conformists. Any gathering of local reporters was tantamount to a verbal revolution against the owners and directors of these two institutions.

The third English language paper is Lord Rothermere's *Paris Daily Mail.* Rothermere's paranoiac brother, Lord Northcliffe, originated more fake news about Germany and Russia than any ten newspapers, and the present *Daily Mail* still gets the same kind of Russian news out of Riga that made possible the Lippmann-Merz disclosures fifteen years ago. In 1933 the *Daily Mail* went over, news and editorials, to the Japanese. It even tore from their context several phrases from the Lytton report on Japan's aggression in Manchuria and Jehol and printed them as a vindication. The *Daily Mail* reader got the impression that the Lytton inquiry justified Japan whereas exactly the opposite is written into the report. Lord Lytton arrived in Paris. He addressed the Nouvelle Ecole de la Paix, vigorously attacking the Japanese general staff which he compared to the Prussian staff of 1870 and 1914. The press generally published this news item. Even the French newspapers, subsidized by the money of the munitions makers who were thriving on Japan, printed part of the speech. The *Herald* gave it place on page one. The *Daily Mail* suppressed it.

These papers affect the thought of about half a million Americans and many Britons who must rely upon them while abroad. There seems no means of getting reliable and unprejudiced news reports for this segment of American life which is supposedly more intelligent than the usual mob of tabloid readers. The wise Britons wait for the London papers.

The only satisfaction in the situation is this: the majority of readers of the English language press in Europe are intelligent enough to mistrust such exponents of freedom of the press.

CHAPTER XIV

THE POISONED SPRINGS OF WORLD NEWS

FROM where do newspapers get the news? Largely from the press services. American news comes from special correspondents and from the newspapers which the agencies serve, and the European news from the newspapers there and the affiliated agencies.

The European sources of news were fairly pure before the war; today they have been turned into political instruments by the parties in power, by Fascist and Communist parties, by semi-Fascist and semi-Communist parties. Journalism must serve the state. They make the announcements openly. Newspapers and the official, semi-official and so-called independent press bureaus do serve the state. Journalists would be shot or exiled if they did not.

They may, in fact, serve the state well. But the better they serve the state the less do they serve us, the citizens of nondictatorial lands, who are confronted with the problems of Fascism and Communism and who want to know the truth about them. From our point of view the news in the dictator countries is poisoned at the source.

The foreign correspondent assigned to Germany or Italy or Russia cannot really "cover" the country by himself. He can, and usually does, attend the main event in the capital, but for the rest, frequently the bulk of the cable to America, he must rely on two sources, the local newspapers and the governmental news bureaus which have their representatives everywhere. The journalist is on hand for the assassination of Dollfuss (although he has to ride or fly to Czechoslovakia to spread the news), but when Hitler strikes in Munich or Mussolini in Florence, the reporter in the capital has to rely on others for the story. These others are usually natives, and whether native or not, they are subject to censorship, its excisions and its delays.

239

My Vienna colleague, John Gunther, took exception to the foregoing statement when I first made it in *Harper's*. He pointed to the fact that improved telephone communications have given foreign correspondents a new means of beating the censorship. Since then I notice that in the 1934 Spanish uprising the government cut the telephone wires which the journalists used the first day or two, and from then on only fragmentary and distorted reports came to us. Not for weeks did we learn the facts about the terrorism and bloodshed with which the present government put down the revolt, and then only in letters to a few papers and the liberal weeklies.

Moreover, it is only possible for a correspondent to do this trick once. Bolitho in Italy telephoned or smuggled his news out under three different names, but that did not prevent the Fascist foreign office from threatening not only the *World* but the *Chicago Tribune* and the numerous papers who used the *World* service. The dictators dare not allow free transmission of news and the telephone is not the permanent means of breaking this rule.

A large part of the news America reads comes from our three press associations: the Associated Press, the United Press and the International News Service. The first is a co-operative of some one thousand three hundred papers; the second its greatest rival, a private enterprise, and the third is one of the Hearst organizations. The United Press, which is liberal in its viewpoint, and which serves all the Scripps-Howard papers, is giving the A. P. a good race although it may never displace it from the position as the largest and potentially most powerful news organ in the world. And it is this very fact, its possession of this vast potential power, that makes its union with the official and semi-official news agencies of the dictator countries so important. The Associated Press serves and is served by the following national news services:

Austria:	Amtliche Nachrichtenstelle.
Belgium:	Agence Télégraphique Belge.
Bulgaria:	Agence Télégraphique Bulgare.
Canada:	Canadian News.

China:	Reuters.
Czechoslovakia:	Bureau de Presse Czechoslovakia.
Denmark:	Ritzaus Telegraphic.
Esthonia:	Esthonian Telegraphic Agency.
Finland:	Finska Notisbyran.
France:	Havas.
Germany:	Wolff.
Great Britain:	Reuters (Ltd).
Greece:	Athena.
Holland:	Nederlandsch Telegraaf Agentschap.
Hungary:	Agence Télégraphique Hongroise.
Italy	Stefani.
Japan:	Nippon Shimbun Rengo.
Latvia:	Latvian Telegraph Agency.
Lithuania:	Agence Télégraphique Lithuanienne.
Norway:	Norsk Telegram Bureau.
Poland:	Agence Télégraphique Polonaise.
Rumania:	Rador
U. S. S. R. (Russia)	Tass.
Spain:	Fabra.
Sweden:	Tidningarnas Telegrambyra A. G.
Switzerland:	Agence Télégraphique Suisse.
Turkey:	Anatolia.

The above bureaus, the Associated Press, the United Press, the Hearst service and a few minor press associations practically control the news of the world. All the official and semi-official bureaus mentioned supply news to the Associated Press and control almost all the news appearing in the press of these twenty-seven nations. In addition to the American organizations, the most important bureaus are Reuters, Havas, Wolff (now joined by its rival, Hugenberg's Teleunion), Stefani, Tass and Rengo. Of this list Reuters alone can escape the charge of being in control of a dictator, an absolute ruler or a hidden group which regard the press as an instrument for political and private profit.

Stefani is Mussolini's big stick for the control of Italian journalism, just as the Wolff bureau is always the main source

of German news. By it Hitler has made all German newspapers think, act and print alike, and incidentally cause between five hundred and one thousand of them to die from
similarity. Communism and the Soviet Government rely on
Tass. (Under its former name, Rosta, it had an exclusive
agreement with the U. P. for several years.) Rengo represents the royal Japanese house and the interests of Baron
Mitsui, reputed sole owner of sixty per cent of Japan's industries and all its munitions plants. Havas claims it is an
independent agency, but the official documents released by the
Soviet Government and the budget of the Tsarist finance
ministry show that large sums were paid this bureau monthly
from 1905 to 1917. Before Havas or ninety per cent of the
French press can make any claim to honest newspaper reporting they should at least attempt to answer the Russian documents which Arthur Raffalovitch, the Tsarist economist and
resident official subsidizer, published in his book, *L'Abominable
Venalité de la Presse.*

In addition to these "great" press bureaus there are the
Bulgarian, the Hungarian, Polish, Rumanian and Turkish
agencies which are mere tools of the dictators, and the Greek,
Finnish, Spanish and others which change colors with democracy and absolutism.

So it comes about that if three hundred million people in
ten countries have lost their rights, and if sixty million additional people in six additional countries are in danger, these
three hundred and sixty million or three-fourths of the population of Europe, are being kept in a state of political ignorance
largely by their press bureaus, and these ten and six press
bureaus pour forth the great stream of corrupt news which
is offered to the American people. With the best intention in
the world the representatives of our press bureaus and newspapers cannot escape this flood. It is physically and mentally
impossible. The American correspondent is usually aware that
the official press bureau today is unreliable and he knows that
every continental newspaper in order to exist must be a propaganda sheet for the regime, but this knowledge, even with a

desire to fight the situation, cannot, day after day, year after year, keep his reports free from the influence of this overwhelming dictatorial propaganda machine.

Here is an example: between 1920 and 1925 the present writer, visiting Italy for the stirring events of the so-called "Red uprising," the seizure of the factories, the so-called march on Rome, the consolidation of Mussolini's power, the massacre of the Freemasons, the assassination of Matteotti, reported to his paper the following facts: the Red uprising in 1920 was bloodless; the labor unions refused to accept militant Communism; after the liquidation of the uprising the minority Communistic element dwindled; when Mussolini came to Rome in 1922 there was no Bolshevism, as he himself wrote in his newspaper; Mussolini did not march on Rome but came in the Pullman sleeper as he himself admits in his autobiography; having made public speeches in favor of a "bloodbath," the dictator did not hesitate to let his followers "purge" the city of Florence; between four thousand and eight thousand men lost their lives in the so-called Fascist revolution of 1920-1926.

But on advice of American public relations counsel, the Fascist Government, forced to seek loans in America, created the myth of Mussolini, "the slayer of the red dragon of Bolshevism." The Stefani bureau daily issued nicely colored news. It put in the word "Italy" in a speech of ex-premier Nitti which criticized "Europe," and the result was a Fascist attempt to murder the Nitti family. It suppressed Croce's famous speech in the Senate after the Fascist newspapers themselves announced that Stefani was issuing it for a later edition. It completely changed the text of Lloyd George's and other speeches in the British Parliament which denounced Fascism as a regime of "suppression, repression, menace, incendiarism, and assassination as instruments of government." It announced the happiness of the Italian people at the time the labor bureau of the League of Nations announced extreme suffering among workmen and peasants because Italy has fallen into the next to last place in the European standard of

living table. It announced balanced budgets annually at a time
American economists were desperately unable to obtain reliable Italian statistics.

What is the result of this perverted, distorted and colored
flow of news from this bureau which supplies its wares for
cabling to America by the Associated Press? One result is that
one of the very papers which the present writer represented
and which once published exactly the opposite, later wrote—
July 15, 1934, to be exact—that "Mussolini took a frantic
and prostrate Italy and in ten years made it over into strong,
united and reasonably happy nation, without shedding blood."
(Why not consult your own columns of, say, July 15, 1924,
Mr. Editor?) Nine Americans out of ten—an actual test
was made by the writer among the leading citizens of a typical
American town, Brattleboro, Vermont—believe that Mussolini
saved Italy from Bolshevism, that he led the march on Rome,
that he made Italy a strong and happy nation, that he balanced
the Italian budget, that he raised the standards of living, that
he is in short a great man and that Italian Fascism is bloodless, non-violent and noble, and might be a fine thing for
America. Brattleboro reads the Boston, New York, Springfield and other big papers as well as its own *Reformer*. The
nine-out-of-ten got their views from the metropolitan press,
which got its news from the A. P.

America's views on Communism have also been established
by the news largely furnished by governmental press bureaus.
The correspondents of the *Times* did not make up the dispatches from which Lippmann and Merz wrote their analysis
of the news; they got their information largely from the
Havas bureau which has the blessings and the francs of the
Quai d'Orsay, and from the Latvian and Esthonian and other
official agencies, and despite such governmental sponsors the
news was not true.

More recently the Tass agency has reported the successes
of the 1928-33 Five Year Plan, the general rehabilitation of
Russia, the progress of the second plan. It has never mentioned a famine. Last year there were again rumors that a
second famine had claimed many victims. The government

denied, the Tass denied, the American journalists and press bureaus spread the dictator's denials. Yet a few days ago the *New York Times,* which had printed many dispatches denying or minimizing a famine, said unqualifiedly, as if it were a generally accepted fact, that "there died in Soviet Russia in the Winter of 1932-33 a minimum of 6,000,000 people by starvation, typhus and other diseases." What then, in this plethora of official statements and paucity of fact, can the average newspaper reader make of the Russian food situation and the success of Communism?

The point is that the average reader is asked to take a stand. Despite the premature explosion of Doctor Wirt, there remains a faction in America that is afraid the policies of the Roosevelt administration are tainted Red—it no doubt prefers the taint of Black or perhaps even Hitlerian Brown. It is a fact that America has been made conscious of the dictatorship idea, and that citizens are being asked to choose. "Are you a Fascist or a Communist?" enthusiasts ask, and they insist that you answer on the spur of the moment, because "there is no time to lose" inasmuch as (they say) the split second of decision has arrived.

It is certainly conceivable that such a decision will have to be made by all Americans and by the American Government, and our choice of Communism or Fascism, based on which system we think the ideal and which has accomplished more for humanity, will be influenced by our knowledge which we have gained from the daily press. It is true that the very small minority which reads books, magazines and weekly reviews understands the aims and methods of the opposing systems quite well, but the decision in America will be made by the masses whose emotions, rather than minds, are worked up by the indirect power of the Tass, Stefani, Havas, Wolff and similar institutions. The masses, not Mr. Wilson, declared war on Germany, and the masses, we can admit twenty years later, were greatly influenced by anti-German propaganda. In the years 1914-1917 Crewe House, the Maison de la Presse, Reuters and Havas beat Wolff and Amtliche Nachrichtenstelle for America's sympathy and participation. Tass and Stefani and Wolff and other agencies are contending for our support today.

From the foregoing the reader may gain the impression that the American correspondent abroad, in addition to being wary of the constant attack upon his integrity, is waging a daily battle against the corrupting powers. This is unfortunately not always the case.

It has always been the custom of European governments, notably dictatorships, to employ the family method, rewards and punishments, in dealing with American journalists. Nothing is too good for the press representative who represents the views of the foreign office. Between 1914 and 1916, when America was still nominally neutral, European governments were bestowing the ribbons of the Legion of Honor, order of the crown, commendatore, etc., on war correspondents and Germany was about to give two men the iron cross. In almost all instances such rewards must be asked for. Had the two men with the German army received the iron cross they would have been self-crucified. But the recipients of the Allied decorations were proud of their service to these nations. Now, in peace time, these honors, which are a reward for service to a foreign country, are still being sought and still being given.

But, all in all, decorations, entrée into society, handshakes of dictators, flattery, free use (up to a maximum of five thousand words daily in Italy) of the government radio or telegraphs, and other rewards are minor elements compared to the major fact that newspaper men, like other human beings, are capable of love and hate, or sympathy and revulsion toward men and things and the dictatorial system. Two of the series of United Press correspondents assigned to Moscow were sympathetic to Bolshevism. But the majority in my time were either cynical or inimical.

The Soviets in 1922 told us we must consider Russia in a state of war—surrounded by capitalist enemies, blockaded materially and morally, and liable at any moment to be invaded. That was why there was censorship and suppression of news.

I know now that this was true. To a great extent it is still true. But in 1922 and 1923 all I cared about was breaking the censorship. Employing the usual skulduggery expected and appreciated by the home office, I was able to scoop the sympathetic United Press man on quite a big story. The news was obtained from a carbon sheet officially issued by the Rosta and therefore passed by the censor. The U. P. man at that time had an exclusive contract with the Rosta, and when he was severely reprimanded by New York he made an investigation and found the "leak." When, however, I asked him why he had not sent the item he had received hours before I had, he replied: "I know the Rosta issued it and the censor would pass it, but I thought it was their mistake, that it would harm the Communist cause, therefore I suppressed it myself."

The American foreign news services employ three classes of men: the few but nevertheless tremendously influential who favor the foreign nation, usually without the inducements of flattery or more tangible reward, to the extent of joyfully coloring the news in a friendly way; the great majority who make the best of the situation and retain their American fairness and objectivity but have to trim sail frequently; and. the few who fight.

In 1923, with the famine waning, the Soviets, which had been forced by the Hoover agreement to permit the entry of a heterogeneous group of American reporters, became more stringent with them; and when Colonel McCormick sent the "ultimatum" to Chicherin demanding the lifting of the censorship, there was a crisis. The Associated Press, on instructions from New York, refused to join a united front. The result was that four correspondents, almost half the American strength, were expelled.

In 1924 the long series of troubles between the German Government and the Foreign Press Association in Germany resulted in a letter signed by A. Del Vayo (of *El Sol,* Madrid, and now a Spanish ambassador) which the government rejected. This time, when the American group was able to put through a vote of confidence in President Del Vayo, the representatives of the *New York American,* the *Journal* and the International News Service refused to join and resigned.

In 1925 the Associated Press and the *New York Times* refused to join a delegation which demanded the repeal of an expulsion order by Mussolini. In this instance, moreover, Press Attaché Cocucione informed the delegation that the A. P. correspondent, as dean of the American corps, had been consulted and had approved the expulsion, and a month later a high executive of the press agency expressed his approval. In April, 1933, the Nazi Government asked Mowrer to resign as president of the Foreign Press Association in Berlin, but this time the American corps supported him. But he had to leave Berlin because Hitler refused to guarantee safety of life and limb.

Whether or not the Americans stick together, flatter the dictators or fight them, the latter employ espionage as well as censorship and threats of expulsion. There were cheka spies under the windows of the Savoy Hotel when the Americans made it their headquarters in 1921, and there are Ovra spies spearing letters out of mail boxes in Rome—and occasionally dropping a fork! Worse still, there are police spies working in American newspaper offices in Europe and there are Communist and Fascist journalists who, after their day's work as assistant to American employers, hasten to the political police to report against them. Recently, Mr. G. E. R. Gedye, of the *Times,* in a somewhat surprised tone reported "evidence of the wide extent to which British and American correspondents here [Vienna] are subjected to espionage" after he had seen a confidential report by the secret police which had been made for Chancellor Dollfuss's press department. Austria, like Italy, Russia and Germany, was found engaged in tapping correspondents' telephones, steaming open their letters, reading their private telegrams, and inspecting their office wastebaskets. "The inaccurate and scurrilous remarks about individual correspondents are so libelous," Mr. Gedye says of the Austrian document, "as to make it impossible to reproduce them. They show that not even the most intimate side of the private life of newspaper correspondents in Vienna is immune from espionage and eavesdropping." The diplomatic advice in the report's conclusion is of great interest. After expressing the hope that "we can easily win over the English and American press representatives in Vienna," the police author adds: "It should be quite easy so to deal with correspondents that they change their attitude. They offer a fruitful field for systematic manipulation provided they are suitably approached."

This, then, is the situation in the brutalitarian states: the dictators "make" the news by controlling the main source of world news, the governmental press bureaus; and they control every word in their own nations' newspapers, the second important source used by the foreign correspondent; they install an official censorship, as in Russia, or they deny a censorship and employ it just the same, as in Italy; finally they offer financial inducements, as free telegrams in Italy, and refund on all cable tolls, as in Yugoslavia, Bulgaria, etc., and they have other awards, such as ribbons for those Americans who work for them, while for the others they have imprisonment, expulsion, threats of physical violence (Italy and Germany), and a system of espionage which weakens the nerves of any man.

Opposite this black picture of perversion of the free international flow of news there is the bright picture of the Pulitzer foreign service prize winners, the latest of whom is Frederick T. Birchall of the *Times*. How, lay readers ask, can one maintain that dictatorial press terrorism exists in the face of the past year's daily dispatches in which Mr. Birchall has exposed the cruelty, stupidity and bloodthirstiness of the Hitler regime as fearlessly as any famous journalist in history?

The explanation of the Birchall case also implies the chief remedy for an intolerable situation. The fact is that the *New York Times* backed Mr. Birchall. It was Napoleon who said "I fear the *Cologne Gazette* more than three army corps," and Hitler might well say he fears the *Times* as deeply. This same *New York Times*, which apparently was so lax about its Italian news that it permitted that grand journalist William Bolitho to expose the Matteotti assassination in the *World* while its own correspondents merely glossed the matter, and which printed little more than official apologies for the massacre of the Freemasons in Florence, stood as a great power behind its Berlin correspondent, and this power even Hitler could not smash.

Again, the Foreign Press Association in Berlin after standing by Mowrer protested in a body sinister charges against it made by Propaganda Minister Goebbels, and showed itself at all times united in its fight for the freedom of the correspondents. Birchall could count on its support. In Moscow, in Rome and elsewhere the foreign association, the Anglo-American organization and the American corps never united in similar action.

Mr. Birchall came to Berlin rather suddenly, right from the managing editorship in New York. He and Hitler arrived simultaneously. Birchall was free from the entangling alliances which almost every journalist must make in order to do his work satisfactorily, and still more important, he belonged to category three, the reporter who does not accept favors, who does not trim his sails and who is by nature a fighting personality. When the time comes for him to write his memoirs he will have a splendid tale of Nazi threats and intimidations, and how he beat them and became famous.

The three important lessons which will save the few free and democratic countries from the perversion of world news by dictators' press bureaus can be drawn from this one case. If we value the liberty of the press we must have:

1. Correspondents willing to fight for the news.
2. Newspapers which will stand behind their men.
3. A united front of the press corps against the dictators.

It is not enough that the *Times* in this case supported its representative; the three American news bureaus and the six or seven great American papers which have foreign services should act as a body in the future. The thirteen hundred American editors who support the Associated Press could, if they were interested enough, request that organization to co-operate with individuals, such as Mowrer and Birchall, instead of maintaining the usual policy of neutrality. If the A. P. took a stand for freedom of the press, its two rivals, which are already of that opinion in affairs abroad, would join it.

The American editors might also consider canceling the contracts, which they made through their co-operative, the Associated Press, with the dictators' news bureau. If a considerable part of our news comes from these bureaus, and these bureaus are little more than propaganda organs of terroristic states, then they are obviously harmful. If, on the other hand, little press bureau news is sent, as some A. P. men claim, then why continue the contracts? Cancellation would demand strengthening the force abroad, and a resulting increased cost of news, but the dollars so spent would be well worth it.

The American public knows almost nothing about the source of the news it reads and believes, and which influences the American mind on all great international questions, on war and peace, on Communism and Fascism. Our public believes in a free press. The American editors, in their sensational battle with General Johnson of the NRA, have never in their history been so enthusiastic for a free press. It is therefore up to the American editors to free their press from the influences of European press bureaus and save the American people from the daily flow of poison on which unfortunate Europe feeds.

PART FOUR

THE STRUGGLE FOR A FREE PRESS

Chapter XV

THE PRESS AND THE INDIVIDUAL

> There is nothing covered, that shall not
> be revealed; and hid, that shall not be
> known.

THE laws of most countries provide for redress when a citizen or subject is injured by the newspapers. In almost every suit, freedom of the press, its rights and privileges, are argued before judge and jury. Almost always the newspaper wins. Almost always freedom of the press is recognized, and this is as it should be, and no better fight can be waged than that for its maintenance since all other liberties depend upon it.

But freedom of the press is one thing and the invasion of the home and the privacy of the citizen is quite another, as the elder Bennett discovered (when he engaged in the so-called new journalism) and the recently departed *Graphic*—which Ring Lardner immediately called the porno-*Graphic*—later attested. The best proof of the matter is the appearance in all journalistic codes of ethics of planks respecting personal liberty and private rights.

The question is well put by a leading American journalist, William Allen White. Newspaper men, he says, are expressing deep concern nowadays over the invasion of the privacy of individuals by the press. "Is there no self-respect in our profession?" he asks. "Are we all quacks? . . . Have we purified our columns by refusing to accept the bribe direct only to take the bribe indirect in seeking circulation through the salacious and the pornographic? Is journalism a whited sepulchre proudly calcimined outside by our probity in the matter of control by coarse and direct influence of advertisers while inside we are a charnal house of corruption through the circulation department? Isn't it as bad to sell a family's privacy, a man's individual rights to self-respect in order to gain circulation and so acquire higher advertising rates, isn't it as bad, I repeat, to do this as to take money directly from interested parties for perverting the news?"

In a more bitter mood Sinclair Lewis declares that recent newspaper publicity has gone mad; its "sunset wonders," he believes, are worse than honest paid advertising: "Lindbergh cannot become engaged without 110,000,000 people leeringly looking on; . . . that not unromantic figure Queen Marie was turned into a clown; . . . the judicial murder of our murderers holds daily the front page. . . . For this is perhaps our greatest achievement over Europe; not our electric irons nor our concrete skyscraper constructions, but our changing of the ancient right of privacy so that the most secret and perhaps agonized thoughts of any human being are the property now of any swine who cares to read them."

Another aspect of the matter, newspaper trial of accused persons, brings similar pessimism from Clarence Darrow. "Trial by jury," he believes, "is being rapidly destroyed in America by the manner in which the newspapers handle sensational cases. Of course it could not happen in England, as far as I know, or in other European countries. It is a species of mob law more insidious and dangerous than the ordinary mob law. I don't know what should be done about it. The truth is the courts and the lawyers don't like to proceed against newspapers. They are too powerful. As the law stands today, there is no important tribunal case where the newspapers are not guilty of contempt of court day after day. All lawyers know it, all judges know it, and all newspapers know it. But nothing is done about it. . . . No new laws are necessary. The court has full jurisdiction to see that no one influences a verdict or a decision. But everyone is afraid to act!"

The journalistic holiday which is being made nowadays out of a personal fortune or misfortune is thoroughly discussed by Silas Bent in *Ballyhoo,* which is required reading for those who are interested in the press generally. Louis Weitzenkorn has dramatized the tragedy of a family whose home a newspaper of the *Graphic* type has invaded. Here, as in many other instances, it is a matter not of freedom but of license of the press. In the four instances which follow in some detail will be told the history of men of more or less fame, who, becoming national figures, naturally had to endure a certain amount of legitimate invasion of their privacy; but at least three of these men were antagonists of the American press, and the fourth hated a large part of it, and all have suffered abuses from it.

The four examples are Lindbergh the Bolshevik, Lindbergh the Hero, La Follette, Sr., and Upton Sinclair, the Don Quixote of our journalism. In the case of Lindbergh, Jr., and Sinclair, privacy was invaded; in all four cases the journalistic canons—Accuracy, Impartiality, Fair Play and Decency— were violated many times.

When Charles A. Lindbergh, Sr., in 1918 was defeated for governor of Minnesota, Eva Lindbergh said: "Father had no adequate means of combating a hysterically lying press."

The newspapers of America had reason to hate Lindbergh. He was a great enemy of the bankers, he believed in the public ownership of the power companies as well as the public ownership of natural resources, he was an enemy of the Montana copper magnates and the Montana copper members of Congress, he fought the flour millers, he believed in the farmers' co-operatives, and in December, 1915, he warned President Wilson that "speculations and loans in foreign fields are likely to bring us into war. . . . The war-for-profit group has counterfeited patriotism."

There was also a private and financial reason for national journalistic opposition. In 1911, when the packers and millers and steel and wool and other interests had got or were getting what they wanted from a business men's Congress, the newspapers joined in the game. The question of reciprocity with Canada had come up and suddenly the national press began a campaign to make this measure popular. It contained two important points: it freed from duty type-casting and type-setting machinery, and pulpwood and news print paper.

There were native industries which would be hurt, of course, and these succeeded in having the Senate Committee on

Finances look into the matter. One of the disclosures was the following telegram:

> "New York
> "February 17, 1911
>
> "By request: private to editors:
> "It is of vital importance to the newspapers that their Washington correspondents be instructed to treat favorably the Canadian reciprocity agreement, because print paper and wood pulp are made free of duty by this agreement.
>
> "Herman Ridder
> "President, American Newspaper
> Publishers' Association."

The plan was for all papers to co-operate in putting through the reciprocity bill so they could get news print free of duty. Ridder's telegram was addressed to Democrats and Republicans, high tariff and anti-tariff advocates. In other words, at least half of the American press, which was Republican and pledged to tariff, was to run a campaign for free trade in those things which concerned their own pocketbooks.

Lindbergh opposed and voted against the bill the editors of America favored.

Practically the entire press of Minnesota opposed Lindbergh's bill to tax iron tonnage. St. Paul, Minneapolis and Duluth newspapers were almost solid against him. In 1918 he ran for governor on the Nonpartisan or farmers' ticket. On one occasion he was arrested and jailed.

Lindbergh's platform (as given by Walter Quigley in a post-bellum introduction to *Your Country at War*) included conscription of wealth in time of war, elimination of the profiteers, price-fixing for farm produce. The campaign was vicious. Quigley arrived one day when Lindbergh was about to address ten thousand persons gathered in a grove. A sheriff and thirty sworn deputies tried to break up the meeting and the crowd wanted to fight, but Lindbergh protested it would do the party no good if blood were shed. "I suggest we adjourn a few miles south into the state of Iowa which still seems to be part of the United States," said Lindbergh. Later he was charged with conspiring to obstruct the war, but was not prosecuted.

"The defeat of Lindbergh again became a national affair," Lynn and Dora Haines, his biographers, write. "He was the one who must go down and every possible weapon was used against him. Never had such a campaign been waged in the state; never one more unfair. As one editor said, 'This campaign is in no sense a local Minnesota affair; beneath the furious battle special privilege is waging in this state lies all the combined power of entrenched politics and wealth from Wall Street to San Francisco.' " A choice sample of the journalistic campaign against Lindbergh is this editorial from a St. Cloud newspaper: "A vote for Burnquist will cheer our soldiers in France. A vote for his opponent [Lindbergh] will be sad news to them and will bring a smile to the Kaiser."

The press ruined Lindbergh. In a speech in Congress in 1916 he had said: "The public gets no information from the press about it [the money system, his favorite object of attack] for anyone who dares uncover the system and expose the schemes for deceiving the public finds that a certain part of the press will attack him and call him a radical and obstructionist, and excoriate him in every way possible. If to tell the truth about things makes him a radical, then radicals ought to be at a premium. But they have not been so far politically."

After his defeat Lindbergh wrote *Your Country at War.* Government agents raided the printing shop and destroyed the plates, also the plates of *Banking and Currency* which attacked the big banks and the Federal Reserve Law. Lindbergh was by now known as a dangerous citizen, a Bolshevik to the Red-baiting press. The reason is obvious. Here are some of the opinions, mostly about the newspapers, he dared express from 1916 to 1918:

"It is impossible according to the big press to be a true American unless you are pro-British. If you are really for America first, last and all the time, and solely for America and for the masses primarily, then you are classed as pro-German by the big press which is supported by the speculators. . . .

" 'Big Business,' washing the hands of their captains: In all issues of their big press and other publications, you can read about what noble patriots we have in the men who profit by the war, while it is the plain, toiling people who are really supporting the entire system, including the payment of the profits to the big fellows. . . .

"It has indeed been humiliating to the American people to see how the wealth grabbers, owners of the 'big press,' really attempt by scurrilous editorials and specially prepared articles to drive the people as if we were a lot of cattle, to buy bonds, subscribe to the Red Cross, to register for conscription and all the other things. The people will do their duty without being hectored in advance by the 'big interest' press. What right, anyway, has the 'big press' to heckle the people as if we really belonged to the wealth grabbers and were their chattel property? . . .

"The attempt has been made by the press to make the farmers believe that the officers of the Nonpartisan League were selfish and later that they were not loyal Americans, also that they were Socialists, as if Socialists were criminals. Not many of those who criticize Socialists know the first principles of Socialism. Socialism and Socialists are libeled and slandered by the false and by the ignorant only, for no one who has studied Socialism can for a single moment question that it has a program whereby, if it could be followed out and put into execution, this world would be cleared of much of its misery and degradation. . . ."

Quoting parts of this book in May, 1918, the *New York Times* said: "Such is the gospel which Duluth refused to hear. Such is the platform of this candidate of the Nonpartisan League. More fortunate than many of the managers and orators of that concern, Mr. Lindbergh, so far as we know, is not under indictment for sedition."

In the *Chicago Tribune* a staff writer, Arthur M. Evans, in June, 1918, wrote, "The reader looks instinctively to see if it bears the German copyright. It doesn't, but it contains many choice morsels of thought that might be gobbled with relish in Potsdam." The *Tribune* Washington correspondent, according to Margaret Ernst, telegraphed a report that in the House Representative Miller said that "because of the attacks he had made upon the American Government" Lindbergh should be called "a friend of the Kaiser."

In 1923 when Lindbergh went campaigning again, his son, "Slim," took him from place to place in an airplane. They were almost killed one day when an unidentified enemy cut a cable on the machine. The elder Lindbergh was still known as a "red-hot Bolshevik."

Lindbergh was one of many victims of an unfair press. The Nonpartisan League, headed by A. C. Townley, had only its weekly magazine to answer the attacks of its political and economic enemies. When the Lindbergh campaign began the members of the League were called "everything under the sun,—anarchists, I. W. W.'s, pro-Germans, disloyal. They [the opposition] used the press, the power of their money and position—every force they could muster to fight the farmers' league."

Although Lindbergh lost, North Dakota went Nonpartisan. Said the official League journal:

> "The part the big daily press of Minnesota played in the political campaign in North Dakota was contemptible. For weeks before the vote, which resulted in the complete and sweeping victory for the Nonpartisan league, the *Pioneer Press* and *Dispatch* of St. Paul and the *Journal* and *Tribune* of Minneapolis were full of poisoned news and perverted editorial comment to the effect that if North Dakota voters returned Governor Frazier and the League to power it would be a 'German victory.' Every day these papers carried great headlines and editorials declaring that a victory for the farmers' administration would be a victory for disloyalty. They said that the only way North Dakota could 'purge itself of disloyalty' would be to restore the old political gang of North Dakota to power and turn out the farmers' administration.
>
> "This version of the North Dakota campaign was spread all over the United States through the activities of the poison press of Minnesota."

One of the typical stories during the campaign was that in the *St. Paul Dispatch* "to the effect that Mrs. Townley had told a woman in Detroit, Minnesota, that she had deposited $60,000 at a Detroit bank, money that Mr. Townley had stolen from the farmers." (I am quoting the words of the *Nonpartisan Leader*.) The Associated Press sent this by wire to all the country. It was printed in thousands of papers. Other papers copied verbatim the *Dispatch* story, which took up nearly a page. "No deposition of this kind was ever introduced in court. No woman of the name given ever existed. . . . It was just a hoax. . . . The story if true could have been verified in an hour by the Associated Press and the *Dispatch* lie nailed. . . . [The hoax was exposed by the Detroit banks.] So far as the *Leader* knows, no paper in America that published the original lie has yet retracted it. . . ."

During the Lindbergh campaign the organ of the League further charged that "practically every weekly and daily newspaper in Montana which is fighting the League is either a debtor to the copper trust or is owned outright by them." And again, "The newspapers do not attack the National Nonpartisan League because of any principles or convictions of their own, for they have none. They are merely the tools of those higher up, of the big business interests who are their masters. Think of the fight the organized farmers are making against war profiteering and you will see one reason for the frantic, lying articles in the poison press."

The campaign against Lindbergh, Townley, La Follette, was largely a press campaign. Wherever the progressives got a hearing they were fairly certain of making converts, but with the entire press of that section of the country against them they were terribly handicapped. As it was so much a journalistic war, the Nonpartisan League was fortunate in the midst of this campaign in gaining as a convert Walter W. Liggett who came out of the editorial office of the *St. Paul Dispatch*. He had been discharged for "disloyalty," it being alleged that he had attended a Nonpartisan League meeting and applauded. For the League Liggett wrote:

"A newspaper is a double-barreled weapon. It can suppress news entirely or distort it under misleading headlines in its news columns. If this fails to have the required result it often will continue publishing unfair attacks in its editorial columns. The editorial columns of the *St. Paul Dispatch* and *Pioneer Press* are even more unfair than their alleged news columns.

"The *St. Paul Dispatch* and *Pioneer Press* are notorious for their subservience to the great special interests—the railroads, the steel trust, the packers, the millers, the bankers and the Twin City Rapid Transit company. They have served these interests for years and done their bidding on every occasion. The *Dispatch* and *Pioneer Press* can not deny that they have fought for the corporations and fought against the people every time there was a real fundamental issue involved. . . ."

Lindbergh, Sr., made no distinction between the newspapers which were fair to him and those which were unfair. He lived and died believing that the entire press was contemptible. Lindbergh, Jr.—the aviator—has always tried to distinguish between the newspapers which treated him well and those he thinks treated him badly. Moreover, on more than one occasion he issued statements in which he absolved the actions of reporters, saying they were only doing the work assigned them by the newspapers. In other words it is the so-called rules of the so-called newspaper game which Lindbergh was challenging as much as the things done to him.

When he married privately, the tabloid press felt itself insulted. When he tried to take his honeymoon without benefit of publicity, the sensational press hounded him. One tabloid called him a "Grade A celebrity," therefore a public commodity, like gas or electric light.

The case of Lindbergh the Hero involves canon 6 of the code adopted by the American Society of Newspaper Editors: "A newspaper should not invade private rights or feelings without sure warrant of public right as distinguished from public curiosity." To Marlen Pew, Lindbergh said that several New York newspapers, five of which he named, do not respect this rule. In July, 1930, Pew and Lindbergh discussed the press and privacy, and here is Pew's story of the famous interview:

"Lindbergh draws the line strictly between the right of the press to report his activities as they relate to the scientific development of air travel and what he calls personal curiosity. He said in sincere terms that he valued and deeply appreciated the 'remarkable liberality' of the press in support of what he terms his 'work.' 'The constructive press has been both kind and generous to me ever since I have been flying,' he said, and he mentioned newspaper men who have been helpful, intelligently critical, fair in their reports and considerate of his private rights.

"Col. Lindbergh, without the slightest hesitation, but with no show of anger, also mentioned five New York newspapers which he said Mrs. Lindbergh and he had decided they could not 'co-operate with and maintain our self-respect.' These newspapers, he said, represent an idea of journalism to which he cannot subscribe. He called their practices 'contemptible' and thought them to be 'a social drag,' 'non-constructive,' and 'a waste of time.' He minced no words in condemning newspapers which, in his view, cater to morbid curiosity and are concerned with private gossip to the exclusion of matters in the realm of 'things, ideas and ideals.'

". . . Reporting their courtship, marriage, honeymoon, and recently the expectancy and arrival of their infant son. Col. Lindbergh admitted these activities had been the bane of his life, that they had been 'disgusting' and 'humiliating,' but contended that his feeling was not against individual reporters, though he thought they might be engaged in 'some more decent business.' His expressed resentment was against editors and publishers who 'force reporters to do these unjust and intolerable things.' He said he had become fairly used to indignities from a section of the New York newspaper press and was past personal feelings in relation to them, 'only I wish they would give me time to do my work,' but he felt as a citizen he had to 'protest against such journalism in behalf of other persons who are similarly plagued and cannot defend themselves.' He thought it weak merely to grin and bear injustice. Col. Lindbergh asserted he was 'through trying to deal with them,' meaning the five New York newspapers he had mentioned.

". . . He did not want to blame specific newspaper men. He did admit he felt outraged when some reporters followed him and Mrs. Lindbergh on their honeymoon and 'for eight straight hours circled about our boat, at anchor in a New England harbor, in a noisy motorboat and occasionally called across the water to us that if we would pose for one picture they would go away.' He thought that particularly mean and unworthy. He considered it absurd that he should have been forced to keep a guard constantly at duty at the gate of his wife's home, and told of an incident wherein a reporter had attempted to bribe a servant with $2,000 to 'betray the secrets of the household.' He also mentioned, with resentment, the publication of Mrs. Lindbergh's expectation last Spring. On no ground, in his view, could this be justified. He spoke of other disagreeable matters. . . ."

Lindbergh had forced every reporter and photographer to sign a pledge that he would use the baby's photograph only in his own paper or his own service, making sure that the following newspapers did not receive a copy: *Graphic, News, Mirror, American* and *Journal*. When the photograph appeared in the *Daily News,* Lindbergh ascertained that it was from the copy furnished the Associated Press. *Time* reported (July 21, 1930) that several days later when an airplane belonging to a company of which Lindbergh was a technical adviser ran into a crowd, the *Daily News* headline read:

LINDBERGH LINER KILLS 2

At the next regular meeting of the board of directors formal protests against the Associated Press action in accepting a picture for distribution to clients on condition that it would not be released to certain ones were made by the editor of the *News* and the general manager of the Hearst newspapers.

On the other hand, the liberal weeklies called upon the society of editors to explain "what justification it has for existing when in the face of this monstrous persecution of Col. and Mrs. Lindbergh no voice has yet been raised by it or any of its members in any of its sessions against this degrading of their profession." Colonel Lindbergh's constitutional right to liberty and the pursuit of happiness were held infringed.

When the Lindbergh baby was kidnaped the press descended upon him again. Mitchell Dawson, Chicago lawyer, speaks of "an army of enthusiastic ghouls . . . prying, spying and trespassing in a ruthless stampede for news," but Pew believes this report false. We do know, however, that all Colonel Lindbergh said was, "Please go away." The Lindbergh case has been summed up by Silas Bent as follows: "Charles A. Lindbergh has suffered more, probably, than any other citizen at the hands of newspaper men. They capitalized for revenue only (their revenue) a stunt flight to France, they built up about his personality a myth which he has never been quite free to dissipate, they outrageously invaded the privacy of his honeymoon, and now they have made more difficult the return by kidnapers of his son. Colonel Lindbergh has an ugly score against the daily press."

In April, 1932, Colonel Lindbergh was forced to issue a statement that "the continued following of our representatives by members of the press is making it extremely difficult, if not impossible, for us to establish contact with whoever is in possession of our son . . . our attempts are still greatly hampered or made impossible by press activity. . . ." And in August, upon the birth of another son, Colonel Lindbergh issued the following statement which can leave no doubt in anyone's mind that he feels bitterly about the press:

"Mrs. Lindbergh and I have made our home in New Jersey, and it is naturally our wish to continue to live there near our friends and interests. Obviously, however, it is impossible for us to subject the life of our second son to the publicity we feel was in a large measure responsible for the death of our first child.

"We feel that our children have the right to grow up normally with other children. Continued publicity makes this impossible. I am appealing to the press to permit our children to lead lives of normal Americans."

Robert M. La Follette fought "invisible government." He attacked all the business interests which were supporting the Republican and Democratic parties. His financial support came largely from the Pinchots, Gifford and Amos; Charles R. Crane, William Kent, Alfred L. Baker. He had a naïve belief that the Progressive Party was different from the two major parties, that it had no financial roots in the same invisible government, and he even asked Theodore Roosevelt to endorse him for the presidency in December, 1911.

The Progressives, however, had decided on Roosevelt. Medill McCormick, one of the heirs of the *Chicago Tribune,* the Pinchots and others, asked La Follette on January 29, 1912, to quit in Roosevelt's favor, but La Follette refused. He began his campaign for nomination. Twelve years later Colonel Dickinson, retired from the State Department, wrote in the *World* that Roosevelt's campaign had been underwritten "just as they would underwrite building a railroad from here to San Francisco." The underwriters were given as James Stillman, then head of the National City Bank (father of the James Stillman of divorce notoriety); E. H. Gary; E. H. Harriman; Daniel G. Reid, railroad manipulator, founder of American Can; Charles F. Brooker, vice-president of the New Haven; George W. Perkins and Robert L. Bacon, Morgan partners. To fighting these very men and interests La Follette had dedicated his platform and career.

On the second of February La Follette delivered an address to the Periodical Publishers' Association, banqueting in Philadelphia. He made his usual attack on Wall Street, Morgan, the Rockefellers, the trusts, big business in general, and said that the money trust

". . . controls the newspaper press . . . newspapers of course are still patronized for news. But wherever news items bear in any way upon control of government by business, the news is colored, so confidence in the newspaper as a newspaper is being undermined. . . . The control [of the press] comes through that community of interests, that interdependence of investments and credits which ties the publicity up to the banks, the advertisers and the special interests. We may expect this same kind of control sooner or later to reach out for the magazines. But more than this. I warned you of a subtle new peril, the centralization of advertising that will in time seek to gag you. . . ."

La Follette was on the verge of a nervous breakdown. According to the *New York Sun* he "would recover a page, divert to explain a page discarded a half hour ago," etc. He himself said later, "I talked too long without realizing it. I went home, really ill from exhaustion." There is no doubt that he acted in a muddled manner, that his speech became a tirade, but there is absolute proof that this confirmed buttermilk drinker was not maudlin, that he had not touched a drop of alcohol, as was alleged for years afterward.

A few days later the *New York Herald* reported that La Follette "is being hustled ruthlessly inside the hearse, although he still insists that he is strong enough to occupy a seat alongside the driver." A few great papers were lenient if not impartial in their attacks upon him, but generally speaking the press of the nation smashed his career. Whether or not the publishers in Philadelphia got together and decided upon united action is not so important as the fact that the press never forgave his attack, and either by innuendo, charges of drunkenness, or by silence, for several years made it impossible for him to have a fair hearing from the reading public.

Naturally enough La Follette fought back. If he could not make himself heard in the nation, he could at least let himself go in the Senate, and he did. When the press asked for an appropriation of five million dollars to advertise the Liberty Loan in 1917, La Follette struck at the publishers' pocketbooks.

He called theirs "a business that is already subsidized by the United States government to the extent of ninety million dollars a year," meaning of course the loss the post office incurs annually in carrying second class mail. On that subject and the loan advertising he said:

> "While engaged daily in impugning and questioning the loyalty and patriotism of others, the newspapers went to Congress and asked to be paid for being patriotic.
>
> "The debates on the recent revenue bill throw some interesting light on the 'patriotism' of newspapers,—particularly when the kind of patriotism applied affects the cash register of business offices.
>
> "For years and years it has been a known fact in Washington that the government has been carrying second class mail,—newspapers and magazines, at a huge deficit. Because of the tremendous influence wielded by newspapers among politicians nothing has ever come of any efforts to reduce the deficit and place the charges on a business basis. Government estimates show that it costs 8 cents a pound for the government to carry second class mail. The remuneration received is 1 cent a pound from the newspapers.
>
> "When members of Congress began scanning about for sources of revenue to meet the huge war appropriations the second class postage was hit upon. Members argued that at a time such as the present no business should be subsidized. It developed that the government is paying $100,000,000 for carrying second class postage and they were receiving in return from the newspapers about $11,000,000—a subsidy of $89,000,000. . . .
>
> "The 'patriotism plus profit' policy of the newspapers is most sordidly illustrated by the history of the attempt to get a $5,000,000 slice of the government money for advertising the Liberty Loan. . . ."

The Senator, however, pointed out that when the question of raising rates on second-class matter was before Congress, and when the big New York newspaper publishers adopted a resolution against any change in rates, two leading papers, the *New York Tribune* and the *Brooklyn Daily Eagle* refused to subscribe to such a move, the first named editorially calling the government loss of millions "a clear subsidy to the publishers."

Shortly after this attack on the press, Senator La Follette made a speech at St. Paul in which he favored high increases in the taxes on the war profiteers. The story which follows was compiled by Senator La Follette from the *Congressional Record* and published by him shortly before his death in 1925:

"The body of Senator La Follette's address, as submitted by the official stenographer to the Committee on Privileges and Elections of the United States Senate, was a discussion of progressive policies and the necessity of organization by the farmers. In the midst of the delivery of the speech, Senator La Follette was interrupted by questions from the audience concerning the war. In response to these questions, Senator La Follette declared at one point in his speech:

" 'For my own part I was not in favor of beginning the war. I don't mean to say that we hadn't suffered grievances; we had—at the hands of Germany. Serious grievances!'

"In reporting this speech to more than 1,200 newspapers in as many cities throughout the country, the Associated Press quoted Senator La Follette as follows:

" 'I wasn't in favor of beginning the war. We had *No* grievances.'

"It was this false report which appeared in the *Chicago Tribune,* the *New York Times,* the *Washington Post,* and more than 1,200 other newspapers in their issues of September 21, 1917. It was reproduced by publications in every part of the country. . . .

"This speech, as reported by the Associated Press, was the immediate cause for the introduction in the Senate of a resolution to expel Senator La Follette from that body as a disloyalist.

"The storm broke on Senator La Follette after the publication of the report of his St. Paul speech, quoting him as saying 'We had no grievance' against Germany.

"As early as October 11, 1917, Senator La Follette in an open letter to the Chairman of the Senate Committee which was investigating his right to his seat, branded the Associated Press report of his speech as 'wholly false.'

"It was not until May 23, 1918, however—eight months after the delivery of the speech—that the Associated Press took any action on the matter. On that date, Frederick Roy Martin, Assistant General Manager of the Associated Press, wrote a letter to the Senate Committee, apologizing for the misquotation and specifically retracting the erroneous report.

"Admitting that the Associated Press had 'distributed inaccurately one important phrase' of the St. Paul speech, Mr. Martin concluded his letter:

" 'The error was regrettable and the Associated Press seizes the first opportunity to do justice to Senator La Follette.'

"Thus, eight months after the delivery of the speech, the Associated Press repudiated as false and untrue the statement credited to Senator La Follette and played up in the headlines of newspapers in more than 1,200 cities throughout the United States. . . ."

"Why was it that Robert M. La Follette was singled out for the most savage and relentless abuse ever directed against a public man in the history of the United States? [he himself asks, and replies]: The answer is clear to every fair minded person who will examine the official records.

"Senator La Follette was pilloried and persecuted because for twenty years in Wisconsin and in the Senate he had been fighting to protect the American people from the unjust exactions of powerful corporate interests; because he had organized and led the Progressive movement; because in the midst of war he fought to lay upon organized wealth and war profiteers a fair proportion of the enormous cost of paying for the war. . . .

" 'The record shows that the resolution to expel La Follette from the Senate was based on the distorted reports of the St. Paul speech, and that after an investigation of more than fourteen months, the United States Senate voted overwhelmingly to dismiss all the charges against La Follette. . . .

". . . La Follette's St. Paul speech was falsely reported to the people, and immediately made the basis of an organized demand from Chambers of Commerce, Dollar-A-Year Men, Bankers' Associations, state Councils of Defense and other bodies, that La Follette be driven from the Senate, under the blot of treason to his country."

La Follette for years alleged that there was a conspiracy of silence against him in the press. As the official record shows, he did not obtain a retraction for eight months. That the *New York Evening Post* was ignorant of the fact that the Senator had challenged the Associated Press immediately after it made its error and that he had requested the newspapers of the country to correct it, corroborates La Follette's charge. Said the *Post:*

"The Associated Press has handsomely and promptly admitted its grievous fault in misreporting Senator La Follette . . . but the fact remains that irreparable injury was done to the Senator, and that a large part of the outcry against him was due to this misstatement in the one thousand newspapers which are served by the Associated Press. Senator La Follette declared at the time that the press had misquoted him, but the matter was never brought to the attention of the Associated Press until Mr. Gilbert E. Roe, his attorney, stated the fact before the Senate Committee of Inquiry on Tuesday. Why the Senator delayed so long is a mystery; but the serious wrong done by this error needs no expatiating. No amount of apology can undo it. . . ."

No, replied Senator La Follette, he did not neglect nor delay,

"but the newspapers neglected to make any correction but on the contrary continued for months afterwards to use the false report as a text upon which to base arguments condemning the Senator and creating public sentiment against him. The Senator had no adequate opportunity to give to the public the truth of the matter. The press was not open to him. As the *Post* says, 'the thought that unintentionally so extreme an injustice may be done a pub-

lic man is one to sober all responsible journalism.' The
injustice done the public is far more serious.   If public
men fighting in the interest of the public may be ruined
and discredited while the fight is on, the public may lose its
fight and its servants become intimidated and afraid to
make any real fight in its behalf."

In the 1922 campaign Senator La Follette said that the
press of Wisconsin with two exceptions was opposed to him,
and that inasmuch as the press of his state usually opposed him
his election was an interesting proof that the press had lost
political influence and that readers mistrusted their newspapers.

In 1924, however, all commentators agreed that while the
smaller papers suppressed the news of the La Follette campaign, the larger city papers, notably the *New York Times,*
covered it completely and objectively.

The case of Upton Sinclair has been brilliantly illuminated
by President Theodore Roosevelt who said to him: "Mr. Sinclair, I have been in public life longer than you and I will give
you this bit of advice: if you pay any attention to what the
newspapers say about you, you will have an unhappy time. . . ."

Upton Sinclair has had an unhappy time.

The latest episode of which was his candidacy for governor
of California in 1934.   Then, as ever, Sinclair got a raw deal
from so many newspapers that there is hardly an exaggeration
in saying he got a raw deal from the press.

A newspaper man should not attempt to sit in judgment on
the case of Sinclair vs. the *New York Times.*   The complain-
ant has stated his side in a pamphlet he calls *The Crimes of
the Times,* and the defendant usually has chosen the role of
silence.

Relations between the two began most favorably following the publication of *The Jungle.*   A stockyards investigation
was ordered by Theodore Roosevelt.   Sinclair, who knew the
contents of the report, offered a story which the Associated
Press refused.   It probably did not believe in its authenticity.

Sinclair says that "throughout the campaign against the Beef Trust they [the A. P.] never sent out a single line injurious to the interests of the packers." But Managing Editor Van Anda, of the *Times,* not only trusted Sinclair but received him with joy and made a three-day sensation of the story. It certainly was news.

During the Colorado bloodshed Sinclair, with the cunning of an Ivy Lee, conceived the idea of breaking the silence of the newspapers by putting on a stunt in front of the Rockefeller offices in New York. It was known as "the mourning pickets." The eastern press saw it as a human-interest story and published news which counteracted the tainted stories or the silence from Colorado. Several of the reporters, says Sinclair, "were men of conscience. One, Isaac Russell of the *Times,* became our friend and day after day he would tell of his struggles in the *Times* office, and how nearly every word favorable to myself or to the strikers was blue-pencilled from his story. So during the Broadway demonstration . . . we lived, as it were, on the inside of the *Times* office, and watched the process of strangling the news."

But now the case becomes more complicated. The mourning pickets were a news item. Sinclair, however, believes that the fact that he wrote a letter to Vincent Astor chiding him about his million-dollar recreation building, is equally news. And every newspaper man knows that such a letter is not news. The *Times, Herald, Press, Tribune* did not print his letter, Sinclair complains, but it is not a fair complaint, journalism being what it is and was.

On the other hand, Sinclair charges the *Times* with failure to review his *Brass Check* and with refusing money for an advertisement for that same book. Here again it seems to me he has no case. But later when James Melvin Lee of the New York University school of journalism denounced the book the *Times* published two columns of vitriol and refused to give Sinclair the equal opportunity of rebuttal. In this point I believe Sinclair is right.

He has a much better case against the Associated Press although here also it is his failure to understand the American principle of what constitutes news that leads him into error. We know that the news out of Colorado was perverted. We know that Sinclair accused the A. P. of poisoning the news there and that after a fanfare from the A. P. the cases against the *Masses* were dropped. But when Sinclair bases a test of the news on the fact that the Associated Press refused to send as news a telegram which he himself sent to President Wilson, newspaper men know that the A. P. was right, because no telegram which an individual sends is necessarily news. On the other hand, that telegram contained a serious charge of corruption which the A. P. may or may not have investigated. It certainly should have done so and published the result.

In the mourning pickets story Sinclair says, "The United Press, which is a liberal organization, sent out a perfectly truthful account of what had happened. The Associated Press, which is a reactionary organization, sent out a false account."

He enlisted the aid of John P. Gavit, managing editor of the *Post,* who wrote to Melville Stone, saying that the matter "on its face . . . certainly created a *prima facie* case of suppression of important facts regarding the situation in Denver," and Stone replied he would investigate. Nothing ever happened, so far as I can find out. The A. P. still, apparently, owes Sinclair an apology.

One Chicago newspaper reviewer said of *The Jungle* that it showed Sinclair knew more about the inside of brothels than the stockyards. I do not think any large paper in America would employ a book reviewer today who reviewed in that manner.

Bennett, of the *New York Herald,* ordered a story from Sinclair, *Packingtown a Year Later,* but neither paid for it nor used it. Incidentally the *Herald* did pay him twenty-five hundred dollars for personal libel.

That Sinclair was hounded by the press and frequently libeled is an indisputable fact. He had become a public figure when he founded Helicon Home Colony which the newspapers used as a butt for jokes, just as they always use Utopian, idealistic, socialistic, "brain trust" and reform theories. The papers which cater most to the masses delight in ridiculing any action by an individual which is outside conventional mass life. It is the snobbery of the vulgar. The yellow press in its time and the tabloid press today not only cater to the *polloi* but the publishers instead of being leaders of public opinion are merely leaders of herd prejudices. A reporter from the *Sun* told Sinclair he liked Helicon Hall, its people and its idea, and "I feel like a cur to have to write as I do, but you know what the *Sun* is." The *Sun* was then still the newspaper man's newspaper. The reporter asked for an amusing story and Sinclair said his collie dog had disappeared. The *Sun* story said that even a dog refused to stay at the Sinclair Utopia.

In Los Angeles one day Sinclair unwisely remarked he could not find a barber shop because the city was so beflagged. The *Los Angeles Times* thereupon called his speech "prattlings of an anarchist."

The 1934 campaign certainly has furnished Sinclair with a grand concluding chapter to a new edition of *The Brass Check*.

No sooner had he received the nomination for governor on the Democratic ticket than the Democratic newspapers deserted him. And this is a significant fact. It brings up the whole question as to why certain newspapers are Democratic and certain newspapers are Republican, and who gets paid for being what it is, and what are the benefits, financial or otherwise, for representing a party.

Although a Democratic party candidate, Sinclair also had a program which big business disapproved. When big business disapproves anything party lines disappear. It was so with La Follette in Wisconsin and it was so in Washington when Ridder told the Republican and Democratic press alike to support the bill making news print free from Republican tariff. "To my knowledge no daily newspaper in the state is supporting me. I believe this situation is unique in political history," sighed Sinclair.

Immediately afterward he found that "masses of falsehood" were poured over his campaign "by newspapers and radio and pamphlets." Heywood Broun's "magnificent articles exposing the California reactionaries were appearing in the *New*

York World-Telegram, but were not wanted in California."
There is no law requiring subscribers to Broun's column to
print them, but there is an agreement that the column must not
be cut or distorted and Broun himself has complained against
certain papers for doing so.

Sinclair had another unhappy experience with the *San Francisco News.* He claims that he told one of the editors a story
in confidence and that that confidence, which journalists respect fanatically throughout the world, was broken when the
story appeared in the paper under the signature of another staff
member.

Summing up the reports in the eastern press regarding his
campaign, Sinclair says:

> "The great newspapers of the country also reported the
> battle, mostly according to their prejudices. The *New
> York Times* gets its California stories from George P.
> West of the *San Francisco News* and Chapin Hall of the
> *Los Angeles Times.*
>
> "West, who used to be a civil liberties man, has become
> a tired liberal, and talked to me sadly about his lack of
> faith, and the inevitability of Fascism in America. In
> his writings he did his best to equal the *Los Angeles
> Times* in depreciation of our movement; but Chapin Hall
> ran clean away from him in the last couple of weeks when
> he sent to the *New York Times* a story about the Com-
> munists supporting us in California. What do you think
> was his sole bit of evidence? That fake Communist cir-
> cular which had been got out by Creel headquarters two
> months back, and was now reproduced on the front page
> of 'Ham' Cotton's newspaper! Not merely had this
> wretched piece of trickery been exposed in the EPIC
> News, but a facsimile of it had been reproduced in *Today*
> of October 6, with a statement of its fraudulent nature.
> 'All the News That's Fit to Print,' says the majestic *New
> York Times.*"

It is not necessary to go to the liberal weeklies for proof that
Sinclair got a raw deal. After the *Nation* called it "one of
the nastiest campaigns on record" and the *New Republic* said

that the press lied about Sinclair, the *New York Daily News* reported the tricks of the Hollywood movie producers; Broun in the *World-Telegram* mentioned the "dirty tactics" and "wilful fraud"; the Scripps-Howard papers printed the statement from Los Angeles that "local newspapers have struck a new low in political reporting. The big dailies make little pretense of printing both sides of the conflict and most of them have passed the sentence of silence on the big Sinclair meetings. The *Los Angeles Times* displays daily a box quoting from Mr. Sinclair's earlier writings on marriage, the church, the Legion, other American establishments. The series has proved damaging to Mr. Sinclair. . . ."

Early in the campaign the *New York Times* had reported that a west coast newspaper had headlined it,"This is not politics. This is war." When the battle was over Sinclair had polled more than eight hundred and seventy-five thousand votes, which every fair-minded man admitted was a remarkable showing when the money the Republicans had spent and their control of the press is considered. Many eastern newspapers thought it quite a victory for Sinclair. But the *New York Times* began its editorial the next morning with these remarkable words: "The total failure of the Sinclair campaign" and concluded with "the people of California . . . attacked the entire Sinclair plan and repudiated it emphatically. . . ." Several days later the *Times* reported in its news columns that the governor-elect was using Sinclair platform planks.

The hysterical Red-baiting *Los Angeles Times* naturally enough called Merriam's victory a "retreat from Moscow." It said that the state had "served notice on the world yesterday that she has not gone crazy. There was nothing uncertain or equivocal about her answer to Upton Sinclair's invitation to forsake her proven paths for the red route of radicalism. . . . It has given the nation-wide radical movement a set-back from which it will not soon recover. The retreat from Moscow has started."

But the unfairest document, in my estimation, was the front-page interview of the *New York Times* of September 2,

1934, in which William Randolph Hearst denounced Sinclair, Communism, Socialism and Bolshevism. The cable contained the statement that the *Times* "invited" Mr. Hearst to interrupt his vacation in Bad Nauheim to comment on developments at home. It seems to me that the *Times* has gone very far afield when it chooses, of all men in the world, the rival publisher Hearst as a stick with which to beat Sinclair. This is a continuation of the feud with an amazing weapon. It is reminiscent of the James Melvin Lee attack on *The Brass Check*. The *Times,* refusing to review the book, published Lee, then refused Sinclair space to reply. Now it called upon the man the *Times* regards as holding the lowest place in American journalism to join in a common attack upon the enemy. It parallels the interview other papers had with Al Capone in which the gangster denounced Bolshevik methods.

And yet "Fair Play" stands high in the code of the American Society of Newspaper Editors.

Chapter XVI

FREE PRESS VS. FREE LABOR

THE first thing a dictator does is abolish the free press. Next he abolishes the right of labor to go on strike. Strikes have been labor's weapon of progress in the century of our industrial civilization. Where the strike has been abolished, as in Italy, labor is reduced to a state of medieval peonage, the standard of living is lowered, the nation falls to a subsistence level. (An impartial international investigation by the League of Nations supplies the documentary proof for these assertions.)

In free countries, notably England, France, Sweden, the United States, labor is still fighting for more rights and privileges. It uses the strike weapon less and less. It realizes that strikes cannot be successful unless there is public sympathy, and that public sympathy or antagonism is manufactured by the press. When the press supports a strike it is sure to win; when the press is honest and impartial it has a fair chance to win, but when the press unites against labor its chances to win are very small.

As a reporter on a newspaper which supported labor I had the opportunity for several years to compare our news with that of the papers owned and directed by politicians and banks. Later, working for a newspaper owned by a bank, I saw the other side of the case. But in both experiences I found that the reporters generally were on the side of labor while their own newspapers directed the news as well as the editorials against labor.

As a reporter I suspected that the antagonism of publishers to the women's clubs, church and other organizations which led the fight for abolition of child labor was prompted by financial interests. Cheap newsboys are necessary for increased profits. But one thing I never suspected, never heard discussed either in the editorial or the composing-room, was the employment by the publishers of a strikebreaking organization.

There are three subjects, in their relationship to the so-called freedom of the press, that I must discuss here: child labor, the press as strikebreaker, the publishers as employers of a strikebreaking agency. First of all the San Francisco strike of 1934 when the press itself played the role of strikebreaker. This was something new. I had known that all Pittsburgh papers could more or less suppress news of a strike, but so far as I knew there had never been a planned campaign by united publishers. (It did of course happen in the early days of Fascist Italy.) But San Francisco of 1934 in my opinion has written the most shameful page in the history of that city's journalism.

San Francisco was not friendly to organized labor; naturally the press was unfriendly. In May, 1934, the longshoremen went on strike and in the course of several months gained the sympathy of many big unions who voted the general strike. It was called. In the first three days the city was in a holiday mood and there was no real suffering from lack of food deliveries. The strikers did not stop the rounds of the milkmen.

Those same three peaceful days the press of San Francisco, augmented by the voice of paid radio orators, preached fear and hatred. News was distorted, invented, colored with propaganda; radio speeches were pure demagoguery, and the villains were always the "Reds" and "foreign agitators."

Labor was smiling, quiet; the newspaper-reading citizenry and the radio masses were quick to respond to hysterical suggestions, when as a climax General Hugh Johnson, arriving as mediator, delivered himself of a senseless blast against labor which became the newspaper signal for hysteria. "When the means of food supply—milk for children—necessities of life to the whole people are threatened, that is bloody insurrection," Johnson said.

Not a hand had been raised, not a shot fired, not a milk delivery missed, no one had gone hungry for lack of transport, and all the fundamental public services were functioning. The general strike began peacefully. It followed the police attack and the shooting of two men several days earlier. Labor had surprised itself and the press with the spontaneous march of twelve thousand men behind the victims' coffins. Despite the press, union after union enthusiastically declared for the strike. When it came, labor permitted the press to function, the telephones to ring, the deliveries of bread, milk and ice to continue and nineteen restaurants were allowed to remain open the first day, fifty the second. Doctors received gasoline for their cars. The few instances of violence, a truck overturned, an altercation between a picket and a strikebreaker, were unimportant. To the press, however, they were sensations worth headlines. As in Italy in 1922, and in Germany in 1933, the politicians of big business, big business itself and the newspapers it controlled were united in San Francisco, but having no Fascist Duce or Fuehrer they called upon the mayor to ask for national troopers to put down the Red Revolution. In the offices of the *Chronicle,* the *Call-Bulletin* and other papers which raised the Red scare and defeated labor, type was being set by members of the typographical union.

The publishers, minor Machiavellis, gave the union men a raise in wages on the eve of the strike. And union labor, here as elsewhere, scabbed on its fellow men.

As a preparation for the general strike the majority of newspapers of San Francisco began a series of inflammatory editorials and distorted news items calling it a revolution; on the other hand, many newspapers failed to print even the official declarations of the strike committee giving the reasons, causes and grievances. A Hearst paper under a headline

"SHOOT, KILL,"
FRISCO RIOT
TROOPS TOLD

reported that Colonel H. H. Mittlestaedt, commanding the soldiers, had ordered the court-martial of any man who fired a shot into the air and told them "in case the strikers attack again, that they would first clip their opponents with the butts of their rifles, then bayonet them, and finally shoot them."

The people of San Francisco were completely befuddled by the press, which was itself hysterical and which raised the usual Red banner to pass its hysteria over to the masses. "Deliberate journalistic malpractice" is the characterization of San Francisco's editors by the correspondent of the *New Republic,* Evelyn Seeley, who exempts only one newspaper, the Scripps-Howard *News.* But even this journal, which is known as friendly to labor, omitted from a late edition the column in which Heywood Broun had said: ". . . and so I still think that the lawless employers should be restrained, and if they don't like it here I see no possible objection to sending them back where they came from."

The *Chronicle,* for example, went in for rabid expressions like these: "The radicals have seized control by intimidation. What they want is revolution. . . . Are the sane, sober working-men of San Francisco to permit these communists to use them for their purpose of wreckage, a wreckage bound to carry the unions down with it?"; while the *Los Angeles Times* stated that "the situation in San Francisco is not correctly described by the phrase 'general strike.' What is actually in progress there is an insurrection, a Communist-inspired and led revolt against organized government. There is but one thing to be done—put down the revolt with any force necessary and protect the right of ordinary people to conduct their ordinary occupations in security. . . ."

The *Sacramento Bee* informed Mayor Rossi that his program had the united support of the law-abiding citizens and spoke of the strikers as persons seeking to overthrow the government of the United States. The *San Francisco Call-Bulletin* upheld the "conservative union men [who] have been shouted down by an element bent seemingly on strife and self-aggrandizement." The *Oakland Examiner* said: "If the small group of Communists, starting with their control of the longshore and maritime unions, extend their power over the community of the bay area—and thence into the whole or even part of the State—California would be no more fit to live in than Russia."

The *Oakland Chronicle* said, "The radicals have seized con-

trol. . . . The radicals have wanted no settlement. What they
want is revolution." The *Portland* (Oregon) *Times* said the
strikers were refusing the public the necessities of life and
blamed "rampant radicalism for unrestrained rule or utter
ruin."

The editorials in the press range all the way from falsehood
to hysteria; they unite in raising the Communist scare;
throughout the strike they blamed the strikers daily for law-
breaking and general violence. The eastern press reprinted
the editorials and the news which came largely from the offices
of the California papers. The East naturally believed that a
revolutionary uprising was occurring in San Francisco. Yet
the question of veracity and integrity of the press must certainly arise in the mind of any man who reads the following
dispatch from America's national humorist and generally admitted unprejudiced observer. Will Rogers telegraphed from
California to the scores of newspapers which take his daily
idea:

> "In 1926 I was in England during their world-famous
> general stike. And brother it was general. Not a paper
> printed, not a train, not a bus, not a wheel turned. Well,
> I never got through telling of the composure of those
> level headed people.
> "Well, I went to San Francisco, and I tell you we are
> not so 'nutty' under stress as you might think. It was as
> quiet as the British. The only thing went haywire was
> the headlines in the out of Frisco papers. I hope we never
> live to see the day when a thing is as bad as some of our
> newspapers make it.
> "There is lots of sense in this country yet."

Again, for his Sunday readers, Will Rogers, whom no one
has yet called a Bolshevik, summed up San Francisco. Saying
as usual that all he knows is what he reads in the papers, he
added that everything in San Francisco was quiet, that eighteen
restaurants were open, that "all the trucks you saw on the
street was either ice, milk, bread or bare necessities." Rogers
concludes that, inasmuch as manufacturers and bankers have

associations, "there is nothing fairer than workmen having unions for their mutual benefit . . . but when the people felt that the Reds were running the thing . . . they turned against 'em. . . . But what I want to get over is that the people were just as down to earth, as peaceful and law abiding as you ever saw. Again, a dog fight would have constituted excitement. There is lots of Reds in the Country, but you would be surprised at the amount of Whites. . . ."

On the subject of violence either the majority of California papers or Mr. Rogers is not telling the truth, and knowing both, I would say, even if I had no other evidence, that the facts are those given by the latter.

The strike was smashed. The press announced that the public was to be congratulated upon this action. "The truth, born of long experience, that a great strike cannot be won if it outrages public opinion," said the *New York Times,* "has apparently been grasped by the strategy committee. . . ." Does or doesn't the *Times* know who makes and controls public opinion? Has or hasn't the *Times* ever heard about the "power of the press"?

Two days later, July 22, 1934, the *Times* under an editorial headline "The American Way" was jubilant. "This country may rightly take satisfaction at the way in which the general strike at San Francisco was met and conquered . . . the local authorities stood fast. . . . Best of all, perhaps, was the spirit displayed by the citizens near whom the danger pressed. They were not thrown into a panic. . . . Doubtless there must be some 'mopping up' in other cities before troubles are over. But what has already been accomplished is sufficient demonstration that Americans will not harbor anarchists, nor tolerate revolutionists, and are still able, as Abraham Lincoln said, to 'keep house.' "

The mopping up, which the *Times* foresaw, took another direction. Thanks to the daily dose of anti-Red poison administered the public by the press, groups of business men, thugs, morons and super-patriots did exactly what the Reds had been accused of doing: they took the law into their own hands and indulged in violence. They broke into private homes and offices, confiscated and destroyed property, wrecked, stole and burned. This rioting by the Vigilantes was too much even for the *Times* which reported that "constitutional rights were disregarded outright" by the mob, "or lightly brushed aside by the constituted authorities." It is a fact that the San Francisco police followed the thugs, entered the wrecked buildings, destroyed what was left undestroyed, and arrested the victims, not the aggressors. Four hundred men and women, described as "Reds," were thrown into prison but not one thug was touched. An attorney for the Communists, George Anderson, whose life had been threatened by the Vigilantes, demanded jury trials. For this invocation of constitutional rights Municipal Judge George Steiger threatened him with contempt action.

This exhibition of lawlessness was hailed with delight by several newspapers. They were the inspirers and did not disown their handiwork. Some of them commented bitterly, moreover, on the apologies of Municipal Judge Sylvian Lazarus, made to the four hundred victims when he released most of them the next morning. "I am disgusted to think that this good old town should have acted like a pack of wolves," he said. "I don't know who is responsible, but it should be traced back to its source." The source confronted the judge from every news stand.

The part the press played in San Francisco is, of course, a mystery to that general public which it either deceived or turned into a wolf-pack. In labor circles there had from the start been rumors that the Chamber of Commerce, the Industrialists' Association, and the big-business organizations, notably those which advertised in the daily papers, had threatened the press if it supported the workingmen. The facts in the case have now been told. Although written in a tone of gratification, it is more in the nature of an exposure of a conspiracy.

On the eve of the strike, Earl Burke writes in the *Editor & Publisher,* Clarence R. Linder, general manager, *San Francisco Examiner;* George T. Cameron, publisher, *San Francisco Chronicle;* Robert O. Holliday, publisher, *San Francisco Call-Bulletin;* Joseph R. Knowland, publisher, *Oakland*

Tribune; Richard A. Carrington, Jr., publisher, *Oakland Post-Enquirer,* and John Francis Neyland, general counsel of the Hearst newspapers, who had just returned from a Hawaiian vacation, met and formed a publishers' council for the purpose of united action. "Their first big effort was to prevent martial law being declared," continues Mr. Burke. "That would have meant that thousands of men on sympathetic strike could not have returned to work, while the community would have been progressively paralyzed as more and more businesses would have to close, thus aiding the announced objective of the strike." The committee decided to support Mayor Rossi who naturally "welcomed" their plans. "On Sunday, July 15, the *Examiner* and the *Chronicle* published front-page editorials stating that radicals had seized control by intimidation and that the general strike was a revolution against constituted authority. William Randolph Hearst telephoned from London to Clarence Lindner, saying a story was being cabled telling how the general strike in England in 1926 had been crushed when the government took control of the situation. This was published on Monday in the *Examiner, Chronicle, Call-Bulletin, Post-Enquirer* and all Hearst papers. The *Oakland Tribune* ran a similar story based on other sources. The *News* sounded warnings to unions not to paralyze the vital processes on which the lives of all depended."

The Red scare proved as effective in San Francisco in 1934 as it had in the 1920's in other parts of the country. ". . . The general public, which had generally been sympathetic towards the alleged wrongs of the longshoremen, awakened to the menace which caused public hardships and threatened citizens' rights and that the general strike was a 'revolution,' " Mr. Burke writes approvingly. To "crush the revolt" the committee, headed by Hearst's Neyland, decided to divide labor into two groups, good and bad, conservative and radical. "Conservative leaders welcomed this help. . . . Newspaper editorials built up the strength and influence of the conservative leaders and aided in splitting the conservative membership away from the radicals."

Possessing the best journalistic brains in San Francisco, the committee then hatched another idea: having failed to get the nation excited about the impending Red revolution with resultant action from Washington, the newspapers screamed about a conspiracy to hide the truth from President Roosevelt. (Always on the side of truth, is the motto of several of these papers.)   General Hugh Johnson arrived.   He had in the past proved rather difficult for the newspaper proprietors. Says Mr. Burke:

"It was evident to the publishers that he might undo all the publishers' council was trying to accomplish.   He proposed to grant the request of the general strike committee that the longshoremen's demands for complete control of hiring halls [be accepted] as a condition before any discussion of arbitration should occur.   But he was informed this would be a compromise with a revolution. Mr. Neylan and the publishers' council sat up with General Johnson until three o'clock Tuesday morning giving him a picture of the crisis. . . .

"The General quieted down when specifically informed that his tactics had been such that the people of California might have to decide to get along without him.   In fact, had decided to get along without him and inasmuch as he had no credentials authorizing him to act for the President in this matter they might even have to ask him to leave San Francisco. . . . He [later] remarked this was the first time he had 'ever been up against a newspaper oligarchy.' "

This is the inside story of the San Francisco press as a strikebreaking agency.   Whether or not the newspapers were the most powerful element in this success is not so important as the means they used.   "They did their best," comments the *New Republic* on the foregoing exposure, "and lied ruthlessly and repeatedly in the endeavor to fan the flames of hostile public opinion. . . . Since the end of the strike they have helped on the campaign of terrorism in every possible way, both by suppressing the facts about what has happened and by continued false statements about the extent of radicalism and pretended 'revolutionary purposes' of the strike leaders."

Rarely has the press of any city been so bitterly accused. Yet the facts justify it. Bitter and tragically pessimistic is the judgment passed by Heywood Broun when he addressed a meeting called by the American Civil Liberties Union to protest the San Francisco terrorism.

"I am not being fantastic but literally truthful [said Broun] when I tell you that a newspaper editor in San Francisco informed me that he considered the news dispatches in the *New York Times* concerning the general strike distinctly 'red' in their leanings. If the threat of Fascism seems to you remote in California, consider the role played by the newspapers in the general strike.

"I have heard many publishers talk about the freedom of the press. They mean the freedom to use child labor. They mean the freedom of a newspaper owner to print what he pleases and throw away the rest. They have said that a free press was the greatest protection of America against Fascism, but we have not got a free press."

Ever since the strike the reporters of California have realized how the press, with one or two exceptions, betrayed its readers, violated its code of ethics and played the game of the advertisers and big business. Chapters of the Guild, which now represents the best part of the newspaper fraternity, have condemned the publishers of California. The Oakland and East Bay Building Trades Council and Central Labor Council of Alameda County have passed the following resolution on the San Francisco press:

"Whereas, the *Examiner, Post-Enquirer, Tribune, Call-Bulletin* and *Chronicle,* daily papers published in the Bay district, have been exceptionally unfair to organized labor in the handling of strike news items; and . . .

"Whereas, organized labor has repeatedly put out truthful and conscientious statements for publication which have been ignored or distorted to our great discredit,

"Therefore, be it resolved, that each and every member of every affiliated local of unions in the building trades council and the Central Labor Council of Alameda

County, be hereby urgently and sincerely requested to immediately cancel their subscriptions to the above-named papers; and

"In view of the friendly and truthful attitude of the *San Francisco Daily News* (Scripps-Howard), to immediately subscribe to or buy only the *San Francisco Daily News* in place of the above-named papers . . . and

"Be it further resolved, that we also withdraw our united patronage from any and all advertisers of the before mentioned unfriendly papers."

Peter Gulbrandsen, journalist, writes in the *San Francisco News* that "the so-called vigilante raids are a disgrace to the community. The newspaper editors who have allowed the whipping up of insane anti-red hysteria have shown a decidedly un-American behavior. . . . It has been a sad spectacle during this crisis to have the large San Francisco dailies, with one solitary exception, indulge in the encouragement of these abominable raids. . . . I am not a Communist myself, but I want to register an emphatic protest against the disgusting vigilante tactics and the tacit approval of such Hitlerian violence by certain San Francisco dailies and the dailies of the East Bay cities as well. . . ."

The employment of a strikebreaking organization by the newspaper publishers of America is probably no secret to some reporters, but the discovery, in the minutes of the annual A. N. P. A. convention, was a shock to me. All reporters look upon scabs, blacklegs or strikebreakers as a low form of animal life and as a rule newspapers have nothing but harsh words for this type of labor. The public, too, hates it.

In the 1929 special standing committee report of the A. N. P. A. there is mention of a strike of two hundred union printers in Albany which gives credit to the mailers, photo-engravers, stereotypers and pressmen "who refused to participate in the bludgeon methods adopted by the Typographical Union, despite the pressure brought to bear upon them." A choice bit of news for Messrs. Green and Woll of the American Federation of Labor. One union struck; the others scabbed. An old but interesting story. The report goes on to say the typos "thought the strike would terrify the publishers into servile obedience to the Typographical Union mandates." Altogether an interesting document. If it shows anything it shows hatred between employers and employees.

Next comes the report of the open shop committee signed by Charles A. Webb, chairman, Harry Chandler, H. H. Conland, E. H. Harris, J. S. Parks, Robert L. Smith, J. L. Sturtevant and L. K. Nicholson. It tells of the employment of a strike-breaking crew in many parts of the United States and Canada. For example: "Two newspapers in New Jersey changed from union to non-union and crews were supplied by the Open Shop Department." H. W. Flagg, manager of this business, sums up his activities as follows: "First, the strength of the Open Shop Department of the A. N. P. A. was demonstrated . . . second, newspapers, from the smallest to the largest, can handle a situation of this kind without undue interruption of business; third, any publisher can maintain an open shop if he so desires; and fourth, enough first-class men can be secured at any time to man an office. . . . This Department is better equipped today to handle any situation that may arise in the departments of a newspaper than ever before and no member need have any fear in negotiating with the union, that if he fails to make a satisfactory agreement he cannot be expeditiously taken care of by the Open Shop Department."

In 1933 Mr. Flagg reports more victories to his masters. More non-union shops were opened in that year than in the past twenty, because this meant paying lower wages "as a result of which many strikes took place." The most important were on newspapers in Orange, New Jersey; Hackensack, New Jersey; White Plains, New York; Middletown, New York; Waukegan, Illinois; and Pawtucket, Rhode Island. . . . Crews have been taken to Wichita, Kansas; Paterson, New Jersey; Springfield, Illinois; Holyoke, Massachusetts; Bayonne, New Jersey; Minneapolis, Minnesota; New Haven, Connecticut; Gloversville, New York; New Bedford, Massachusetts; and San Francisco. These crews ranged from ten to three hundred men, the latter for use in San Francisco.

Truly a remarkable showing. Strikes everywhere, newspaper workers against newspaper owners, the owners breaking them with scab labor while editorially the majority of newspapers proclaim their friendliness to labor, to the rights of collective bargaining, to the American Federation of Labor, today the greatest organized enemy of the Red menace of Bolshevism. And that fine old phrase, "the interests of capital and labor are identical," is still in newspaper service.

Some time before the New Deal, Chairman Hewson, of Typographical Union No. 6, remarked on an arbitration board decision to reduce wages ten per cent. without decreasing hours, that "the decision absolves the publishers from all social responsibility." Further evidence of the "friendship" between newspaper workers and publishers was given by President Davis of the A. N. P. A. who, when President Roosevelt ordered a newspaper code, submitted the following anti-union paragraph:

"The right of employer and employe to bargain together free from interference by any third party shall not be affected by this code, and nothing herein shall require any employe to join any organization or to refrain from joining any organization in order to secure or retain employment."

This was in the summer of 1933; in the autumn Charles P. Howard, president of the International Typographical Union of North America, declared that the American Newspaper Publishers' Association was

"resisting every effort of the government and labor union to shorten working hours and increase wage scales. All this fuss and bother about the freedom of the press has been initiated by the publishers to becloud the real issue. They are trying to avoid any code which will force them to reduce hours and elevate wages in the printing trade. . . .

"The A. N. P. A., if its policy is to be believed, still hews to the conviction that its prosperity is founded on long hours and small pay for its workers. The code they want does not contain one single provision for shorter hours or more money for the printer. In fact, the one they submitted was so absurd that the government turned it down summarily."

Arthur Markel, deputy president of the Commercial Telegraphers' Union, makes the statement that the Associated Press has refused all negotiations with his union and has threatened with dismissal any employee suspected of union sympathies.

Indisputable fact: the United Press and Hearst men were unionized; the A. P. men were not.

From the minutes of the A. F. of L. reports I take a later statement: "The Associated Press shows no sign of receding from its granite faced opposition to the rights of its workers to organize."

In "backward, degenerate, uncivilized and dying Europe" newspapers are sold by grown-up men and women; in God's country several hundred thousand children are employed by the newspapers to sell and deliver the morning and evening editions. Inasmuch as the publishers prefer to employ children at a small wage rather than grown-up men and women at a living wage, the Child Labor Amendment to the Constitution has met with tremendous opposition. The press is against it and the press is the greatest power in America.

President Roosevelt is against child labor. As we have already seen, his early declarations on this subject were either suppressed or buried among the advertisements. Most NRA codes abolished child labor, but the NRA did not last. For the time being children were taken from the mills in the South, the factories in the North and the canneries. But if the publishers succeed in their big propaganda and lobby war for "freedom of the press" in exploiting children, they will be back in the mills and factories eventually.

The fight of the publishers against progressive civilized social labor legislation is no new thing. Publishing is a business and social legislation entails using some profits of business for social welfare. It is an attack on the old rugged profit system—which made our civilization the finest in the world—up to 1929.

The Child Labor Amendment, the Publishers' Association bulletin warned its membership in 1932, "would seriously affect the newspapers' present system of using newspaper boys as a part of their distribution and sales methods." Immediately the papers mobilized. "The full force of organized newspaper publishing" was exerted. Likewise the A. N. P. A. was not caught asleep when the Wagner Labor Bill was introduced in 1934. Publisher W. F. Wiley of the *Cincinnati Enquirer,* chairman of the committee on federal laws, demanded immediate action to prevent "enactment of such repressive and destructive legislation." The association voted a resolution against the bill.

For downright hypocrisy the action of the International Circulation Managers' Association against the child labor amendment takes the prize. The passage of the law, says a resolution this branch of the publishing business adopted, would "breed indolence and dependence, deny . . . equal educational opportunities . . . and add to the cost of government." Furthermore the myth about America's greatest men having been newsboys is incorporated seriously in the next paragraph which calls paper peddling "a boon in the past" which has "helped many of our leaders in the state and nation, in achieving success."

The I. C. M. A. furthermore claims it presents the "truth" concerning newsboys. But the documented truth is told by Warden Lewis E. Lawes of Sing Sing prison: "Recently I had a census taken here in Sing Sing to determine the number of inmates who had sold newspapers in their youth. . . . Of the 2,300 men, over 69 per cent had done so. These figures support my contention, based on nearly thirty years of experience, that juvenile delinquency and so-called criminal tendencies are largely the result of detrimental influences and associations that can often be corrected. The use of youngsters below the age of fourteen in selling newspapers, particularly in cities, is not at all calculated to correct such conditions."

The conclusions from the foregoing facts are obvious. The press insists on its freedom but denies labor—whether radical or conservative A. F. of L.—its freedom; where it announces friendship to organized labor such declaration does not interfere with the employment of strikebreakers; it supports the continuance of child labor for purely financial reasons, frequently raising moral banners to cover up, just as it raises Red scares against strikers.

Of course it would be unfair to let the word "press" in this or in any other chapters mean the entire industry. There are always exceptions. Although the Publishers' Association demands a united front, there is as high as fifty per cent insurgency in many cities, notably in New York, on the child labor question. In Pennsylvania, after an investigation of sweatshop child labor by Mrs. Pinchot, the *Philadelphia Record* and the *Pittsburgh Press* (Edward T. Leech, editor), each the leading paper in its city, took up the crusade and won minor victories immediately. On the other hand the *New York Herald Tribune,* predicting the collapse of the New Deal, said editorially that time will show that "no other item was more fatally destructive than Section 7-A and the support given under it by the administration to the unionization of industry. . . ."

Labor had taken 7-A as a Magna Charta of liberty—the equivalent of No. 1 of the Bill of Rights, under which the publishers fight valiantly whenever increased wages, shorter hours of labor, unionization and new taxations threaten "freedom of the press."

CHAPTER XVII

THE NEW BATTLE FOR PRESS FREEDOM

THE tree of freedom of the press more than any other in the garden of liberty, needs to be refreshed frequently with the blood of martyrs which Jefferson believed its natural nourishment. Men have risked their lives and fortunes, shed their blood and died for the free press. Colonial history records many instances of sanguinary violence. Zenger remains the symbol of the everlasting struggle. More recently Don Mellett lost his life defending the public.

With the arrival of Franklin Delano Roosevelt, however, the United States of America was shaken with the thunders of a new war. All the Big Berthas of journalism went into action. Commander-in-chief of the government forces was General Hugh Johnson of the picturesque word. And who of the other side was to leap first into the trenches, first into No Man's Land, first into the enemy line, ready to water the tree of liberty with his heart blood, but Colonel McCormick, of the *Chicago Tribune,* Ogden Reid, of the *New York Herald Tribune,* William Randolph Hearst, veteran of the Spanish-American War, and Elisha Hanson, attorney for the publishers and veteran of dozens of battles for the power and paper companies?

While the war raged, however, something took place which in a relative way resembled the Kerensky revolution in Russia. The newspaper men of America—not the editors of America and certainly not the publishers of America or the newspaper owners of America—suddenly caused a revolution. The significance to America of this extraordinary turn of events I must leave to the following chapter.

The battle to end all battles for a free press began early in 1933. If the reader can think back that far he will remember that the nation had collapsed and that President Roosevelt had saved it. At least the great majority of people thought and felt that way about it then. The President had closed the banks and opened them again. That period had been called a "holiday." The depression, which the press had hinted at sometime in 1930 or 1931, was now an acknowledged crisis in the affairs of the world. Sir Montague Norman declared it was the greatest crisis and that it showed the capitalist system was dead, but this statement was made by a foreigner and may have had an ulterior motive. We in America did know one thing—that the situation approximated a state of war—and we felt that a great leader had arisen whose New Deal, Blue Eagle and NRA would win the field.

In 1933 there was a unanimity of opinion for a while that was phenomenal. For a little while the nation went over as one man to the side of its leader. It was the days of 1917 all over again, Roosevelt was as sacred as Wilson, and to criticize the NRA was tantamount to treason.

The accomplishments of the Roosevelt administration early in 1933 resembled a miracle. The Blue Eagle appeared everywhere and men's hearts beat with a fine free rhythm. F. D.'s in the White House, all's well with the world. The stock market jumped forward; business picked up; the codes for industries were formulated and put into action; a wave of optimism engulfed the nation and the press unanimously headlined its applause.

Then came a black day for the Blue Eagle. Almost everyone had been mobilized behind its victorious banner but the newspaper publishers. And at the end of the glorious summer they arrived in Washington with a newspaper code they themselves had written. Their committee consisted of Howard Davis, chairman, Amon Carter, of Fort Worth, and John Stewart Bryan, of Richmond, and their attorney was that same Mr. Hanson whose firm, reported Paul Anderson, "distinguished itself a few years ago by lobbying against the late Senator Tom Walsh's resolution for a Senate investigation of the power trust, and was conspicuously successful during the Mellon regime in obtaining tax refunds for wealthy clients. A noble representation of the vaunted guardians of our liberty."

Their code, again in the words of Mr. Anderson, was "the

most dishonest, weasel-worded, and treacherous document," yet presented to Johnson. "It was loaded with all sorts of exemptions and jokers, all carefully designed to enable the newspapers to escape the obligations which their editorial pages were clamorously urging all other employers to assume. Compared with it the codes proposed by the steel and coal barons were charters of liberty and enlightenment."

General Johnson was disgusted. He ordered his legal department to draft another. Meanwhile a large part of the press announced their codes as accepted and gave little publicity to Johnson's denial. This was the first but not the last ambush against the General. The publishers' next unpublished move was to ask Jim Farley to give Johnson "the works," but Farley merely told Johnson, over the telephone, what he had been asked to do.

When the committee returned to Washington it found a new code had been prepared. And this was the signal for the firing of the big guns marked "freedom of the press." The code, said the publishers, violated the Constitution, notably the Bill of Rights. (The First Amendment provides that "Congress shall make no law . . . abridging the freedom of speech or of the press. . . .") Johnson and Richberg added a provision that nothing in the code should be construed as modifying, qualifying, amending or repealing the Bill of Rights, and this was accepted.

The *Washington Post,* recently purchased by Eugene Meyer, led the attack in the capital. A New York tabloid published an untrue story saying Johnson and some ladies had crashed a speakeasy. But not all the newspapers joined in this sniping. The *Milwaukee Journal,* angrily attacking the American Newspaper Publishers' Association, disclosed the following message which that body had sent its membership:

"Following careful consideration of all aspects of the present situation, the A. N. P. A. recommends that newspaper publishers do not at the present time prepare or subscribe to a code under the National Industrial Recovery Act, and further recommends that because the publishing of newspapers is not an industry but an enterprise of such peculiar importance as to be especially provided for in the Constitution of the United States and of the several states, whose independence must be jealously guarded from any interference which can lead to or approximate censorship, the situation be given further consideration before determining upon the course to be ultimately taken for the benefit of the country at large."

According to the *Journal* this was a plea for special privilege, self-centered and self-seeking, an attempt to stand aside and apart from a movement for general recovery. It notes that whereas the first duty of a paper is to print the news, its other character is the employment of men and women, the buying of materials, the sale of its services and its products. But "we cannot see that in this character it is exempt in any degree from the duty of being a good citizen. . . ."

However, in making his annual report to President Butler of Columbia, Dean Ackerman stated his belief that the press had prevented a dictatorship under the NRA; inasmuch as the Roosevelt administration controlled radio, was powerful in motion pictures, etc., "the only possibility of the United States escaping a dictatorship was inherent in the fight of . . . journalism for public recognition of freedom of the press. . . ." But apparently the war was far from over. Press and public had won but the first skirmish. Celebrating the two hundredth anniversary of the establishment of a free press on this continent, James M. Beck, authority on the Constitution and lawyer for corporations, Myron C. Taylor, chairman of the board of the United States Steel Corporation and Colonel McCormick, chairman of the committee of freedom of the press of the A. N. P. A., warned the nation that the situation was still threatening.

Alone, Mr. Stern, publisher of the *Philadelphia Record,* disagreed with speakers at the memorial meeting honoring John Peter Zenger. "The same kind of Tories who sent him to jail," he wrote, "now gather to do him honor. All the NRA provides is that publishers must pay minimum wages and observe maximum hours in operating their business. That power is in no wise different from that of the fire marshal or the building inspector. And the wage and hour provisions of the NRA have no more to do with what a newspaper prints than the fire and building regulations of the city of Philadelphia. Lip service from autocratic steel barons and Red-baiting publishers is no honor to Zenger. The same kind of Tories sent him to jail."

While in Washington President Roosevelt, asked by John Boettiger, of the *Chicago Tribune,* about freedom of the press, replied, "You tell Bertie (Colonel McCormick) he is seeing things under the bed."

Then the violence of San Simeon broke loose. Full-page advertisements in Hearst's own and other newspapers, costing thousands of dollars, were headlined:

"W. R. HEARST DISCUSSES FREEDOM OF THE PRESS AND INDIVIDUAL LIBERTY

"William Randolph Hearst, who was one of the first to enroll his papers and magazines in the NRA and operated them strictly according to its provisions, nevertheless has come to the conclusion that the NRA, in the militant manner by which it is conducted, is a menace to liberty and a hindrance to recovery."

According to Mr. Hearst, the meddlesome NRA was interfering with business

"and will interfere in our business to our serious detriment; . . . we cannot sacrifice our own interests and our own independence without sacrificing the interests of the public, whose welfare it is the duty of the public press to consider first in all ways and at all times. . . . In view of the fact that the NRA is a menace to political rights and constitutional liberties, a danger to American ideals and institutions, a handicap to industrial recovery, and a detriment to the public welfare, . . . the publishers of a free press ought to tolerate it less and expose it more. . . . The examples of the *Kansas City Star* and the *Chicago Daily News* is an inspiration. Surely, this is the time when a free press should not only preserve its freedom but justify by conscientious service and courageous action the independence which the founders of the Republic bestowed upon it."

The honeymoon was over. The truce was broken. The era of good feeling came to an end. The war was on again.

The most vicious counter-attack came from General Johnson. In two speeches, Chicago, November 6, and Minneapolis, November 7, 1933, he let flow the famous language. Months before he had predicted that "dead cats" would fly; now he said:

> "We do not mind really honest and substantial dead cats, and I have some justly coming to me. My only complaint is that most of these dead cats are synthetic. The biggest imitation dead cat is the one about the freedom of the press. . . .
>
> "We are entering a new era—an era of profit for industries and decent conditions for labor. We are entering an era ushered in by the leading men in industry and labor who are on our staff. That is the New Day and Deal and the whole trouble with our few opponents is that they are seeing things under the bed. Certain sections of the press are inciting these jitters by headlines. My only request is that the gentlemen of the Fourth Estate [the General referred to them as the Third Estate] give us a chance and not lend themselves to this primitive witch-doctor-dancing. . . .
>
> "We were ready for the dead cats. But let's have some real ones. Let the few powerful men who have opposed this law step out and give their real reasons. Not freedom of the press, but their real, honest-to-goodness reasons. They want the benefits of this act, but not its burdens. They want to take everything and give nothing. . . .
>
> "Why do they not say now what fair criticisms they have, instead of crying out about freedom of the press and dictatorships? What is the real reason for these complaints? Is it that we have raised wages and reduced hours of work in order to relieve the despair of 4,000,000 bread-winners, and that this is contrary to the

best interests of the nation? What better have they to
offer? What have they done and what are they willing
now to do to help? . . ."

In Minneapolis his subject was *Beneficiaries of the Old
Deal.*

"They are few in number, but ruthless in method. Some
of them control powerful newspapers and they are using
these papers to misrepresent every development of NRA.

"It is no longer possible to get a square deal in truth
and accuracy for the President's program from the management and policy of those papers."

Among the issues in this journalistic war which were not
brought to the front-page trenches were:

A union or guild embracing newspaper workers.
Child labor of newsboys.
Reduction of hours of employment.
Increased wages in the newspaper trade.

The Scripps-Howard papers, in a statement signed Robert
P. Scripps, said the issue is a double one.

"In the economic philosophy which the code symbolizes,
we believe sincerely. . . . As publishers we are willing to
pay our full part toward NRA success, whatever the price
may be, as the newspaper code relates to the manufacturing and the industrial phases of newspaper making. As
to the second element—freedom of the press—. . . we say
with equal emphasis . . . we will support to the limit the
retention of a clause which will prevent any debate about
the right of the newspapers of this nation to publish facts
and express opinions. . . ."

In the view of the American Civil Liberties Union, as sent
to President Roosevelt, freedom of the press does not depend
upon legislative enactments, "but upon the ability of the press
to fight for its own rights. Where freedom of the press has

been attacked in recent years, as in the case of certain radical publications or little papers without influence, it has been largely due to the failure of the powerful and influential papers to come to their aid." The *Nation* also fired a broadside which was heard by at least the reporters in all the newspaper offices that December. "The newspaper publishers, now suddenly awake to the freedom of the press though nine-tenths of them have connived at innumerable interferences with personal liberty, freedom of speech, and public assembly ever since 1917, ought to adopt a code of fair practice without a day's delay."

In hundreds of newspaper offices according to Hart Girland, the betting was ten to one in January, 1934, that the Big Steamroller, as represented by the American Newspaper Publishers' Association, would crush General Johnson, the President himself, and everybody connected with the NRA. Edwin Baird, editor of *Real America,* made the statement that "all their bombastic thundering about 'freedom of the press' was, and still is, nothing more than a black smoke screen to hide their real motive, which is to avoid paying a decent wage to their editorial staffs."

On February nineteenth President Roosevelt approved the compromise code. Article VII stated that the publishers do not thereby "waive any constitutional rights or consent to the imposition of any requirements that might restrict or interfere with the constitutional guarantees of the freedom of the press." President Roosevelt in his executive order calls Article VII "pure surplusage." "While it has no meaning it is permitted to stand merely because it has been requested. . . ."

But the concluding words of the President's letter were a bombshell or earthquake or what you will. "The recitation of the freedom of the press clause in the code," he said, "has no more place here than would the recitation of the whole Constitution or of the Ten Commandments. The freedom guaranteed by the Constitution is freedom of expression and that will be scrupulously respected—but it is not freedom to work children, or to do business in a fire trap, or violate the laws against obscenity, libel and lewdness."

Which the publishers thought more than "pure" surplusage.

The *New York Herald Tribune* called for an apology.

G. B. Parker, editor-in-chief of the Scripps-Howard papers, said since the Constitution guarantees freedom and the newspapers enjoy it, "so, as the saying goes—What the hell?"

The *New York American* thought the attack "rather unwarranted and somewhat vindictive" and reminded the President that "the Hearst papers and the greater part of the papers of the United States had been crusading for the abolition of child labor long before Mr. Roosevelt was of age."

The *Chicago Tribune* thought the charges against publishers "unjust." Its attack on the NRA continued and Paul Anderson reported in the *Nation,* February 7, 1934, that he was pleased "that literally thousands of letters are pouring into Washington from persons stating they have canceled their subscriptions to the *Chicago Tribune* because of its scurrilous attacks on the NRA. This was the sheet which introduced the delectable practice of employing known criminals and racketeers. By every standard of professional decency and public morals, Colonel McCormick has earned the right to retire from the publishing business. I hope the people of Chicago will help him to exercise it."

Curiously enough the *New York Daily News,* edited by Captain Patterson, one of the heirs of Joseph Medill, founder of the *Tribune,* supported the NRA.

Heywood Broun chided the *Herald Tribune* for its phrase "government by insult." "I watched the conduct of the newspaper publishers from the very beginning of the NRA hearings," he wrote, "and their record was of a sort which would make 'government by insult' a feat unparalleled in the entire history of lily-painting."

The *Los Angeles Times* was particularly angry over the child labor business, warning Roosevelt not to abolish "what long experience has demonstrated to be, without exception, the greatest training school for city-bred boys in existence." (Cf. Warden Lawes' statement on Sing Sing.)

On the other hand, Mr. Stern in his *New York Post* said, "O. K. MR. PRESIDENT" in large type; the *Milwaukee Journal* spoke of the "camouflage" of the freedom of the press banner, and Mr. Anderson gave honors for decent handling of the question to Messrs. Paul Patterson, Roy Howard, David Stern and Captain Patterson "and many others," whom he did not name; but he insisted that "there is no industry in the country which has exploited its employees more harshly, or resorted to more ruthless and unscrupulous methods to get what it wanted" than the newspaper industry. He even alleged that some newspapers use their "pull" to break the fire and building laws. Could he have been referring to my old *Pittsburgh Leader?*

Came April. Came the annual convention of the American Newspaper Publishers' Association. Came four-column reports of speeches about "loss of freedom, loss of manhood, financial oppression and NRA poisoning." No one could complain, opined Guy Fawkes, that the news was withheld from us.

To the sniping from housetops and machine-gunning all along the line, was added the sound of new batteries. In addition to discussing the basic principle of American Liberty and Democracy there appeared matters like wage scales, the newsboy delivery problem, child labor, and last, but a million miles from least, the new Guild of editorial employees. Said the chairman of the committee on that last subject:

"The freedom of the press would be abridged by any law passed by congress, whether by the exercise of a code or otherwise, which would do any of the following things:

"First, unreasonably raise the cost of production. Plainly that would abridge the freedom of the press. Secondly, unreasonably decrease the return from publishing. That would be just as much an abridgment as excessive taxation."

(Among the members of the freedom of the press committee is Harry Chandler, of the *Los Angeles Times.*)

The next address was delivered by President Davis, chairman of the code committee, who said that the three new problems were the maintenance of newspaper-boy delivery and sales; the demand of certain representatives of organized labor that the code should include a scale applicable to all the daily newspapers of the United States; and the request of the newly organized Newswriters' Guild for recognition in the code.

> "It was the committee's position from the outset that the newspaper-boy delivery system should be maintained. . . . With respect to the demand of certain labor leaders for wage scales, your committee from the outset took the position it was impossible to accede to such a demand, insisting that the difference in the cost of living conditions, respective earnings and established trade customs made it impossible to do more than follow the maximum hours and minimum wages contained in the code. . . ."

Among other speakers who supported the views expressed was James Francis Neylan, head of the Hearst newspapers on the Pacific Coast.

Who, asked Guy Fawkes, is to decide what is reasonable and unreasonable in raising costs of production or decreasing profits?

> "If we know our newspaper owners, the forced installation of a new toilet in the city-room could easily be hailed as 'unreasonable.' Obviously, any attempt to raise reporters' salaries, reduce their working hours, eliminate child labor, improve working conditions, install new typewriters, limit patent-medicine advertising, prohibit too-personal 'personals,' or in any way 'decrease the return from publishing' is going to be hailed henceforth as an abridgment of the Freedom of the Press."

Prophetic words. *Vide* the next chapter.

Following the publishers, the American Society of Newspaper Editors drew up a report congratulating themselves, the publishers and attorney Hanson "for having rescued the press from the malign clutches of Franklin Roosevelt and Hugh Johnson." For this noble work Anderson offered them "the annual award for hypocrisy, smugness, intellectual dishonesty, and general misrepresentation"; he called theirs the most "sanctimonious, self-righteous, or self-laudatory document" ever struck off the mimeograph machine. The Society, he continued, "has never been more than a poor joke. For seven years, led by the wizard of the ouija board (Casper Yost, of the *Globe-Democrat,* who sponsored a book of verse he avowed had been received over the ouija board by the wife of a commercial printer), it blocked an amendment to its constitution enabling it to punish members for blackmail or other crimes. . . . I do not minimize either the gravity or the imminence of the danger which confronts freedom of the press. . . . But it does not arise from any hocus-pocus on the part of Roosevelt and Johnson. It arises from the fact that so many of the men who have been entrusted with—or have acquired— the privilege of exercising that freedom have used it to grasp special privileges and profits for themselves. . . ."

Addressing the *Yale News* staff, of which his son Whitelaw is a member, Ogden Reid, of the *Herald Tribune,* said freedom of the press has been challenged in the licensing provision of the NRA; censorship is not the only danger; among others are "demands to make expenditures which are not economically desirable or possible." President Roosevelt told the University of Missouri School of Journalism that such talk was "silly." General Johnson in a radio talk offered a new sensation. "I have seen," he said, "instructions to reporters [in Washington] to send in no news favorable to NRA. Recently in several instances disturbing news stories have been published by them which have not one ounce of factual foundation—pure fabrications. We can't even get the truth."

Throughout the United States the Argonne Offensive of the press against the cohorts of General Johnson began. In August, 1934, when the code administrator arrived in Chicago he found Colonel Knox's *Daily News,* Colonel McCormick's *Tribune* and Citizen Hearst's *American* and *Herald and Examiner* closing in, center, right and left flanks. The General, in the Century of Progress Lagoon Theater, made his last desperate stand. Among his remarkable utterances were:

"I protest that it is not freedom of the press to suppress or garble important news which happens not to be in accord with some editorial policy or opinion. . . .

"That is domination of the press and when it is practiced by a great chain of newspapers under one-man control it becomes a public menace. . . . I wish the newspapers would submit a code containing provisions which would leave elimination of such practices to their own self-governing bodies. They are the only industry that has declined to do so. . . .

"In my opinion . . . the NRA retains the bulk of the public support. Why, in such a situation, we do not have an undivided press is beyond me. I have seen news garbled, suppressed and colored and I have seen able young men prostituting their talents in libelous and misleading stories pandered as news at the behest of opinionated bosses.

"The whole vast humanitarian surges for the elimination of the sweatshops and child labor are perverted in such a cartoon as appeared in yesterday's *Tribune,* which advertises a non-existent situation to become stark propaganda for the return of both sweatshops and child labor.

"It is a weariness of the heart and a grievous ailment of the stomach. If I did not know how little that editorial page has come to mean to the citizens of this district, I might feel desperate about it. As it is, it is a mistake to dignify that stewing pot by mentioning it.

"It is not the professors in government that we have to fear. . . . It is the scum of intellectual prostitutes—the academic mercenaries who write for a controlled and dominated press the thing that is not—in utter disregard of the welfare of the country."

This was the Balaclava charge of the doughty General, his Hundred Days rolled into one, his early morning of Waterloo. All that the publishers had to do now was "mop up," or consolidate the trenches taken, because the enemy was beaten. "Freedom of the Press" won the field. Among the victors were the gentlemen who approved the denial of civil liberties in California, who gave Mr. Sinclair the rawest deal a candidate for office has had since La Follette and the senior Charles Lindbergh made their campaigns; gentlemen who employ Fascist propaganda agents and raise the Red flag whenever liberal thought makes its appearance in the universities; employers of labor who proclaim themselves friends of labor and keep an organized force of strikebreakers handy; editors who approve the arrest of men for picketing or for reading the Constitution of the United States in a public place.

Celebrating the one hundred and forty-seventh anniversary of the signing of the Constitution in Philadelphia, the NRA was still being peppered by its victorious foes. Bainbridge Colby, Colonel McCormick, Commander Edward A. Hayes, of the American Legion, and James M. Beck spoke for the Constitution.

On October 23, 1934, "the long controversy between the authority administering the Daily Newspaper Publishers' Code and the Newspaper Guild" was set for a hearing. A rumor of "treason" befouled the victorious air.

Chapter XVIII

IF THIS BE TREASON!

THE arrival of the Newspaper Guild gives national importance to the problem of the free press and the free reporter. The reader may remember that the writer, on the very first day of his employment, twenty-five years ago, heard from his own editor the lowest word in the English language. Mr. Eagle said that newspaper men were prostitutes.

This reporter never quite agreed with his editor. But other editors have said even worse things regarding the most glamorous and romantic if not the oldest profession in the world. For example, John Swinton, when editor of the *New York Tribune,* speaking on *The Independent Press* to the New York Press Association, made the following alarming confession:

> "There is no such thing in America as an independent press, unless it is in the country towns. You know it and I know it.
>
> "There is not one of you who dares express an honest opinion. If you express an honest opinion you know beforehand it would never appear in print.
>
> "I am paid $150 per week for keeping my honest opinions out of the paper I am connected with. Others of you are paid similar salaries for doing similar things. If I should permit honest opinions to be printed in one issue of my paper, like Othello, before twenty-four hours, my occupation would be gone.
>
> "The business of the New York journalist is to destroy the truth, to lie outright, to pervert, to vilify, to fawn at the feet of Mammon, and to sell his race and his country for his daily bread.
>
> "We are the tools and the vassals of rich men behind the scenes.
>
> "We are intellectual prostitutes."

Years ago Frederick Lewis Allen gave his judgment on the journalistic problem in a magazine article entitled *Newspapers and the Truth.*

". . . Editors and reporters find out that what pays is to write the sort of news-stories which pleases the man at the top. In rare cases, of course, there may be actual corruption; but more often what puts bias into the news is merely the permeation of the staff by a sense of expediency. They put their jobs first and the truth second. . . .

"And the whole process of corrupting the news, where corruption to-day exists, is less often the deliberate work of men bent on falsehood than a process of drifting before the winds of circumstance, timidity, and self-interest."

Robert Allen and Drew Pearson, once the anonymous collaborators in *The Washington Merry Go-Round,* have this to say for the highest placed of all newspaper men, the Washington correspondents:

"As long as the preponderant majority of American newspapers are trivial, reactionary and subservient, the work of the Washington press corps will reflect these debasing influences. . . .

"The reporter working for a paper dominated by water power, financial, or political interests writes what these interests want to appear and not what he knows is the truth. . . .

". . . In the atmosphere of reaction, cowardice, bigotry, incompetence, and even worse, that pervades the capital to-day, a militant and fearless press could render invaluable service to the cause of a desperately needed political and economic reformation."

Finally I quote from Ralph Bayes, once city editor of the *Los Angeles Record:*

"The bitterness of our portion is this precisely: that we are hired poisoners. . . . In my ten years of experience on various sheets as reporter, editor and news agency representative, I have come to know the masses with whom I had to deal. . . . It was my tragedy, as it is the tragedy of the majority of my fellows, that this knowledge . . . must be used not for the uplift, but for the further enslavement, the drugging of the minds of men. . . . The press, at least, isn't any more rotten or venal than the rest of the system. In the editorial rooms of the country there are good fellows and true, sheer tired of the daily assassination in which they participate. . . ."

I quote all these opinions and I add my statement that in all the barrooms where newspaper men have grown maudlin, and in all the press clubs where there has been serious talk, for a quarter of a century I have heard similar expressions. The older men were usually cynical. Those whose cynicism was redirected by an urge for material success usually went into press agentry or purely commercial businesses, but the younger men sometimes worried about fantastic things such as Truth, and Integrity, and Honesty, and Freedom of the Press; and not once but a million times the words "journalistic prostitute" have been heard in the profession.

And now, a change has come in journalistic America.

In August, 1933—it seems like a millennial time—with codes to the right of them, codes to the left of them, volleying and thundering, one of the most exploited classes in the world and notable upholder of exploiters, the newspaper men of America, began to organize. The NRA permitted unionization but newspapermen preferred a "Guild." They were seeking better working conditions, pay commensurate with their labor—which never in modern history had been paid any of their number except those whose names were salable in syndicate features; they wanted shorter hours in addition to a minimum wage, the right of collective bargaining, a little economic security in their haphazard lives. In other words, they sought at long last some of the things labor had been winning, through strife, for several hundred years.

There had been many feeble attempts at unionization before, the idea being an old one and a plan similar to the present having been advocated by Upton Sinclair whom the Guild ought to honor in some way for his long single-handed fight for a free press. Credit for the creation of the present Guild goes to Heywood Broun, who under the heading "It Seems to Me" has for years given the readers of the *New York World-Telegram* and other papers his uncensored views on everything in this world including his own character and capabilities.

Apparently the journalistic "slaves" were ripe for the call of the leader. The word went out to the city rooms and young and old were excited by the prospect. The enthusiasts everywhere immediately planned branches of Broun's proposed Guild, the conservatives sought the views of the controlling powers. In most instances the editors and proprietors said nothing, remained neutral, because they had heard the same sort of noise before, had seen unions or clubs established, had a memory perhaps of one or two newspaper strikes called by writers which ended in worse than fiasco; in other instances the evident antagonism of the majority was voiced by the few. The *Philadelphia Bulletin,* the *Philadelphia Inquirer* and other papers warned their writers that it was best they refrain from guilds and from discussion of their rights under the newspaper code.

In September *Editor & Publisher,* which had told the publishers of America of "unrest among editorial workers without parallel in our memory," debated the guild question, saying it had its doubts about the unionization of editorial craftsmen. That month the hearings were held in Washington. Broun addressed to the code officials a challenge to the publishers.

"Quite inadvertently I am sure," he said, "some of the publishers have allowed the feeling to grow and spread that newspaper men and women who join organizations of their own creation will be subject to penalties. The penalty may not be dismissal. All newspaper men know of an institution known as the Chinese torture room. A reporter who incurs the displeasure of the boss by organizing activity may find himself writing obits for the rest of his life.

"You cannot have a free press which rests upon the

fears and apprehensions of reporters who are frightened and who feel that they have good reason to be frightened. I may add that if a writing guild cannot obtain those things which seem to us fair, then news-writing unions will."

On the question of wages, Frank Morrison, Secretary of the American Federation of Labor, proposed higher minimums than had been suggested, and the following significant amendment: "Those employed in the gathering, the writing, or the editing of news shall receive a minimum weekly salary of not less than the wages paid to the highest class of skilled mechanics employed in the production of the same news publication, and the same hours averaged over a period of six months as provided for skilled mechanics." It was an ironic commentary on American journalism. The reporter, the journalist, usually equipped with superior education and many talents, has to get his news, sometimes risking his life, and always using up considerable shoe leather, then write a story to the best of his ability—while the linotype operator merely touches the keys of a machine. The latter usually get double, or more, than the former, and here at last the union was proposing equal pay!

"American editorial workers [said *Editor & Publisher*] have always been willing to accept what was offered without thought of bargaining. This came to a tragic climax when depression struck, and editorial men, as in Cleveland, saw their pay drop 30 or 40 per cent, while organized printers were cut only 6 per cent between 1929 and 1933. For the whole country, according to Lloyd White, one of the promoters of the Cleveland Guild, union rates dropped 7.7 per cent during the depression, while unorganized factory workers' wages dropped 40.9 per cent.

"We have been shouting in *Editor & Publisher* for many years for a square deal for editorial workers. Particularly were we made indignant by the unequal drift during the boom period, when newspapers were vastly better able than now to pay fair wages, work men reasonable hours and protect them from the tyrannies of ruthless office despots, each intent on his own private score. The high professional or artist ideal, to put one's whole being into the job and let the rewards take care of themselves, was disgustingly exploited."

Within a few weeks the Guilds had enrolled twenty-five hundred men and women. New York had between five hundred and one thousand members, Newark reported one hundred and twenty-six, Cleveland two hundred and five. The Cleveland organization showed its militant character immediately. The New York Newspaper Guild resolved that "the freedom of the press is one of the essential foundations of human liberty," a phrase which the group of newspaper publishers who were fighting the NRA code were also employing while they waved the star-spangled banner and restated the Declaration of Independence, the Bill of Rights and the Constitution of the United States. But the reporters indulged in no such ballyhoo or buncombe. They also resolved, ". . . That we do not believe, however, that the newspaper industry, which asserts its freedom from governmental interference with the news, or free comment on the news, can rightfully evade its responsibility to assume, by organization under a code of fair practice, the same responsibilities for public welfare that other industries are being called upon to assume."

In Washington, on December fifteenth, representatives of thirty newspapers met and organized the American Newspaper Guild for the purpose of preserving the vocational interests of newspaper editorial workers, "and to improve the conditions under which they work by collective bargaining, and to raise the standards of journalism by such measures as may be deemed advisable by the national executive committee of the Guild."·

The national Guild elected Broun president and the following officers: Lloyd White, *Cleveland Press,* first vice-president; Andrew McLean Parker, *Philadelphia Record,* second vice-president; Edward D. Burks, *Tulsa World,* third vice-president; R. S. Gilfillan, *Daily News,* St. Paul, fourth vice-president; Adoniram Judson Evans, *Richmond Times-Dis-*

patch, fifth vice-president; Emmet Crozier, *Newark Star-Eagle,* treasurer; Jonathan Eddy, *New York Times,* secretary; Doris Fleeson, Washington correspondent *New York Daily News;* Ruth McKenney, *Akron Beacon-Journal,* and Thomas Brown, *Buffalo Evening News,* executive committee.

In April, 1934, the American Society of Newspaper Editors voted thirty-seven to ten to empower its directors to express the organization's attitude toward the Guild and to create a committee to act as liaison officer; it objected, however, to a motion of the resolutions committee which said in part:

> "We are in sympathy with the rapidly spreading movement to improve the economic security and ethical standards of the men and women in reportorial work. We do not believe that the guild movement should be a part of the trade unions. . . . If the mutuality of interests between publisher, editor and reporter is lost by an editorial swing to organized union labor, it will be impossible to maintain open, free-thinking channels of news."

The keynote of opposition was struck by Stanley Walker, city editor of the *New York Herald Tribune* (now of the tabloid Hearst *Mirror),* who declared the Guild "unprofessional in its philosophy, unsound in its leadership and a menace to the well-being of reporters. It has been one of the tragedies of this business, game, profession, craft, racket or whatever you want to call it, that no group of newspaper men, certainly not more than six or eight, can agree among themselves on any project."

Particularly disturbing, thought Mr. Walker, was "the plain threat of a strike" contained in a Guild suggestion that contracts with the publishers run the same term as typographical union contracts. He also brought the cheerful news that a large part of the Guild membership was on the point of deserting owing to "interminable arguments" over "fantastic demands."

Allen Raymond, reporter, representative of the New York Guild, said to the editors: "To whom it may concern: There is today and always will be one basic determination of the Guild against which no decent newspaper man can stand—the protection against all tyranny and oppression of the right of this craft to organize. . . ."

Editor after editor replied. Some viewed with alarm, others were indifferent, a few thought the boys were acting foolishly, a few were favorable; but the great fear in the hearts of the majority was that the Guild would "degenerate" into a labor union.

One of the few newspapers which frankly and editorially endorsed the Guild was the *New York Daily News* but it also showed the union idea worried it. Under the heading *Birth of a Newspaper Union* it said in part:

". . . The *News* signed the blanket code without a quibble, and is living up to it at an added cost of $200,000 a year.

"Some other papers proudly flying the Blue Eagle are chiseling. In one office, for instance, a reporter must ask for his extra day off if he wants it, and he soon suspects he is in disfavor if he does ask for it. . . .

"There is also the question of the freedom of the press. Would the press be as free if reporters and editorial writers belonged to a union? It is possible that at some future time, if the writers were thoroughly organized, they might object to writing news from an anti-union point of view. That is something which can only be speculated about.

"It is also a question in our minds whether the press is as free when it is subsidized by the Government as it is when it pays its own way 100 per cent. The American press is subsidized by the Government to the reported extent of $100,000,000 a year, in Post Office transportation and delivery below cost. So we sometimes wonder just how free the press in the United States is, anyway."

The first clash between publishers and writers occurred in San Francisco. A strong chapter of the Guild had been organized in the office of the *Examiner*, a Hearst paper. In New York the Hearst papers had jubilantly published editorials on the front page boasting how they had increased wages and lessened working hours, above and below NRA requirements; the Guild had replied by stating the fact that there had been three ten per cent wage cuts throughout the Hearst system which were still unrestored, that staffs had been reduced and that hours were still long.   William Randolph Hearst, Jr., became very angry, so angry in fact that thirty writers of the *New York American* not only resigned from the Guild but sent a letter to President Broun saying, "It was with astonishment that we learned recently of the high-handed, arbitrary and impudent action of the Guild in endeavoring in a left-handed manner to bring reproach upon Mr. Hearst, whose kindness and generosity toward his employes has been of the highest order."   Broun replied, editorially, that this was a remarkable document, that it showed the men running for their lives, that Naaman in Biblical times had bowed his head in the House of Rimmon, but "he did not smear his mouth with shoe polish," and he concluded by naming the thirty the "Pieces of Silver Association."

However pyrrhic the victory had been, it was a victory for Hearst; Edmond D. Coblenz, editor of the *American,* brought its fruits to the proprietor at his castle at San Simeon, where Clarence Lindner, editor of the San Francisco paper, also reported.   The conference was short and decisive: a telegram from headquarters directed the discharge of Louis Burgess for reasons of "economy."   Mr. Burgess was the leading spirit of the Guild in the San Francisco *Examiner* office.   The next day all Guild notices on the *Examiner* bulletin board were torn down and a sign "For *Examiner* business only" was posted. A telegraphic request to Mr. Hearst for a "plain statement" was ignored.   Mr. Broun thought the principle of collective bargaining, the keynote of the NRA, had been violated, and Mr. Burgess, who had been an editorial writer for seven years, filed a formal complaint with the NRA regional labor board under Section 7-A of the law.

At this time the Guild boasted eight thousand members, one-fifth the estimated total of newspaper workers in the United States.

Opening its first national convention President Broun made the announcement that the Guild in six months had grown "from nothing to the largest organization of its kind in the world"; it had beaten the long established British newspaper men's union by some three thousand, but the growth had been "amorphous," and the purpose of the meeting was to crystallize its character. On a motion of the president, Louis Burgess was hired (for seventy-five dollars a week, the same salary he got on the *Examiner*) as national organizing secretary. Mr. Broun called this action a challenge to Mr. Hearst: "You have fired him, we have hired him."

The message of greeting from President Roosevelt was very moderate: ". . . It affords me real and personal pleasure to send a word. . . . newspaper men have been and are rendering real and valued service to the nation. . . ." But among the first actions taken by the Guild was the passage of two resolutions, one urging the immediate release of Tom Mooney, the other calling upon the Guild to use "every means for obtaining additional legislation to protect collective bargaining and to outlaw company unions."

Here, I believe, is the best proof of a theory that I have always held. I have given evidence in previous chapters of what I believed to be the unfair treatment of men, ideas and organizations by the press, particularly of radicals, labor leaders and labor unions. I have maintained that the Associated Press has been unfair to labor and that the newspapers of the nation, with notable exceptions, have been unfair to organized labor, have attacked collective bargaining, and have on many and tragic occasions supported their advertisers and the Mellons, Fricks, Carnegies, Rockefellers and other great employers of labor, and also the private and brutal coal and iron police, the various militias, the bloodthirsty vigilantes and other terroristic, extra-legal, vicious and at times murderous forces against labor unions on strike and the labor movement in general. In the whole history of labor violence in America I have felt that the newspaper men were not to blame for the attitude of the newspapers. Individually the writers have always expressed themselves either in favor of labor or at least

a fair deal. Labor has not had a fair deal. Now organized
newspaper men for the first time went on record in favor of
labor.

Nor was this all. The suppression of news, the distortion
of news, the abuses of advertising, the invasion of private
rights and many other failings of modern journalism for
which the reporter is frequently blamed, were discussed by the
convention and answered by resolutions. The news writers of
America went on record for not only the freedom of the press
but the freedom of their own conscience in telling the truth
accurately, without that distortion and suppression which might
be the cause of economic, industrial and military wars. A
code of ethics was written. Its main points are:

> A newspaper man's first duty is to give the public ac-
> curate and unbiased news reports.
> The equality of all men before the law should be ob-
> served. Newspaper men should not be swayed by political,
> economic, social, racial or religious prejudices.
> News accounts dealing with persons accused of crime
> should be in such form as not to mislead or prejudice
> public opinion.
> Sources of confidential information should not be re-
> vealed.
> Guild should work against suppression of news by
> privileged persons or groups, including advertisers, com-
> mercial powers and friends of newspaper men.

In resolutions the publication of propaganda in the guise of
news was severely condemned, likewise the publication of false
and misleading information oppressive to persons or groups,
the payment of money to newspaper workers for publicity and
the employment of reporters for other than editorial work.

This is the voice of American newspaper reporters. It is
not the expression of the thousands who are indifferent, nor
the few who are crooks, but the majority who are intelligent
and apparently at last awakened. It is a direct answer to H. L.
Mencken, who about a decade ago, discussing the problem of
false news, said it got into the papers "because journalists are

in the main, extremely stupid, sentimental and credulous fellows . . . because the majority of them lack the sharp intelligence that the proper discharge of their duties demands."

The approval by the leading eight thousand newspaper workers of America of a new code of ethics is a landmark in journalism. It is also the cause of a terrific storm. My friend, Marlen Pew, whom I have quoted approvingly on every occasion, and who in 1933 approved the Guild, was now among the snipers. "It smacks of class-conscious propaganda, irresponsible romancing and is crusted all over with hate," he said of the code. "Most of the charges are false, many are half truths, as every newspaper man knows. . . ." Admitting that no one disputes the fact some papers are edited by the business office, that some are deliberately false to public trust, that some are anti-social and exploit and foment social, political and military wars, some practice distortion and deceit, and that some reporters have fallen into disrepute, degraded as hirelings compelled to play the games of public enemies, Mr. Pew added, "It took a poison pen to indict the whole press and all newspaperdom, in generalities. . . ." Other editors expressed varying opinions:

George F. Milton, *Chattanooga News:* "It is a challenge to publishers, this call for strict adherence to truth in news columns. They cannot afford to lag behind their reporters on this principle."

Hulbert Taft, *Cincinnati Times-Star:* "A restatement of truisms."

M. E. Foster, *Houston Press:* "I do not believe in the Guild. . . ."

Fred Fuller Shedd, *Philadelphia Bulletin:* "I see nothing in the code . . . to which any newspaper interest should or can object."

Walter M. Harrison, *Oklahoma City Oklahoman:* "In my opinion ethical standards are unimportant. If the Guild affiliates with the A. F. of L. it has no future."

Arthur J. Sinnot, *Newark Evening News:* "The ethical code is commendable. . . . I hope the Guild does not intend to arrogate to itself the right to say, you shall print this or that. . . ."

William E. Gonzales, *Columbia* (S. C.) *State:* "No point . . . conflicts with the *State's* standards."

Charles K. McClatchy, McClatchy Newspapers: "Contract provisions show extreme radical elements in saddle in Guild. . . . Another instance of radicalism—this time coupled with ignorance—is in the resolution demanding immediate pardon for Thomas Mooney, who stands before God and man as a convicted professional dynamiter. He was fairly tried. . . ."

A. H. Kirchhofer, *Buffalo News:* "The Guild code . . . should command confidence."

Mr. Hearst was caught by the ship news men.

Hearst: "I have sympathy for NRA. . . . Frankly I do not believe in a newspaper guild. Maybe I am old fashioned. I have always regarded our business as a profession and not a trade union . . . I believe in the main objects."

Reporter: "And what are those, Mr. Hearst?"

Mr. Hearst: "Well, better working conditions and proper compensation. I like to feel that a newspaper man is like a soldier in war. He should be ready to go out whenever there is a call and willing to work all day and all night on his assignment if it calls for it."

Reporter (cynically): "Work for love of it and starve?"

Mr. Hearst (laughing): "I don't think they ought to starve. It's not happened on our papers. We have tried to pay good workers a decent compensation. The Guild, if it is to be like a union, will attempt to dictate policies, putting itself above the public. It would also tend to deprive the reporter of the character which makes a newspaper man a romantic figure."

Mr. Hearst then proceeded to Bad Nauheim and an interview with Hitler.

From San Francisco the Hearst lawyer, reviewing the case of the discharged writer, Burgess, sent a letter to the regional labor board saying that an order to reinstate would infringe on freedom of the press!

Arthur Hays Sulzberger, vice-president of the *New York Times,* declared that this newspaper "is always ready to discuss with its employees any matter of mutual interest."

Captain Patterson of the *News* and Stern of the *Post* immediately notified the Guild they would talk business.

The *Standard-Times* of New Bedford, Massachusetts, dismissed two men as soon as a Guild chapter was formed. The *Rochester Journal-American* posted a notice saying, "Any negotiations must be with elected representatives of the editorial employees . . . regardless of membership in any outside organization." Paul Block, of the *Newark Star-Eagle,* was forced to recognize the Guild after a bitter fight over his firing seven members; he also had to reinstate a seventy-six-year-old newspaper man who had been with the paper fifteen years.

The *Philadelphia Record,* owned by David Stern, was the first newspaper in America to sign a Guild contract.

And now a most amusing incident occurred. The *Long Island Daily Press* (Jamaica, New York), S. I. Newhouse, publisher, had discharged several employees and, according to the Guild, forced others to quit that organization. A strike was called. Heywood Broun, carrying a placard, picketed the plant by land and Jonathan Eddy, national secretary, picketed it by air. Then Mayor La Guardia of New York stepped in and an agreement was signed which the Guild considered a victory. The event marked the first appearance in history of reporters on the picketing line. The epilogue was a letter, written by managing editor, Philip Hochstein, to the *Times, Herald Tribune, World-Telegram, Post* and *Brooklyn Eagle,* in which he complained that all the accounts of the picketing of the *Press* plant and the agreement had been biased in favor of the Guild!

The next skirmish involved the *Staten Island Advance* published by the same Mr. Newhouse. This too was a minor engagement in the revolution which was going on in the journalistic world. Its larger issues were raised by the *Editor & Publisher,* which now said its subscribers need no longer regard the Guild "as an independent body of responsible professional news writers and editors," because "it is a radical trades union, at least in so far as its national officers are concerned. . . . Heywood Broun, national President, speaks in favor of the strike weapon. He, the pacifist, itches for a knock-down fight." The *Guild Reporter* is compared with the Communist *Daily Worker*. "Indeed, the tone of the two is so nearly identical that they might be issued from the same desk."

Carl Randau, president, called a New York Guild meeting in which he charged the publishers with raising the Red scare to attack the newspaper men. Something new in Red scares! He denied that the *Daily Worker* unit had gained control; Jonathan Eddy, national secretary, reported that the A. N. P. A. had sent out a confidential bulletin throughout America labeling the Guild "very dangerous." Although the Guild denied radical tendencies Mr. Eddy declared New York members "at last realize that their interests are largely the same as those of all other wage earners." The majority of publishers "have either openly refused to cooperate, or pretended to cooperate with no sincere intention of arriving at the one real basis for such cooperation, a collective agreement. . . . We now have gone to the unions. We expect and have already received a different kind of cooperation from them."

The American Association of Schools and Departments of Journalism in its brief to the code authorities said that ". . . no business which depends for its existence on paying less than living wages to its workers has any right to continue to exist in this country . . ."; furthermore, that the minimum wage set for staff and learners is below the standard of decent living.

In New York and Boston the Guild chapters asked the Associated Press for collective bargaining, saying that 73.9 per cent of the A. P. workers in New York and 75 per cent in Boston were members. General Manager Kent Cooper in reply asked for "a list of the employees of the Associated Press in New York and Boston making the request to you and the form in which they made it." This sounded more like a threat than an offer to co-operate, so Secretary Eddy refused, but in a letter to the regional labor board said "press associations have resisted our efforts to induce them to come under codes as have other industries."

Throughout. the long and honorable careers of Melville Stone, Victor Lawson et al., the Associated Press maintained that it was the most honest organization in the world because it was co-operative. Co-operation proved everything. It could not do a Democrat harm or a Republican harm because half its co-operators were Democrats, the other half Republicans. Simple as that. Not a word about the forty gentlemen who controlled the bond votes. No mention of the paradox of the majority of twelve or thirteen hundred co-operators almost daily attacking all other co-operative, community ownership, and socialized public service ideas. Is the co-operative A. P. now co-operating with the co-operative Guild?

In Boston the local Guild filed a brief charging the *Herald-Traveler* with violating the NRA and the newspaper code by attempting to intimidate its employees and refusing to bargain collectively. In St. Louis there was a split in the Guild which the *Editor & Publisher* hailed as marking its break up—its foundering on the rock of New York radicalism. A test case, the contract with the *World-Telegram* of New York, ended in compromise, the leading Scripps-Howard paper declaring itself "entirely sympathetic to the aim of the editorial workers to share equally in the success to which they contribute," but it refused "to become a party to any contract the terms of which would in their execution dissipate authority, disrupt coordinate effort, and ultimately bring about disintegration of the property and loss of both jobs and invested capital."

The first big strike called by the Guild was against the *Newark Ledger,* a tabloid published by Lucius T. Russell, Sr., a booming westerner who posted on his bulletin board his view that, "You can go to all the regional boards you damn please but you will get no relief from the *Ledger* until you come to me personally." Mr. Russell blamed "socialistic propaganda that is trying to make everyone class conscious." Editorially the *Ledger* frequently boomed Il Duce and Fascism. The staff published a newspaper with a leading article headlined *The Ledger Fails You—Its Staff Doesn't.*

Now occurred one of those things which have added comedy and tragedy and vast quantities of irony to the revolutionized journalistic situation. After almost a century of reporting that terrorism or violence is always started in strikes by working-men, the newspaper men in Newark found it on their doorstep. They did not start it, they knew. Now they alleged that the employer had imported gangsters—"a known gangster from Paterson and Detroit and his mob of gangsters to 'protect' him." Win or lose, no Newark reporter will be ignorant of strike tactics in the future.

Meanwhile in Washington the revolt of the reporters was growing into the second world war of the press against the NRA. The case of Dean S. Jennings, the *San Francisco Call-Bulletin* re-write man fired in July, came now in October before the National Labor Relations Board. Its jurisdiction was challenged by Mr. Hanson who wanted it heard by the National Industrial Board set up under the publishers' code. "If," he said for Mr. Hearst, "the National Labor Board issues an order in this case, Mr. Hearst will not comply with it. Mr. Hearst's position is that if the code is meaningless in so far as the government is concerned, it is meaningless in so far as he is concerned."

The publishers, who from the first had yelled they wanted reporters to remain gentlemen rather than join the American Federation of Labor, were of course driving the Guild into the latter's doubtful arms. President Green offered assistance in New Jersey.

On December 3, 1934, the National Board ruled it had jurisdiction over Guild disputes and that "no genuine issue of freedom of the press can be fabricated"; and no sooner said than President Davis of the Publishers' Association made a counter-statement, saying, as the reader has already guessed, that "the decision . . . in the *Call-Bulletin* case is a threat to a free press in the United States." One New York City newspaper came out openly for the Guild. The *Post*, pointing out the fact that Jennings had been officially held discharged because of his activities in connection with the formation of the Guild, said:

"Mr. Hearst who had been hinting darkly that Mr. Roosevelt and Moscow are in cahoots to 'Sovietize' America, will no doubt now find his deepest suspicions confirmed. Mr. Howard Davis, president of the American Newspaper Publishers' Association, leaps into the fray with the declaration that this action violates the 'freedom of the press.'

"The *Post* has said before and says again that collective bargaining, minimum wages and abolition of child labor no more endanger 'freedom of the press' than zoning, health, fire or sanitary regulations. A newspaper could be closed up for violation of sanitary regulations, but who would argue that this endangers the freedom of the press?

"Strange how newspapers which make the least use of freedom of the press do the most talking about it."

This ruling of the National Board was the most important victory in the short Guild history. It occurred on a Monday; on Tuesday all was lost when the Labor Board ordered the case reopened. The Guild's officers were in Washington attending an NRA meeting on editorial wages and hours. On hearing the news they walked out of the conference, headed by Heywood Broun. But not before Broun had issued the first direct declaration of war between the reporters and the publishers.

"As long as the corridors of Mr. [Donald] Richberg [head of the National Emergency Council] are filled with the mysterious, high-pressure representatives of the publishers we feel that we belong elsewhere.

"When and if NRA purges itself we will return. We charge definitely that on this occasion and several former ones NRA has allowed itself to be terrified by the publishers. The American Newspaper Guild is not afraid of the publishers. We have nothing to lose but our jobs.

We are beginning to learn how to fight the publishers at those times when we must fight.

"This is not the battleground. We don't want to be ambushed. We are going back to the picket line in Newark. The air is cleaner there. Good morning."

Hanson, the publishers' counsel, called the Guild representatives "disloyal both to their members and to the publishers of this country." He was told to withdraw his heated remark. "I am willing, now that I have said it," he replied. Later he expressed his amazement that "newspaper writers attack the great heritage which has come down to them from their forefathers." It was assumed that he was again referring to freedom of the press. No matter. From now on the newspaper men of the nation were at war with the publishers of the newspapers.

But it was more than that. It had become a struggle that was to affect the entire NRA, the rights of labor under Section 7-A and the American public. Especially the public. It had up to now stood by the President. Labor had taken the NRA as a new charter of liberty. Although many disputes about company unions and "outside" unions had been compromised unsatisfactorily, there had never been a "show-down," or a decision from the Supreme Court. The anti-administration press and the anti-union labor press were joined in an attempt to destroy the entire Roosevelt program. It now began to appear that the dispute over the Guild was to be made the basis of that action.

This became more apparent when the Labor Relations Board, sustaining its findings, warned the Hearst paper that it must reinstate Jennings or face prosecution by the Department of Justice. The *Call-Bulletin* was invited to challenge in the courts the board's right to remove the fairly well plucked Blue Eagle. Immediately Mr. Davis announced a convention of the twelve hundred members of the Publishers' Association to consider "the gravest problem with which the press of this country has yet been confronted." The New York Guild unanimously adopted a resolution for a conference with American Federation of Labor leaders and a mass meeting with the printing trades unions "to denounce the publishers' action in threatening a breach of the newspaper publishers' code, clarifying the issue of free press to include freedom of newspaper men to join an organization of their own choosing." Again that gadfly of the New York publishers, the *Post,* ridiculed and denounced its colleagues, saying that the misuse of the freedom of speech principle as an excuse to evade the usual regulations of commerce and industry "is rank hypocrisy."

Meanwhile out in the front line the war became a series of trench raids pending the final big push. The publisher of *Il Progresso,* a certain Generoso Pope who once shook hands with Mussolini and never got over it, fired his English page editor, Alphonse Tonietti, head of his office unit of the Guild. The employees of the *Jewish Daily Bulletin* went on strike and won when a Guild contract was agreed upon. Estolv Ward, chairman of the *Oakland* (Cal.) *Tribune's* Guild chapter, was fired, as were Ronald Scofield, its secretary, and Wallace Vaughan, librarian. In a hearing in New York, David Frederick, president of the Boston Guild, and Morris L. Ernst, attorney for the national body, charged the *Boston Herald* with firing John C. Beale and Travis Ingham for organizing activities, which Robert B. Choate denied as the cause. The Guild, he said, "wanted everything under the sun." The Guild said it wanted a minimum wage.

The year ended with the Guild apparently victorious in the diplomatic field. The NRA and the President were on their side. True, Jennings was not back on the job, nor was Alexander Crosby reinstated by the *Staten Island Advance.* Redfern Mason, veteran music critic of *San Francisco Examiner,* had resigned when he was put on the "hotel run" after he had become active in the Guild. In both San Francisco and Chicago the roaring anti-union voices of a majority of publishers had kept the Guild from progressing. However, Madison, Wisconsin, newspapers went over in a body to the Guild and closed the town while in Cleveland the *News* signed a contract with a forty-dollar minimum salary after a strike was threatened. The Guild claimed ten thousand members, or almost fifty per cent. of the profession in the urban centers. Its success in organizing therefore was phenomenal.

With considerable jubilation the Guild entered 1935. President Broun had seen President Roosevelt. The attack on Richberg had reached strategic objectives. The future was indeed bright. And now, as in the past, newspaper men felt that they had some power in America. They had done great things. They had exposed Fall and Teapot Dome and the Ohio gang. They had made and broken famous and notorious personalities. They had created the Coolidge Myth and later they had helped ruin Mr. Hoover. They had had a lot to do with the unanimity with which the United States went over to Franklin Roosevelt in the crisis of 1933.

They thought perhaps they could do something about publishers too.

On January 23, 1935, President Roosevelt reversed the decision of the Labor Board. The Jennings-*Call-Bulletin*-Hearst case was again dumped on the doorstep of the Newspaper Code Authority which the Guild has always said is controlled by the publishers. It was even worse than that. W. A. Harriman, administrative officer of the Blue Eagle, believed that the President's action put the entire NRA "on the spot." There was a rumor that the National Labor Board, headed by Francis Biddle, would resign in a body. Guild Secretary Eddy, asking the national body's permission to resign from the Newspaper Board, said Roosevelt's action "makes my continued presence on the board tantamount to condoning a fraud upon the working newspaper people of this country." This statement was published by the *Times, American* and *Herald Tribune*. The newspapers also published a statement from Heywood Broun, which appeared in various versions, showing excellent editing:

Times and *Post:* "The newspaper publishers having cracked down on the President of the United States, announce that 'a satisfactory adjustment' has been reached. They mean satisfactory to the publishers. . . . We contend that the government of the United States has been held up by the threat and the bluff of the publishers of the United States. That is tragic enough. It is even more so when we consider the fact that the President surrendered at the point of a wooden gun."

In a radio talk a day or two later Mr. Broun accused all the New York newspapers with the exception of the *Times* and the *Post* of censoring the foregoing statement. *Time* commented on this fact. In this way a million newspaper readers were again confirmed in their suspicion that newspapers are not printing all the news, that Mr. Shaw may have been right when he said, "Newspapers all over the world are busy suppressing the news."

In March the *Newark Ledger* obtained an injunction restraining Guild members from picketing, interfering with employees, loitering, boycotting, attempting to dissuade advertisers from using the paper or readers from buying it. It prevented the circulation of the *Guild Reporter*. It restrained the Guild from freedom of speech, freedom of the press, freedom of the air. The Guild thought that an injunction of this nature should rally the Publishers' Association and the Editors' Association in a joint fight against violation of constitutional rights, but no cry of alarm was heard in these journalistic temples. The *Times,* after editorially declaring that "many reporters join with editors and publishers in condemning the biased quality of this publication [the *Guild Reporter*]" called the injunction objectionable. The *Post* asked "the American Newspaper Publishers' Association and Colonel Bertie McCormick" to fight for their favorite tenet, freedom of the press. Even the *Herald Tribune* said this freedom was being violated in New Jersey. The publishers rested on their dignity. But the public responded to an appeal from the National Anti-Injunction League whose treasurer, Quincy Howe, published the fact that newspaper workers had already contributed twenty thousand dollars for the fight.

On March 28, 1935, the strike, which began November 17, 1934, ended with "a substantial victory" for the Guild. Mr. Broun reported that the general public played an effective part

by refusing to buy the *Ledger* while hostilities were on. Shortly thereafter, L. T. Russell was removed as publisher of the
Ledger. The property was sold at auction.

In April Mr. Broun in the course of a speech said that
"labor's public enemy No. 1 is Franklin D. Roosevelt." The
Philadelphia-Camden unit, second largest in the Guild, demanded that the national president of the Guild apologize. In
refusing to do so Broun suggested that the organization elect
some one else in June.

Although the Guild has won many victories there is a noticeable disillusion among newspaper workers. They have realized
that what is called the power of the press is not the power of
the newspaper workers, but that of the owners. Mr. Broun
could well recall the statement made to him by the cynical
gentleman in Washington to the effect that everything the
publishers of America want is accomplished, nothing that the
publishers oppose is ever done. The publishers' use of power
in such matter as private ownership of public utilities, the
rights of labor to organize or strike, the child-labor amendment, the pure food and drug legislation, the handling of
political propaganda, and a hundred and one other things have
substantiated the cynical gentleman. Whether or not the publishers decide to smash the Guild will probably be decided very
soon.

In May, 1935, the Supreme Court ruled against the NRA.
Without losing an hour an official of the A. N. P. A. asked all
publishers to remove the Blue Eagle. Within a week Guild
leaders were being fired on various smaller papers. The same
month the disillusioned workers of the great American free
press at their second convention voted a referendum on joining
the American Federation of Labor. The fight goes on.

Chapter XIX

A ROLL OF HONOR

BEFORE I conclude this inquiry into the integrity of the American press, I must follow my criticism by presenting a roll of honor. First on every roll of honor is the *Manchester Guardian*. I have never heard one severely critical word against this newspaper, although I have talked to say five hundred colleagues about freedom of the press. The *Manchester Guardian,* everyone agrees, is a living example of such a possibility.

But in Germany in my time the *Frankfurter Zeitung* was equally great.

I remember when the French first marched into the Ruhr and then into Frankfurt. British labor and liberalism denounced the occupation, the wanton wreckage of government and materials, mad and unjustified. The *Manchester Guardian* led in protest; the Northcliffe press upheld France in violent editorials and twisted news. It revived the old German-hating days which helped bring on the war.

The French military, accompanied by the *Chicago Tribune* staff car, entered Frankfurt. A number of civilians were shot. A French major, representing the high command, stalked into the office of the *Frankfurter Zeitung* and ordered the assembled editors to print a warning notice addressed to the population. An hour later the French general received his notice back. To it was pinned a printed slip:

"Frankfurter Zeitung
"Editorial Department.
"The editorial board of the Frankfurter Zeitung thanks you for submitting the enclosed manuscript, but regrets deeply that it is not able to publish it. This, however, is not to be taken as a reflection upon the literary value of the enclosed manuscript . . ."

333

The French command was furious. A general in gold braid and medals stormed the editorial sanctum.

"I demand the publication of this notice tomorrow morning, on the front page, in the center, four columns wide, in large type. The safety of the people depends on it," he said threateningly.

"His Excellency misunderstands," the editor replied. "The *Frankfurter Zeitung* in all its history has never been dictated to. The owners have placed this publication in the hands of the editorial board; the board decides on all news. You cannot go above our heads. What you can do is confiscate the newspaper; you can in fact smash the presses, burn down the house, even execute the editors, but one thing no man can do, and that is, tell the editors what goes into this newspaper."

The military raged and stormed and went down in defeat. There was nothing to be done about it. Confiscate the *Frankfurter Zeitung,* destroy it, hang the editors? What good would it do? He had to give notice to the populace.

"Now, if you go about it in a nice way, if you ask us decently to publish the announcement, and if we consider it to the public advantage, we will publish it when and where we think best."

So said the editor. The General apologized. The incident was over.

In all the history of modern journalism, is there another episode to cap this real story of freedom of the press?

It is now my pleasant duty to look at the brighter side of the American picture. The reader will remember that the public utility corporations, for example, never claimed they had corrupted more than four-fifths of the press, and President Roosevelt, when he spoke of the campaign of lies, falsehoods, propaganda, surely did not mean that charge to be universal. And, as already said, whenever the "press" is charged with being "off side," or waging a battle, or maintaining a guilty silence, or doing something noble or ignoble, not all the newspapers of a city are meant because there are usually exceptions, one way or another.

There remains, however, the question of how large a part of the press can be called a free press, what proportion really believes in the freedom of the press, how many obey the code of ethics, how many violate it daily and so on. As it is quite impossible to answer these questions completely, and inasmuch as the cases of control by advertisers, propagandists, big business, etc., in the second section of this book are also not complete, neither, unfortunately, can this roll of honor be complete.

Every newspaper man has his own idea about a roll of honor, as in fact he has about every journalistic question, and I do not expect more than two or three of the forty thousand members of the profession to agree with everything contained in this volume. But, inasmuch as I have had the assistance of scores of reporters in other chapters, I also note their co-operation for this one and I have helped myself to the recommendations of authorities.

What are the outstanding achievements of the free press in America? Colonel McCormick lists them as follows:

Defeat of the Tweed Ring in New York.

Protection of life by safeguards in all theaters, resulting from exposures following the Iroquois Theater fire, which cost five hundred and seventy-five lives.

Disclosures of Ruef-Schmitz municipal looting in San Francisco.

Revelation of Dr. F. A. Cook as an exploration humbug.

Exposure of criminal neglect leading to the sinking of the *Titanic,* with loss of 1,513 lives.

Expulsion of William Lorimer from United States Senate for vote-buying, leading to direct election reform.

Governor Len Small's defeat in public life.

The exposure and routing of the "Ohio gang."

Destruction of the K. K. K.

Don R. Mellett's martyrdom at Canton.

Newton D. Baker's successful defense of freedom of press against a despotic judge in Cleveland and against a Kentucky judge who barred a reporter from his court.

The Minnesota "gag" law, defeated by newspaper action.

Dangers of the sea as shown by the *Vestris* overloading case.

Case of George R. Dale, Muncie, Ind., publisher, sentenced for contempt of court.

Press agitation leading to repudiation of the Eighteenth Amendment.

Exposure of Mayor Walker of New York.

War on racketeering, vice and crime.

The Tweed gang was ruined by the *New York Times,* in those days a crusading newspaper. Lorimer was exposed by the *Chicago Tribune* which presented proof to the Senate that he had bought his seat with one hundred thousand dollars obtained by extortion. The Senate refused this evidence, so the *Tribune* produced more in 1912 and forced his trial in 1914 for mismanagement of a bank chain. The *Tribune* also gets the credit for its fight on Mayor Thompson and the Prohibition Amendment, and to Colonel McCormick go the honors of leading the fight on the Minnesota newspaper "gag" law.

The most notable martyr of the battle for a free press is Donald R. Mellett, editor of the *Canton Daily News.* He was shot to death by gangsters in the middle of his campaign against the police and vice elements of the Ohio city.

From the very first days of the Ku Klux Klan the press was opposed to it. Despite the fact that about eighty per cent of the newspapers declared themselves editorially against the Klan its membership increased by a million or more for several years, but ridicule and public indignation and the press exposure of graft finally killed it. How bitter the fight was is illustrated by the case of George Dale, editor of the *Muncie Post-Democrat,* who in 1922 was attacked by three masked Klansmen and beaten almost to death. He shot one of the attackers with a gun he wrenched from his hand. Although he demanded an investigation he himself was arrested by the Ku Klux municipal officials of Muncie, charged with carrying a gun, with liquor violation, with libel and contempt of a court which was partly composed of Kluxers and entirely intimidated by the organization. The State Supreme Court finally ruled in Dale's favor in 1926.

Annually since 1930 the University of Missouri has awarded bronze medallions "for distinguished work in journalism" throughout the world, and as I believe it is the most important review of the service to the public by the newspapers, I will summarize the citations which Associate Dean Frank L. Martin has sent me:

The first newspaper, in the first award, was the *New York Times* which was characterized as clean, constructive, fair, complete, the leader in thought and opinion, "stoutly maintaining its independence as a newspaper under the fine leadership of Adolph Ochs." *La Prensa* of Buenos Aires, Percy S. Bullen, American correspondent of the *London Daily Telegraph,* and E. W. Stephens, Missouri editor, received the next three medals. *La Prensa* and *La Nacion* are two of the world's finest newspapers; if they were published in the United States or in Europe they would also become internationally powerful.

In 1931 the first award went to the *Manchester Guardian,* "for its brilliant battle for liberalism . . . and for its courageous fight for peace; for its sensitiveness to moral ideas. . . ." The *Baltimore Sun* papers, "two brilliant, fearless and constructively liberal newspapers . . . free from either one-man domination or business control . . ." are next honored and the journalists of the year are Houston Harte, of the *San Angelo Standard-Times,* Robert P. Scripps, and Henry F. Childers of the *Troy* (Mo.) *Free Press.*

The next year Missouri honored its own *Post-Dispatch.* If this newspaper were published in New York its present liberal policy and middle-western influence would certainly become nationwide and America could then boast a rival to the *Guardian.*

In honoring the *Frankfurter Zeitung* the university administered extreme unction: one year later this great journal was Hitlerized.

Casper S. Yost, of the *St. Louis Globe-Democrat,* Frank W. Rucker, of the *Independence* (Mo.) *Examiner,* Miss Malvina

Lindsay, of the *Kansas City Journal-Post*, Charles G. Ross, brilliant Washington correspondent for the *Post-Dispatch*, and J. P. Tucker, of the *Platte County Gazette*, Parkville, Missouri, were the journalists of 1932.

The *Kansas City Star*, *Japan Advertiser* and the London *Times* received the 1933 awards, the *Times* being credited with being "the leading newspaper of the world." H. J. Grant, publisher of the *Milwaukee Journal*, was the only individual honored. In 1934 the *Des Moines Register-Tribune*, the *Melbourne Argus*, and a magazine, *The Churchman*, edited by Dr. Guy Emery Shipler, comprised the university list while the individuals awarded the medals were Colonel Robert Morgan White, of Mexico, Missouri, and Herbert W. Walker.

Whether or not priority means anything in these lists I do not know. Many newspaper men I am sure would place the *Christian Science Monitor* early on any list of important American newspapers, and once the field is open to weekly publications there are dozens of names more important than those of country editors already honored.

For an honor roll of Washington correspondents I go to Mr. Anderson of the *Post-Dispatch* whose name I believe should be put at the head of it. He is frank, fearless and one of the fairest critics of the press. Mr. Anderson writes:

"It required no particular courage to write the truth for the *Baltimore Sun*, the *St. Louis Post-Dispatch* or the Scripps-Howard papers. Such newspapers as these expect it. But what would happen to the correspondent who tried to write the truth about 'Coolidge Economy' for the *Boston Transcript*, or about the Mellon tax refunds for the *Philadelphia Public Ledger*, or about the social lobby for the *Washington Star?* What would happen to any man who insisted on dishing up the bald truth about any Republican administration for such papers as the *New York Herald Tribune*, the *Detroit Free Press*, the *St. Louis Globe-Democrat*, the *Chicago Tribune*, or the *Los Angeles Times*? The Washington corps of correspondents has its inevitable percentage of sycophants, climbers, politicians, and lads with an eye on the main chance, and it has, sad to relate, a solemn bevy of 'gallery statesmen' who have been duped into a bogus sense of being 'part' of the government, and hence bound to conceal its blunders and knaveries. But on the whole they are ten times better men than the owners of their papers. I present herewith my own Honor Roll of Washington correspondents for 1929:

"John A. Kennedy and Edward L. Roddan, of Universal Service. . . .

"Paul R. Mallon and Raymond Clapper, of the United Press. . . .

"Harold Brayman of the *New York Evening Post,* and Phelps H. Adams, of the *New York Sun.* . . .

"M. Farmer Murphy of the *Baltimore Sun.* . . .

"Ruth Finney, of the Scripps-Howard papers. . . .

"Marion L. Ramsay, of Universal Service. . . .

"Drew Pearson, of the *Baltimore Sun.* . . .

"Robert B. Smith, of the *Philadelphia Public Ledger. . . .*"

The following year Mr. Anderson continued his criticism and selection:

"The refusal of the Hearst, Scripps-Howard, and other independent dailies to join in the sycophantic orgy of President-petting and Senate-baiting which attended the power controversy, and their realistic perception of the issues involved, are enough to hearten any newspaper man who cares for the honor and influence of his profession. Incidentally, the moment seems opportune to repeat my ancient annual custom by presenting my own Honor Roll of Washington correspondents for 1930. The flowers are distributed as follows:

"William C. Murphy, Jr., of the *New York World.* . . .

"Ruth Finney, of the Scripps-Howard papers, and Marion L. Ramsay, of Universal Service. . . .

"M. Farmer Murphy, of the *Baltimore Sun.* . . .

"Raymond P. Brandt, of the *St. Louis Post-Dispatch.* . . .

"D. Harold Oliver and Marguerite Young, of the Associated Press. . . .

"William Hard, of the Consolidated Press Association. . . .

"Alfred D. Stedman, of the *St. Paul Pioneer Press.* . . .

"Robert B. (Red) Smith, of the *Philadelphia Public Ledger.* . . ."

This list, thought Ernest Gruening, was incomplete, and he suggested the following names:

Louis J. Heath, of the United Press.
Drew Pearson, of the *Baltimore Sun.*
Theodore C. Alford, of the *Kansas City Star.*
Harry Frantz, of the United Press.
Ruby A. Black, of the *Portland Evening News.*
John Snure, *New York Herald Tribune.*
Franklyn Waltman, Jr., of the *Baltimore Sun.*
Mark Thistlethwaite, of the *Indianapolis News.*
Henry Hyde, of the *Baltimore Sun.*

Annually the *Nation* publishes its honor roll of citizens and institutions. In 1927 its journalism list included:

"The editors of the *New York World,* for the crusading devotion to liberal ideals which makes of their daily the finest public servant in the urban press of the North.

"Julian and Julia Harris, of the *Columbus* (Ga.) *Enquirer-Sun,* for gallantry, wisdom, and patriotism in the conduct of their daily.

"R. Charlton Wright, editor of the *Columbus* (S. C.) *Record,* for his efforts to compel the punishment of the lynchers of Aiken in his state.

"Thomas F. Millard, for telling the truth about China in the *New York Times.*

"Grover Clark, for editing an American newspaper in Peking and keeping it true to the best American traditions."

In 1929 the *Nation* honored my two friends, Silas Bent and Carleton Beals.

In 1932 the *Nation* honored Louis F. Stark for his reports on Kentucky in the *Times*; H. L. Mencken and the *Baltimore Sun* for an article denouncing the Salisbury lynchers, and the *Buffalo Evening News* for work in improving labor conditions.

In 1933 the honors went to "The *New York Times* for printing and Walter Duranty for writing, during the decade and a half of Soviet rule which has now passed, the most enlightening, dispassionate, and readable dispatches from a great nation in the making which appeared in any newspaper in the world." Particularly significant in view of the fact that the *Times* had been the most criticized newspaper in 1920 for its reports on Russia.

In 1935 the *Nation* honored the editorial staff of *Fortune* for articles exposing the munitions industry and stimulating the senatorial investigation; Heywood Broun for his work as president and chief defender of the Newspaper Guild; John L. Spivak, of the *New Masses,* for "a lively and convincing job of muckraking, in nine articles, revealing the extent and character of anti-Semitic Nazi propaganda in the United States"; and John Wechsler, editor of the *Columbia Spectator* for his "able and courageous journalistic attack on all forms of reaction at the university."

The long time editor of the *Nation,* Mr. Villard, deserves a special place in any journalistic honor roll. Technically eliminated from awards by his position as editor of a weekly since his sale of the *New York Evening Post* in 1918, he has been for years the watchdog of the free press, the leading critic of the organs of criticism, and although few newspapers are frank enough to admit it, it is a fact that they have been greatly influenced by his strictures.

Likewise Walter Lippmann and Charles Merz deserve highest praise for their "Test of the News." The *New Republic* of their time called the dispatches about Russia the scandal of our time and the scandal of history. These two journalists not only exposed this scandal but must be credited with the decent reforms which followed.

Marlen Pew has always been one of my newspaper heroes.

His life history is a story of fighting for a free press. In Boston, Philadelphia and New York, wherever he got the job of editing a newspaper, there was sure to be a journalistic civil war, because he took literally the promises of the owners and publishers that he was to have a free hand in producing an honest journal. In every instance his honest intention to tell the news led to conflict.

In Boston, for instance, Pew was told by the wealthy owner of the *Traveler* he need pay no attention to advertisers and big business. The *Traveler* boomed. But big business was angry because the publication of real news in Boston was harmful to special interests.

Pew had a long-term contract. He paid no attention to the report that the *Traveler* had been sold to the shoe machinery trust which with its banks and other business affiliates is a powerful social and political force in New England. One day Pew got a story involving a Boston banker, a brokerage house and a leading law firm, all of whom informed him that the story could not be run because the exposure of corruption would do considerable financial harm to the companies involved.

At the last minute, when the forms had been made up—the scene was similar to the climax of the play *The Fourth Estate* which Captain Joseph Patterson, editor now of the tabloid *New York News,* wrote years ago when he was a young radical— the would-be suppressors appeared in the composing-room. The business manager informed Pew that the shoe machinery company was the real owner of the *Traveler* and wanted the story killed. Pew replied nothing would stop him so long as he was editor. The machinery agent said he would buy up the contract. Pew insisted on spot cash. The shoe man was able to get the cash in time and Pew walked out of the office.

In Philadelphia, as editor of the *News-Post,* Pew was sued for libel after a political exposé, spent a night in jail, and tried for months to persuade the District Attorney to try him. But the indictment was pigeonholed and still remains in some dusty desk.

In New York he managed Hearst's International News

Service, but quit after a quarrel. His life, he says, has been "the most wonderful, glamorous, satisfying adventure that any man can desire."

Gruening has had similar experiences. When he arrived in Portland, Maine, with his *Evening News* he found the press there in control of Guy P. Gannett who was also associated with the Fidelity Trust and with Walter Wyman, representative in Maine for the Insulls. Gruening waded into the situation with an attack on the power interests. The result was a boycott of the *News* which Gruening charged to the Fidelity Trust. Gannett and the bank denied it. Gruening then published the following statement from a representative of the Cumberland County Power and Light Company: "I am extremely sorry, but my orders are not to give the *Portland Evening News* a line of advertising. I got those orders from Mr. Gordon. Mr. Gordon got his orders from Mr. Wyman. Mr. Wyman got his orders from Mr. Insull."

When the *New York Times,* the *Herald Tribune,* the *Philadelphia Inquirer* and other papers published full stories that bonds of the Continental Oil Company had been traced to the Republican National Committee, nothing appeared in the *Portland Herald and Express* and Gruening charged that Gannett had suppressed the news. Said Mr. Pew, who in 1929 was in charge of the *Editor & Publisher:* "The ugliest situation we have noted on the newspaper map of the United States in a long time is reported from Portland, Maine, where Dr. Ernest Gruening and his associates of the *Evening News* have carried their case of alleged advertising boycott and bank and Insull utility oppression to readers, demanding a showdown. . . . The Portland situation possesses certain earmarks which unmistakably point to unfair, even despicable methods to kill a newspaper enterprise. It is no heavy draft on imagination to see the hand of Insull in the picture. . . . Honest newspaper men everywhere will watch the Portland fight with keen interest for a great principle is at stake there. . . . The advertising system is and must be the foundation rock upon which a newspaper is built. To use it to intimidate truth is as wicked and cowardly a perversion of journalism as has been devised. American newspaper men will not tolerate it."

What this country needs is more Pews and Gruenings in editorial jobs.

I am aware of course that ever since the Newspaper Guild began to gain strength there has been a falling off in the universal esteem of the fraternity for the editor of *Editor & Publisher*. It is probably a very painful situation for all concerned. Pew, in my opinion, still ought to be among the first on the newspaper honor roll. He has been more effective in *Editor & Publisher* in criticizing the press, pointing out its faults as well as its glories, than any man in America; he has tried to make a living force instead of a scrap of paper out of the code of ethics; he has published more suppressed news stories than all the weeklies put together and he has been the most important force in the country for the improvement of the newspapers.

With Pew, Villard and Gruening I would include Heywood Broun, William Allen White and Silas Bent: six liberal, critical minds whose criticism has been severe but constructive. These men I believe have been a tremendous factor in bettering American journalism.

Lowell Mellett, editor of the Scripps-Howard *Washington News* and almost all the other members of this chain, which are listed as uncorruptible by the utilities, deserve a place on the honor roll.

The *Newark Evening News* (Arthur J. Sinnott, editor) frequently puts the New York city papers to shame. It has the largest circulation in the metropolis of all outside papers. New Yorkers therefore found in the *Newark Evening News* the complete story of the government order against Bayer's aspirin advertising. The reader will remember that the New York papers either suppressed the item or "buried" it. This publication exposed the canning lobby during the Tugwell episode, and during the Nye munitions hearings the New Jersey paper did not hesitate to print all the exposures of the New Jersey shipbuilders. Editor Sinnott is sympathetic to the Guild and pays wages generally higher than the New York average.

The *Evening News'* Washington bureau is headed by Walter Karig who must be credited with the instances mentioned and given place among the most honorable correspondents.

Among the newspapers which escaped the hysteria of the Sacco-Vanzetti case and gave the two men a square deal are the *Brooklyn Daily Eagle,* the *Milwaukee Leader,* the *New York Telegram,* the *Baltimore Sun,* the *Pittsburgh Press,* the *St. Louis Post-Dispatch,* the *Toronto Mail* and *Empire,* the *New York Times,* and the two Waterbury, Connecticut, papers, the *Republican* and the *American.*

In the Mooney case the *San Francisco News* and the *Baltimore Post* are to be congratulated for finding the missing witness, MacDonald, the only man outside the perjurer Oxman who testified against the accused. He recanted, but remained unfound when the state and defense needed him to repeat his recantation. But the highest honor goes to Ernest Jerome Hopkins, of the *San Francisco Bulletin,* who in 1916 covered the case and wrote news stories expressing his belief in Mooney's guilt and in 1931 exposed the conspiracy which sent Mooney to jail. "Sixteen years of printed poison," wrote this newspaper man, "have convinced Californians that evidence or none, it is better to keep two radicals in prison than remove a nation-wide stimulus to radicalism. . . . 'We got the right men on the wrong evidence. . . . They may not be guilty of the bomb explosion but they belong where they are. . . .' Any governor who pardons Mooney will be digging his political grave." For California's attitude Hopkins blames the state of mind created by the press.

Eugene Lyons "broke" the story of the Sacco-Vanzetti case and Sam Spewack of the *World* made it nation-wide.

Tom Pettey, of the *New York Herald Tribune,* and Russell Porter, of the *New York Times,* early in 1933 exposed Machado's terrorism in Cuba.

Paul Mallon, of the United Press, and Fraser Edwards, of the Hearst Service, defied the secrecy rule of the Senate and reported the vote on the nomination of Lenroot for the federal bench.

Mr. Hearst's Walter Winchell when not writing Broadway

gossip is the most outspoken enemy of the munitions ring in America.

Boyd Gurley, of the *Indianapolis Times,* and Thomas L. Adams, of the *Vincennes Commercial,* exposed the political corruption in Indiana, which was later confirmed by one of their victims, D. C. Stephenson, grand dragon of the Indiana Ku Klux Klan, who went to jail for life.

The *Baltimore Sun, New York World, St. Louis Post-Dispatch* and *Springfield Republican* were outspoken against the President and the Secretary of State in 1927 when all signs pointed to our going to war with Mexico.

The *Chicago Tribune,* suing as a taxpayer, forced Mayor "Big Bill" Thompson and his associates to disgorge $1,732,272 in 1928.

Among the newspapers which fought the utility propagandists are the *Toledo News-Bee* (Harold C. Place, editor) which saved the citizens six hundred thousand dollars a year by defeating the gas company; the *Worcester Evening Post* (George T. Richardson, editor, and John H. Fahey, publisher) which saved the public more than three million dollars by obtaining lower electricity rates; and the *Scranton Times* (E. J. Lynett, publisher) which fought successfully a water rate rise.

In the fight against the utilities and in favor of the Tennessee Valley Authority the largest evening newspaper in the South, the *Memphis Press-Scimitar,* (Edward J. Meeman, editor, and Null Adams, reporter) did brilliant work. In the New Jersey hearings on public service charges, the entire case was fought on evidence and on editorial presentments made by the *Newark Evening News.*

Of the foreign language press there is not much to be said. Practically all the Italian newspapers in America are influenced by the Fascist foreign office either with the free cable service or with Italian bankers' money in America or with decorations, free trips to Italy and interviews with the Duce.

The largest daily labor and Socialist newspaper in the world is the *Jewish Daily Forward* edited by Abraham Cahan, and owned co-operatively. There are no profits. Whatever money is made goes into enlarging the newspaper or into labor unions' civil and cultural institutions. The success of the *Forward* should be an object lesson to those who claim reader or co-operative ownership of a newspaper is impossible.

There are additionally hundreds of smaller newspapers which are as free and independent and courageous and unbuyable as the large city papers. For many years the *Butte Daily Bulletin* which was published in an editorial room in which stood six loaded Winchester rifles and where revolvers lay alongside the typewriters of the reporters, carried on the fight in a state where the copper interests had corrupted the press. It was the sole support of Senator Wheeler. Business men did not like it, nor did the banks, and an advertising boycott broke it in 1930, just as it has broken free and independent papers in many other cities.

"After knocking around the country for years, bowing to sacred cows, writing news to suit the business side of the newspaper, carrying out instructions to color news, and otherwise violating the dictates of my conscience, I have spent the last twelve years on a newspaper which approaches my idea of what a newspaper ought to be," writes W. C. Janson, managing editor of the *Ironwood* (Mich.) *Daily Globe*. Linwood I. Noyes is the publisher.

On the recommendation of Westbrook Pegler the names of Ted Lewis, of the United Press, and William F. Kerby, of the *Wall Street Journal,* are included. These reporters, according to Mr. Pegler, one dull afternoon decided to "make" a story by getting a congressman to insert a ten per cent profit limit in the Vinson Big Navy bill. Result: a saving to the American people of between one hundred million and four hundred and fifty million dollars.

This honor roll is not complete. The Pulitzer journalism prize winners, for example, are not included. They may be found in the *World Almanac*. I am aware that every newspaper man who reads this chapter will disagree with certain choices and propose others. I myself have reserved one addition which is very likely, from the present outlook, to rise to first place on the unanimous honor roll of all journalism workers. I refer to J. David Stern, publisher of the *New York Post,* the *Philadelphia Record* and the *Camden Courier.* In Philadelphia thousands of persons rejoice in the excellent *Record.* How great a part it had in turning out the politicians who made the name Philadelphia synonymous with crookedness I do not know, but there are two facts for your consideration: the *Record* is a crusading newspaper, and "gang" politics in a state known as "Corrupt and Contented" has been defeated.

In New York the *Post* is, in the phrase of one of Mr. Stern's bright young editorial writers, taking the place of the old *New York World* by giving the metropolis the liberal, independent, crusading journalism which it needs. The *Post's* headlines are frequently sensational and misleading, but its editorial page is now the only important one in New York. It has something to say and says it well if at times stridently. The rivalry between *World-Telegram* and *Post* should be encouraged. In its best days the old *World* was the greatest newspaper in America. New York could do with two *Worlds.* In fact nine would not be too many.

CHAPTER XX

IS A FREE PRESS POSSIBLE?

> How can I speak of thee, or thy power
> express,
> Thou god of our idolatry, the Press?
> A fountain at which drink the good and
> wise,
> Or an ever-bubbling spring of endless lies;
> Like Eden's dread probationary tree,
> Knowledge of good and evil is of thee.

NEITHER the honor roll nor the strictures in the preceding chapters have been received with unanimous approval or disapproval by many colleagues. This is not surprising. Newspaper men rarely agree upon anything. That several thousand actually joined a guild and did not disrupt it within a few months is the journalistic surprise of the century.

As for panaceas, or even mild palliatives, I know from experience that every newspaper worker rolls his own and some men may be dictatorial and others fanatic in their views, but all talk about an ideal newspaper with which they can experiment in some far-off idealistic day.

Discussing the forces warring against the free press—advertising, big business, propaganda, social ambitions, human weaknesses, lack of economic security, its resultant atmosphere of fear—and also the standards and qualifications of newspaper men—I said to a friendly critic in explanation of my honor roll: "I suppose I should have included more newspapers from the big cities. I should not judge the entire metropolitan press from my own experiences. I do not suppose that any one of the nine New York newspapers nowadays would suppress a story to please a department store, for example. . . ."

"Don't fool yourself," replied the journalist who is one of the leading members of the *New York Times* staff; "don't you know that there was an elevator accident this week in a department store, three persons were killed or injured, and not one of the nine New York dailies mentioned the accident."

The *New York Times* man continued:

"It so happens that I heard about this case. In a city filled with violence such news is not worth more than a few lines. But the point is that it was suppressed because of fear of offending an advertiser.

"Actually there is not much news suppression nowadays. The present system might be called the funeral march. No metropolitan newspaper can afford to have weekly and monthly magazine critics continually accusing it of unfair practices. So news unpleasing to advertisers, to the owner, to public utilities, to the political and to the hundred and one other powers, is marched silently toward its burial—hidden among the small advertisements, beyond the sporting or the financial pages where few will see and where small headlines will diminish unpleasantness."

The *Times* man went further:

"The real trouble is that much news is suppressed before it is made—I mean, suppressed by the mind—never even set down on paper and submitted to an editor. Frequently no one bothers to look into anything which is harmful to advertisers or friends of the newspaper proprietors. This is due to a state of mind. You haven't written about that. It is important. It is the state of mind of the reporter everywhere. He is supposed to be the investigator; but he is the overlooker; I mean, he overlooks news every day. From the moment he finds how useless it is to investigate and report on certain things and certain men, his mind becomes numb, and he goes through years of work, here in New York too, seeing only what he should see, writing only what he should write. Psychologically he has arrived at a state of mind, however, which makes him believe that he is thoroughly honest, a man of the highest integrity, a powerful instrument for the good of the world, because he feels that he is telling the public the truth that shall set it free."

He went on:

"As for me, I realized that one day. But I have done nothing about it. You see, I am one of the high-priced men.

I have too much to lose. In other words, I am a coward."

Then in reply to a question:

"That's why I joined the Guild. I don't think it will cure everything. Every time it moves left I, who am a conservative, feel very badly about it. All that I want of the Guild is that it should get the reporter out of that cowardly state of mind which has taken the place of a conscience. I think the Guild is succeeding in that. So I go along with it."

But, for the Guild, the going is getting harder every day. The publishers are fighting the Guild. As proof of the old-style system, suppression of news, the president of the Guild points to the hearings conducted by General Johnson on the newspaper code; vital information was presented but "almost nothing was printed about the whole problem. One or two of the New York papers gave fairly full accounts. The rest was silent or, at best, paragraphic"; and furthermore, when Professor Lindsey Rogers who was in charge of the code made a speech in Chicago severely criticizing certain newspaper practices, "every paper in Chicago but one omitted his speech entirely. The one gave him a single line."

Nevertheless the Guild claims ten thousand men mobilized. While it has been my experience to find the majority of colleagues cursed with indifference, I know from contact that every last one of them believes something is wrong with the press and much can be done by the writers. That "the public has lost faith in its daily press" (Villard) can be confirmed with every journalist. Walter Lippmann, now of the *Herald Tribune* and about one hundred and fifty papers which use his syndicated column, once pointed out that "there is everywhere an increasingly angry disillusionment about the press, a growing sense of being baffled and misled," while Broun just after the 1934 newspaper code hearings expressed the view that ever since the crash of 1929 "many things have occurred which have led the average reader to distrust the average newspaper. Never has the phrase, 'Oh, that's just a newspaper story,' carried a heavier ring of cynicism."

Nineteen reasons for public distrust were recently listed by Dean Ackerman of Columbia. (Vide Appendix.) Many have been specifically discussed in the foregoing pages. The nineteenth in the list was: "In all civilized countries at present newspapers exist for the purpose of concealing truth."

In his answers Mr. Pew agreed or explained his disagreement with eighteen; for the last he had but one word: "Nonsense." But surely Mr. Pew was forgetting his own editorials on the dictatorship of Europe, for it was he who first pointed the fact that three hundred and sixty million people live under systems where the press conceals the truth, where dictators make that function the main one of the official press. And this holds for South America and the Far East as well as fifteen nations in Continental Europe. And when you have a majority of the American press publishing utility propaganda advocating private ownership because they are paid to do so, rather than giving the truth about both sides of the question, you cannot include the country of Jefferson and Andrew Hamilton, the defender of Zenger, among those where the truth is not concealed, at least in part. And so long as Northcliffes, Rothermeres and Beaverbrooks with their prejudices and egomanias dominate the British press and the munitions interests and the *Comité des Forges* dominate French journalism, what chance is there for unbiased, impartial, objective facts—let alone the debatable "truth" about men and events—in these democratic countries?

Much better than any answer to the charges gathered and discussed by Dean Ackerman is the view expressed by Mr. Lippmann. Analyzing liberty and the news, he once said of the leading publishers of America and England:

"Judged simply by their product, men like Mr. Ochs and Viscount Northcliffe believe that their respective nations will perish and civilization decay unless their idea of what is patriotic is permitted to temper the curiosity of their readers. They believe that edification is more important than veracity. They believe it profoundly, violently, relentlessly. They preen themselves upon it. To patriotism as they define it from day to day, all other considerations must yield. That is their pride. And yet what is this but one more among myriad examples of the doctrine that the end justifies the means? A more insidiously misleading rule of conduct was, I believe, never devised among men. . . . In so far as those who purvey the news make of their own beliefs a higher law than truth, they are attacking the foundations of our constitutional system. There can be no higher law in journalism than to tell the truth and shame the devil."

How are we to go about that?

Salvation, according to Mr. Lippmann himself, lies in two things: "ultimately, in the infusion of the news-structure by men with a new training and outlook; immediately, in the concentration of the independent forces against the complacency and bad service of the routineers." Sir Norman Angell, foreseeing a socialized state, proposes that it do four things to free journalism:

"1.   While . . . encouraging freedom of the press . . . amend laws with reference to anonymity, libel, and so forth. . . .

"2.   Make of journalism a chartered profession like the law and medicine, demanding certain qualifications and adherence to a certain code of professional conduct.

"3.   Create a state or governmental press, managed . . . by a journalistic judiciary, pledged to the impartial presentation of news. . . .

"4.   Encourage organized labor to create its own co-operative press . . . (via) trade unions and the industrial co-operative societies."

But, on the other hand, Charles Edward Russell is opposed to more laws dealing with the press. Merely to force the newspapers, as is done in France and other countries, to make retractions when they libel persons or interfere with the freedom of individuals, is a small palliative. "There can be no cure for the kept press," Mr. Russell believes, "until there ceases to be a power sufficiently great and sufficiently interested, to keep on keeping the press. . . . The only answer is that we must steadfastly support, further and develop the few publications we now have that are not under the advertising lasso and can therefore tell the truth. Without a free press other free institutions are impossible and so long as nine-tenths of the newspapers are kept as ours are kept, to speak of a free press is a mere mockery."

Professor Ross, of Wisconsin, who believes that "the defection of the daily press has been a staggering blow to democracy," recommends an endowed daily newspaper pledged to the impartial publication of news.

Many, if not most newspaper men, lay the blame on the public. People get the governments they deserve and the press they deserve. A really free people gets a really free press; masses which come under Nietzsche's *Sklavenmoral* heading get a slavish press—one has but to look at the slave-mind of the Italians and the Germans for proof, and compare it to the British, the Scandinavian, Swiss or Dutch mentality. "When enough people are interested in having the truth told," writes Lewis Gannett, "the truth will be told; the real difficulty about getting the truth told in the American press is that not enough Americans care about news from foreign countries." Or their own. "Every editor knows—from experience—that his public wants scandal news more than it wants honest international political news."

Other palliatives and cures suggested by newspaper men, include:

> The small ad-less newspaper at a penny.
> A high-priced newspaper independent of advertisers.
> An endowed newspaper.
> Daily newspapers to be published by the university presses.
> Labor-union newspapers.
> Co-operative newspapers.
> Staff direction of a paper *(Kansas City Star* and *Brooklyn Eagle)*.
> Municipal newspaper *(Los Angeles Municipal News)*.
> Increased rivalry from the radio.
> Increased power of the Guild.
> Support of magazines which are the gadflies of the press.

Ethical courses in the journalism schools.
General education of the public.
Dictatorship.

The ad-less newspaper has been tried twice. E. W. Scripps was the experimenter. The *Day-Book,* Chicago, N. D. Cochran, editor, and the *Philadelphia News-Post,* Hamilton B. Clark and Marlen Pew, editors, were fairly successful and "out of the red" when the war ended their existence. Mr. Pew still believes in this type of paper.

The *Times,* Mr. Bent figures, costs fourteen cents a copy and sells for two. The advertiser pays the difference. If papers like the *Times* sold for five or seven or ten cents, with the number of pages cut down to less than half, the publisher could make a profit on circulation and be free from the advertiser. In Paris, Americans for years have paid three to six cents for a six- or eight-page sheet; in Spain I paid seven to twelve cents for the *Paris Herald* or *Tribune.* There are probably enough persons willing to pay higher prices for free newspapers in America to make several profitable.

The great danger here might be a journalistic Gresham's law. The yellow, sensational, tabloid press and the press subsidized by parties or persons who have a private motive in influencing public opinion, are a cheap press. Cheap money, bad money, drives out the good. Albert Jay Nock, Professor Ross and Sir Norman Angell have expressed similar fears in world journalism.

Rivalry between press and radio was officially ended in December, 1933, when the publishers limited the broadcasters to two five-minute bulletin periods. There are now important signs of revolt. WNAC became Boston's most popular station when it subscribed to a real news service. The Yankee Network, the Transradio Press Service, KNX, Hollywood; KSTP, St. Paul; WLS, Chicago; KWK, St. Louis, are proving that Mr. Ochs was right when he warned the Associated Press its plan to curtail news broadcasting drastically would fail.

Radio is the great modern paradox. A new means of communication with the masses, it has sometimes been used to fight the press; again, to go over the heads of the politicians or of governments. Its potentialities are socially tremendous; they have been used largely to popularize laxatives. Radio is entirely controlled by advertisers and as a result about ninety per cent of its programs range from the imbecilic to the disgusting. Yet radio can be made into a force for enlightenment perhaps even greater than the printing press.

The *Los Angeles Municipal News*, edited by Frank E. Wolfe, had a short earthquake-like existence. It was honest. It drove that tyrannical Tory, General Harrison Gray Otis, almost mad. He and other publishers persuaded the advertisers to boycott the *News* and finally incited the citizenry, which the *News* was serving better than the other papers, against it. The "proletariat" killed its own newspaper. That was a fine ironic ending.

The labor press has not been successful. The *Milwaukee Leader* alone survives. On the other hand the *Forward,* in the Jewish language, is an outstanding success. Many leading newspaper men would like to see organized American labor establish and support great dailies in the big cities; they would prefer the integral bias of this endowment fund to the present multiple, conglomerate and corrupting influences. There is at the moment more than a rumor that such a newspaper is contemplated in New York City.

As for endowed newspapers, they would naturally have some drawbacks, but they might prove better than most present-day journals. We have today the university presses which publish a great many of our best books. In fact, when a writer has done a good work which he knows will have neither great mass appeal nor a chance for commercial success, he offers it to the university presses. The universities publish dailies of student interest only. I would like to see the universities experiment with real newspapers.

Journalism is now being taught in about a hundred schools, but only thirteen offer definitive work in journalistic ethics, according to a report of the University of Missouri. This leading institution suggests the following outline of a syllabus for "Ethics of Journalism":

1. Ethical Problems which confront:
   The publisher: the chief editorial writer, the news editor, the reporter, the circulation and advertising managers, etc.
   Relation of these problems to ethics proper.
2. The Aims of Journalism:
   Its social obligations.
   Legal requirements.
   Questions of news suppression, coloring, faking.
   What the public wants.
3. Allegations Made Against the Press:
   Journalism once a profession, now business.
   Dominated by materialistic considerations.
   Preference shown for sensational over significant.
   Craze for mass circulation—record ad linage.
   Exploitation of crime news—influence of the circulation managers over news and make-up editors.
   Diminution of editorial leadership and influence.

Since the newspapers are employing many journalism graduates nowadays, reporters whose minds have been opened by a course as outlined above would be less likely to succumb to office routine and influence. There is much encouragement in this. In the colleges themselves a journalistic awakening is noticeable. After generations of parochialism the newspapers of the leading universities are learning that the world is just around the corner from their splendid ivory walls. War and peace, militarism, Fascism and Communism and Democracy, great economic problems are beating down upon hitherto secure lives. Columbia, Princeton, Bucknell, Nebraska University papers and now the *Yale News* are open to discussions of these subjects.

This, however, does not make newspapers of these essentially university organs. If they were endowed sufficiently to buy and gather news, as at present the *Christian Science Monitor* is endowed by a church, they could compete with the commercial press in their cities or towns.

I would like to see a Ford or a Rockefeller leave fifty million stringless dollars for the publication of a really independent

newspaper. Better yet, if one day Mr. Hearst or Mr. Chandler
or Colonel McCormick or Captain Patterson or any other of
the multimillionaire newspaper owners were to call in the staff
and say a few simple words, such as:

"From this afternoon on you are free from all outside control; you are to publish a newspaper in strict accordance with
the canons of journalism and the code of ethics and your own
conscience; so long as you do that your jobs are safe. Now
produce a free newspaper."

Is this idea too fantastic? This is exactly what took place
on the *Frankfurter Zeitung*. It became a really free newspaper.

But the result in America might not be the same. In Frankfurt in the free days there was no department-store boycott,
no public-utility boycott, no patent-medicine boycott, no banker
boycott. In America a newspaper publishing news unwelcome
to the advertisers, the chambers of commerce, the national
manufacturers' associations, the American Legion, the other
super-patriotic societies, the financial world, and other ruling
powers, would lose a lot of advertising. The owner would not
be grossing about two million dollars a month. He might, in
fact, have to dig down into his bank balance. But it would be
worth trying.

Among the practical solutions of the problem I think the one
offered by the American Newspaper Guild is the best. The
Guild seeks a greater share and responsibility in newspaper
making today. The difference between the Guild and the publishers is this: the former displays a social conscience while the
latter still live in the golden but dying age of the socially irresponsible profit motive.

The difference between the editors with their canons of
journalism and the news writers with their code of ethics is
the difference between men who are publishers' yes-men to
whom the official protestations of honesty, sincerity, decency
and truthfulness are moribund or forgotten words on a piece
of paper and youthful enthusiasts (of all ages) to whom these
same words are part of the living truth.

The Guild, on the other hand, means what it says, and has
gone much further than its official declarations. On Thursday

evenings over station WEVD representatives of the society can be heard discussing the status of American journalism with the public it is supposed to serve.

In the Jennings case the Guild informed the public about publisher pressure being exerted in Washington; it discussed the "freedom of the press" issue as a "blind," dust in the eyes of laymen. "It is not freedom of the press that is at stake, it is the right of all labor to organize under Section 7-A of the NRA," one speaker declared; "it is a question of power of the press not freedom of the press; it is a matter of wages, hours, the right to organize for everyone, not merely newspaper men." The Guild maintained it believed in the real freedom of the press not the despotism of individuals over workers and that the maneuvers of the organized publishers have made the reporters realize they are not certain glamorous figures divorced from the world but a part of the working community.

This new consciousness is most important. The Guild declared itself interested not only in the rights of its membership but the rights of all men. It demanded a restatement of the rights of labor outside the NRA, especially the following points:

1. Guarantee of the right of collective bargaining.
2. Definitive prohibition of company unions.
3. Clarification of the power of the Labor Relations Board.
4. No discharge of employees for labor activity.
5. Provision for inspection of employers' books.
6. Provision for inspection of books by government agency, regarding hours, wages, etc.

The Guild, furthermore, told the public newspaper men would watch in Washington, Albany and other capitals where laws were being introduced affecting the rights of individuals and labor. It has appointed a legislature committee which is empowered to make recommendations and to prevent the destruction of rights promised under NRA; to prevent the increased taxation of low income groups and the exemption of the high income groups; to prevent a system of jobs at any price and the plans of employers to beat down wage levels and defeat strikes and the right to strike, and to lower the American standards of living.

What the Guild really wants is a say in newspaper making in America.

It is entitled to that. The day of the irresponsible employer is over and the employer who does not recognize this fact is inviting revolution. Even in Fascist Italy where it actually does not exist, the paper plans of the corporative state insist on producers having something to say about production.

In no other industry is the employee as capable of directing the whole works as in newspaper making. All the editors are graduate reporters. The editors and reporters and the typographical and other unions make the newspaper. The publisher or owner has his functions, of course, but his main work is to direct the "policy" of the paper, and every reporter knows that "policy" usually is the thing he·is fighting. The policy may be adherence to the Republican or Democratic Party, or private ownership of public utilities, or war on Mexico, Japan or Russia, or the protection of the medicine men. The less policy the freer the newspaper. If this kind of policy direction by the owners of the press were completely abolished and the journalists whose policy would be merely to publish the news, came into control, then the day of the free press would be at hand.

But whether or not a Utopian day arrives when newspaper men will publish the news, the time has surely come when the economic freedom of the reporter must be guaranteed. Economic security, of course, should be guaranteed for all men. In this machine age when the potentialities of production make possible for the first time in history enough food, shelter and clothing to take care of all mankind, ignorance and indifference stand between the people and the goal. And it is just this ignorance and indifference which the organized newspaper workers would break down.

They cannot begin their work until they themselves are free from fear.

"Closely related to ignorance and inertia, but even more powerful in its influence against complete and impartial truth-telling by newspapers, is fear. Fear is a characteristic not simply of newspapers; it is a characteristic of the American people. It is not physical fear. . . . It is rather intellectual and spiritual fear. . . . Fear in journalism begins with the reporter and permeates every part of the newspaper organization. . . . Fundamentally it is fear on the part of the reporter and employees immediately above the reporter. . . . He believes that the publisher wants only stories with a conservative bias and that if he writes an important political or economic story showing no bias or showing radical or liberal bias, the story will not be printed and he may be fired. . . . There is instilled into the young newspaper man's mind the feeling that the publisher is involved in various capitalistic enterprises, that his business and social associates are all capitalists, and that he is publishing the newspaper in the interests of capitalism. . . . The same reasoning applies to such an organization as the Associated Press. . . ."

Nelson Antrim Crawford, who has been an editor of many publications, secretary of the American Association of Teachers of Journalism and the author of *The Ethics of Journalism,* which is used in many schools, thus sums up the psychological status of the American reporter. In newspaper offices there have never been many men of the Lingle type, but a majority who proved too adaptable, and a minority who come breathing high idealism. These have been so many young Doctor Arrowsmiths. Usually they are soon disillusioned. But worse yet are those who do not realize they are tempered and compromised by the psychological forces, the unseen but ever-present influences and the pressure from the business office which are much more powerful than Arrowsmith found in the highly ethical profession of medicine. Years in a newspaper office are filled with unconscious compromises, with sail-trimming to all the commercial trade winds.

If the Guild idea succeeds fear should be banished. If all men join and none fears for his daily bread, he can, to paraphrase Mr. Shakespeare, keep his foot out of brothels, his hand out of plackets, his pen from lenders' books, and defy the foul fiend. The profession is a small one, and the best part is already organized. Certainly one is justified in regarding this development as the most important of all in the struggle for a free press in our country.

Cynics and realists say that with newspapers as with governments we get what we deserve. The masses are ignorant and vile; recent intelligence tests show them to be little better than morons; to Machiavelli they were "mud," and to present-day Mr. H. G. Wells they are clumsy louts. The prospect therefore of educating "mud" and morons and clumsy louts into an intelligent majority requiring an intelligent government and intelligent newspapers is most depressing.

It is of course very easy to blame everything on the public. The men who govern—dictators, demagogues, politicians—and the owners of the press, most of whom have an abysmally low opinion of the masses, are openly the champions and the upholders of the "common people." The dictators betray them every day, the press sells them at so much per thousand circulation to the advertisers. If, however, the standards of intelligence reach a hitherto unapproached height, it will follow that government and the press will also improve. And when that great day comes we will have an end of exploitation and corruption. We will have nations without war. We will, in short, have the Perfect State. And pie in the sky when we die.

I have listed the plans and ideas of noted thinkers and leaders. They may be palliatives or they may be cures. But, palliatives or cures, if adopted within the century they will take still longer to accomplish much. Among those who are unwilling to wait a long time are the Communists. In Russia you have impatience mounted on a Red horse. You have a ruthless drive forward at terrific speed toward a known goal.

I am well aware, having spent many years fighting and exposing them, that all dictatorships suppress the freedom of the press, and although I have not changed an early conviction (that freedom of the press is the first and most important force working for the liberation of the human spirit), I have realized that a distinction must be made between the Red, the Black and the Brown dictatorial systems. Free printing is abolished in Germany to make possible the rule of fanaticism, bloodthirsty super-patriotism, a self-appointed superior race and the coal and iron barons of the Ruhr; in Italy to carry on the same imperialistic desires of the manufacturers' associations of Milan and Turin and the Italian banks to whom Mussolini's Black Shirts are merely an armed manifestation of power. In reactionary dictatorships there is no intention of future free, dom. In radical dictatorships the opposite is true.

The fact that all dictatorships, military, business or proletarian, suppress the newspapers, must be considered from the standpoint of the ultimate goal. But "ultimate goal" lies in the distant times of mass education and enlightenment. Idealists who find these objectives worth while, therefore give their approval to one form of dictatorship, while they denounce the others where there is no plan, no hope, no liberating future.

For practical men who believe in the free press as the source of all freedom, one step under our present system of government would be to free the newspaper worker. Give him economic freedom and his spiritual freedom may come of itself. That is, indeed, the idea behind the newspaper Guild. Only the other day, to the astonishment of the present chronicler, President Broun repeated in a public address the words which my first city editor used a quarter of a century ago; he said that the newspaper workers of America today were no better than prostitutes, and that when the Guild succeeds in organizing all and they succeed in their program, that word will never again be applied to them.

If, however, the Guild fails as a practical road to freedom of the press, those of us who are interested in getting there will have to turn again to roads which realists call fantastic, impractical, naïve and idealistic, or, in other words, toward changing the order under which we live today.

We have had a very few liberal, fearless newspapers, but we have never had a free press. Many newspaper men believe that when the day comes in which they themselves enjoy economic freedom in a world concerning itself chiefly with profit-making, they will be able to gain a free press from the commercial men who now operate it for their own purposes.

Of course the leaders of the Guild know, as do all intelligent Americans, that we produce enough food, clothing and shelter, thanks to machine and power development, to supply all our people and make everyone economically secure. They know the reasons why such a distribution does not take place. They have committed themselves to a program which envisages this end. Do they, however, believe that they can achieve this economic freedom for one small group which must exist in the midst of a civilization which refuses the same salvation for other groups?

Meanwhile neither the devastating shout of "impractical idealists" nor the waving of the Red flag by multi-millionaire publishers should deter newspaper men and women from continuing their fight. If they win freedom for themselves they will probably find that they have done little to make the press free. But they will be better able to join the other important minorities who also want not only freedom of the press but freedom for all people.

THE END

APPENDIX

APPENDIX

I

THE NINETEEN CHARGES AGAINST THE PRESS

Addressing the American Society of Newspaper Editors, Dean Ackerman, of Columbia, summed up the "charges against the press":

1. That the newspaper standards are determined by circulation. The press gives the public what it wants, rather than what the public needs.
2. The newspaper violates the individual right of privacy.
3. Financial news is promotional rather than informative.
4. News values are often superficial and trivial.
5. Most reporters are inaccurate when reporting interviews.
6. Newspapers do not lead in public affairs, but follow the leadership of organized minorities.
7. Newspapers make heroes of criminals by romantic accounts of gang activities.
8. Headlines frequently do not correctly reveal the facts and the tenor of the article.
9. Newspapers are interested primarily in day by day developments and do not follow through to give the reader a continuous and complete account of what is happening.
10. Weekly newspapers are subservient to local political machines.
11. The press utilizes its freedom as a license to exploit policies which make for circulation rather than for service.
12. The press is not sincere in its attack upon special privilege because it accepts a subsidy from the Post Office Department.
13. The basic fault with the press is its ownership; that the press cannot be impartial and true advocate of public service so long as its owners are engaged or involved in other businesses.
14. News and photographs are sometimes falsified.
15. Many men and women hesitate to express their real opinion to the press because of the uncharitable attitude of editors toward criticism and because of their fear of retaliation.
16. In reporting Sunday sermons and religious meetings, the press seeks sensation rather than knowledge.

367

17. Corporations, private and public organizations, are compelled by self-interest to maintain publicity departments to insure accurate reporting of their affairs and policies.
18. The press over-emphasizes irrational statements of public officials, particularly members of Congress.
19. In all civilized countries at present newspapers exist for the purpose of concealing truth.

II

THE CANONS OF JOURNALISM

ETHICAL RULES ADOPTED BY THE AMERICAN SOCIETY OF NEWSPAPER EDITORS ON APRIL 28, 1923, AND SINCE ENDORSED BY MANY STATE ASSOCIATIONS AND OTHER GROUPS OF JOURNALISTS:

The primary function of newspapers is to communicate to the human race what its members do, feel and think. Journalism, therefore, demands of its practitioners the widest range of intelligence, of knowledge and of experience, as well as natural and trained powers of observation and reasoning. To its opportunities as a chronicle are indissolubly linked its obligations as teacher and interpreter.

To the end of finding some means of codifying sound practice and just aspirations of American journalism, these canons are set forth:

(1) *Responsibility*—The right of a newspaper to attract and hold readers is restricted by nothing but consideration of public welfare. The use a newspaper makes of the share of public attention it gains serves to determine its sense of responsibility, which it shares with every member of its staff. A journalist who uses his power for any selfish or otherwise unworthy purpose is faithless to a high trust.

(2) *Freedom of the Press*—Freedom of the press is to be guarded as a vital right of mankind. It is the unquestionable right by law, including the wisdom of any restrictive statute. To its privileges under the freedom of American institutions are inseparably joined its responsibilities for an intelligent fidelity to the Constitution of the United States.

(3) *Independence*—Freedom from all obligations except that of fidelity to the public interest is vital.

A. Promotion of any private interest contrary to the general welfare, for whatever reason, is not compatible with honest journalism. So-called news communications from private sources should not be published without public notice of their source or else substantiation of the claims to value as news, both in form and substance.

B. Partisanship in editorial comment which knowingly departs from the truth does violence to the best spirit of American journalism; in the news columns it is subversive of a fundamental principle of the profession.

(4) *Sincerity, Truthfulness, Accuracy*—Good faith with the reader is the foundation of all journalism worthy of the name.

A. By every consideration of good faith, a newspaper is constrained to be truthful. It is not to be excused for lack of thoroughness, or accuracy within its control, or failure to obtain command of these essential qualities.

B. Headlines should be fully warranted by the contents of the articles which they surmount.

(5) *Impartiality*—Sound practice makes clear distinction between news reports and expressions of opinion. News reports should be free from opinion or bias of any kind. This rule does not apply to so-called special articles unmistakably devoted to advocacy or characterized by a signature authorizing the writer's own conclusions and interpretations.

(6) *Fair Play*—A newspaper should not publish unofficial charges affecting reputation or moral character, without opportunity given to the accused to be heard; right practice demands the giving of such opportunity in all cases of serious accusation outside judicial proceedings.

A. A newspaper should not invade rights of private feelings without sure warrant of public right as distinguished from public curiosity.

B. It is the privilege, as it is the duty, of a newspaper to make prompt and complete correction of its own serious mistakes of fact or opinion, whatever their origin.

(7) *Decency*—A newspaper cannot escape conviction of insincerity if, while professing high moral purpose, it supplies incentives to base conduct, such as are to be found in details of crime and vice, publication of which is not demonstrably for the general good. Lacking authority to enforce its canons, the journalism here represented can but express the hope that deliberate pandering to vicious instincts will encounter effective public disapproval or yield to the influence of a preponderant professional condemnation.

III

CODE OF ETHICS ADOPTED BY THE AMERICAN NEWSPAPER GUILD

1. That the newspaper man's first duty is to give the public accurate and unbiased news reports, and that he be guided in his contacts with the public by a decent respect for the rights of individuals and groups.

2. That the equality of all men before the law should be observed by the men of the press; that they should not be swayed in news reporting by political, economic, social, racial or religious prejudices, but should be guided only by facts and fairness.

3. That newspaper men should presume persons accused of crime of being innocent until they are convicted, as is the case under the law, and that news accounts dealing with accused persons should be in such form as not to mislead or prejudice the reading public.

4. That the Guild should work through efforts of its members or by agreement with editors and publishers to curb the suppression of legitimate news concerning "privileged" persons or groups, including advertisers, commercial powers and friends of newspapers.

5. That newspaper men shall refuse to reveal confidences or disclose sources of confidential information in court or before other judicial or investigating bodies, and that the newspaperman's duty to keep confidences shall include those he shared with one employer even after he has changed his employment.

6. That the news be edited exclusively in the editorial rooms instead of in the business office of the daily newspapers.

7. That newspaper men shall behave in a manner indicating independence and decent self-respect in the city room as well as outside, and shall avoid any demeanor that might be interpreted as a desire to curry favor with any person.

IV

INTEGRITY OF THE PRESS

RESOLUTION ADOPTED BY THE NEWSPAPER GUILD, IN CONVENTION, ST. PAUL, JUNE, 1934

WHEREAS, freedom of the press is a right of the readers of news and a responsibility upon the producers of news; and is not a privilege for owners of news channels to exploit; and

WHEREAS, reporting is a high calling which has fallen into disrepute because news writers have been too often degraded as hirelings compelled by their employers to serve the purposes of politicians, monopolists, speculators in the necessaries of life, exploiters of labor, and fomenters of war; therefore be it

RESOLVED, that the American Newspaper Guild strive tirelessly for integrity of news columns and opportunity for its members to discharge their social responsibility; not stopping until the men and women who write, graphically portray, or edit news have achieved freedom of conscience to report faithfully, when they occur, and refuse by distortion and suppression, to create political, economic, industrial and military wars.

V

GUILD CONSTITUTION

ARTICLE II—PURPOSE

Section 1. The purposes of the National Guild shall be to advance the economic well being of working newspaper men and women; to guarantee greater economic security for the employed and unemployed members of our craft; to guarantee, insofar as we are able, constant honesty in the dissemination of public intelligence; to raise the standard of journalism and the ethics of our craft; and to foster friendly co-operation with all other workers of the newspaper industry.

VI

THE PRESS AND THE UTILITIES

The Associated Press

The Associated Press is mentioned scores of times in the fifty-two volumes of the Federal Trade Commission's hearings and documents. Three utility men admitted A. P. connections. Among the Commission's exhibits are letters from A. P. men to utilities propaganda chiefs showing friendly co-operation, and asking for more utility stories to circulate.

William C. Grant, director of the Texas propaganda bureau of the NELA, on cross-examination by Judge Healy, admitted that he was still on the A. P. payroll as relief editor; and that he was author of signed stories in the *Dallas Times-Herald* and unsigned stories in the *Houston Chronicle* and *Dallas News* supporting the public utilities. He admitted (Exhibit 2026) that he had written editorials on utility subjects for the *Dallas Times-Herald*, and that he had submitted these editorials to the Dallas Gas Company for revision.

J. B. Sheridan, NELA propagandist for Missouri, testified he had written Major Richardson, propagandist for Pennsylvania, that "the A. P. will prove invaluable to him." To his Texas colleague, George McQuaid, he wrote (Exhibit 2962):

> "The Associated Press sends out practically everything we give them. They have 35 newspapers in Missouri. We get matter printed in them from 1 to 25 newspapers on one story."

Raising the Red Flag

A favorite trick of the utilities propaganda agents was to accuse anyone who spoke or wrote in favor of public ownership of being a dangerous Bolshevik; and the press was usually glad to co-operate. Sheridan testified before Judge Healy:

> "Judge, as I recollect it, getting this rumor and gossip and things that came around, this was an idea to tie up any plan against private owned utilities with the Bolshevist idea; see?"

What $700 Did in Tennessee

Guy P. Newburn, Tennessee public utility information director, reported an advertising campaign in one hundred papers, and said, "We had approximately 40 favorable editorials written on this matter." The only unfavorable ones appeared in the Scripps-Howard papers and in the *Nashville Banner*. "At a cost of less than $700," he said, "we have been able to get our story in papers whose combined circulation is approximately 350,000."

All But Four in Alabama

With the exception of F. I. Thompson's four papers, the *Mobile Register*, *Mobile News Item*, *Montgomery Journal* and *Birmingham Age-Herald*, all the Alabama papers accepted

NELA propaganda, according to the NELA agent in that state. He said that "the *Montgomery Times* uses a good deal without credit as editorial matter." It was always a boast of the NELA that their canned editorials were republished by the newspapers as their own.

St. Louis and Kansas City Papers

There were some newspapers the utility agents could not "reach." Of the *St. Louis Post-Dispatch,* an agent (Exhibit 2954) wrote: "It is the only one of 600 newspapers in Missouri which is opposed to the electric industry." The *Kansas City Star* and *Times* rebuffed the propagandists. The NELA agent wrote (Exhibit 2958):

"The newspapers are the only things of which I fear. To be frank with you they make me sick: but what are we to do; in so much as the Nelson papers make Kansas City ownership of Kansas City utilities a fetish, I suppose we have to be tender with them."

The American Metropolis

The reports and hearings of the utility commission lasted many years, but were little reported in the American press. Ten per cent would be a fair estimate of the papers which reported the hearings as objectively as they would an event not unfavorable to the press as a whole or to individual newspapers. But the *New York Times* did publish most of the evidence involving itself.

In direct testimony J. S. S. Richardson, NELA agent, admitted preparing the material for a *Times* article on the Conowingo power development. Another article, in the *New York Times Magazine* of October 2, 1927, dealing with "The Electric Age" was written by Dr. Frank Bohn while he was in the employ of the NELA (Exhibit 1314).

Yes, If Paid For

One of the most interesting exhibits is No. 3764, the replies to a questionnaire the propaganda bureau sent to all North and South Dakota papers asking if they would use the utility hand-

outs. The majority said, yes, if paid for. Only a few kicked.
Here are some samples:

Henry Jacobsen, *Castle Rock Press:* Yes, if with advertising.

G. G. Warner, *Gregory Times-Advocate:* Yes, if it will benefit us. Send on your propaganda, and if I can use it so that it will
make me some money, I sure am going to do it.

Mandan Daily Pioneer: If current is given free.

Portland International: No. Pay for your advertising.

VII

THE PRESS VERSUS LABOR

The best analysis of the press in a labor dispute can be found
in "Public Opinion and the Steel Strike, supplementary reports
of the investigators to the commission of inquiry, The Inter-
church World Movement, Bishop Francis J. McConnell, chairman, with the technical assistance of the Bureau of Industrial
Research, New York" and the "Report on the Steel Strike of
1919," by the same organization (Harcourt, Brace & Co., publishers).

The following Pittsburgh newspapers were analyzed: The
Gazette-Times and *Chronicle-Telegraph,* owned by the sons of
the late Senator Oliver, colleague and co-worker of Senator
Penrose; the *Post* and *Sun,* owned until his death by T. Hart
Given, president of the Farmers National Bank; the *Dispatch,*
the *Leader* and the *Press,* principal owner Oliver S. Hershman
and circulation manager, William S. Haddock, sheriff of Allegheny County during the strike.

(The present writer would like to say at this point that several of these papers have been killed or absorbed by the others
and the rest have changed owners; Pittsburgh journalistically
is now in the hands of Paul Block, Hearst and Scripps-Howard. The Scripps-Howard *Press* I am sure would not lend itself
to such prostitution as the 1919 investigation revealed.)

There are several hundred interesting pages in the two volumes showing the complete perversion of the seven newspapers,
the power of big business in corrupting the press, the failure of
all seven papers to print any honest news. Of the Associated
Press the report states that in past strikes this organization got
its news already "colored" from the local papers and that the

only safe procedure is for the A. P. to send an independent reporter. Of the seven journals which uphold the freedom of the press in the present writer's home town, the report concludes:

"[The Pittsburgh workers] believe that the press immediately took sides, printed only the news favoring that side, suppressed or colored its records, printed advertisements and editorials urging the strikers to go back, denounced the strikers, and incessantly misrepresented the facts. *All this was found to be true in the case of the Pittsburgh papers.* (Italics ours.)

"The strike was defeated by:

(a) The strike-breaking methods of the steel companies and their effective mobilization of public opinion against the strikers through charges of radicalism, bolshevism and the closed shop, none of which were justified by facts; and by the suppression of civil rights.

(b) The hostility of the press, giving biased and colored news and the silence of both press and pulpit on the actual question of justice involved; which attitudes of press and pulpit helped to break the strikers' morale.

"We recommend to the press that it free itself of the all too well founded charge of bias, favoring capital against labor, and redeem its power as a promoter of truth and a formulator of public opinion by searching out all the facts in regard to industrial questions and publishing them without fear or favor."

VIII

THE PRESS IN WAR TIME

(From the *Congressional Record*, February 9, 1917.)

Mr. Caraway: Mr. Chairman, under unanimous consent, I insert in the Record at this point, a statement showing the newspaper combination, which explains their activity in this war matter, just discussed by the gentleman from Pennsylvania (Mr. Moore):

"In March, 1915, the J. P. Morgan interests, the steel, shipbuilding, and powder interests, and their subsidiary organizations, got together 12 men high up in the newspaper world and employed them to select the most influential newspapers in the

United States and sufficient number of them to control generally
the policy of the daily press of the United States.

"These 12 men worked the problem out by selecting 179 newspapers, and then began, by an elimination process, to retain
only those necessary for the purpose of controlling the general
policy of the daily press throughout the country. They found
it was only necessary to purchase the policy, national and international, of these papers; an agreement was reached; the
policy of the papers was bought, to be paid for by the month;
an editor was furnished for each paper to properly supervise and
edit information regarding the questions of preparedness, militarism, financial policies, and other things of national and
international nature considered vital to the interests of the
purchasers."

This contract is in existence at the present time . . . and it
accounts for the news columns of the daily press of the country
being filled with all sorts of preparedness arguments and misrepresentation of the present condition of the United States
Army and Navy and the possibility and probability of the United
States being attacked by foreign foes.

This policy also includes the suppression of everything in
opposition to the wishes of the interests served. The effective-
ness of this scheme has been conclusively demonstrated by the
character of stuff carried by the daily press since March, 1915.
They have resorted to anything necessary to commercialize public sentiment and sandbag the National Congress into making
extravagant and wasteful appropriations under the false pretense that it is necessary. Their stock argument is that it is
"patriotism." They are playing on every prejudice and passion
of the American people.

BIBLIOGRAPHY

BIBLIOGRAPHY

There are thousands of books and pamphlets on journalism and its problems. Several hundred have been read and consulted. The following are the most important in relation to the foregoing pages.

Ethics

CRAWFORD, NELSON ANTRIM, *The Ethics of Journalism*
FLINT, LEON NELSON, *The Conscience of the Newspaper*
HAPGOOD, NORMAN, *Everyday Ethics*
WILMER, L. A., *Our Press Gang*

Freedom of the Press

CHAFEE, ZECHARIAH, JR., *Freedom of Speech*
ERNST, MORRIS LEOPOLD, AND SEAGLE, WILLIAM, *To the Pure*
HAYS, ARTHUR GARFIELD, *Let Freedom Ring*
LIPPMANN, WALTER, *Liberty and the News*
SALMON, LUCY MAYNARD, *The Newspaper and Authority*
WEINBERGER, HARRY, *Freedom of the Press*

Propaganda and Publicity

BERNAYS, EDWARD L., *Crystallizing Public Opinion*
BERNAYS, EDWARD L., *Propaganda*
CREEL, GEORGE, *How We Advertised America*
LASSWELL, HAROLD DWIGHT, *Propaganda Technique in the World War*
LEE, IVY, *Publicity*
LONG, JOHN CUTHBERT, *Public Relations*
LUMLEY, FREDERICK ELMORE, *The Propaganda Menace*
PONSONBY, ARTHUR, *Falsehood in War-time*
RIEGEL, OSCAR WETHERHOLD, *Mobilization for Chaos*

Utilities Propaganda

GRUENING, ERNEST HENRY, *The Public Pays*
RAUSHENBUSH, HILMAR STEPHEN, *The Power Fight*
RAUSHENBUSH, HILMAR STEPHEN, *High Power Propaganda*
THOMPSON, CARL DEAN, *Confessions of the Power Trust*
UNITED STATES FEDERAL TRADE COMMISSION, *Utility Reports*

379

General

ABBOT, WILLIS JOHN, *Watching the World Go By*
ALLEN, WILLIAM CHARLES, *War! Behind the Smoke Screen*
ANGELL, SIR NORMAN, *The Press and the Organization of Society*
ANGELL, SIR NORMAN, *The Public Mind*
PEARSON, DREW, AND ALLEN, R. J., *Washington Merry-Go-Round*
BENT, SILAS, *Ballyhoo*
BENT, SILAS, *Strange Bedfellows*
DEWEY, JOHN, *The Public and Its Problems*
GREENWALL, HARRY J., *Scoops*
HOLT, HAMILTON, *Commercialism and Journalism*
LIPPMANN, WALTER, *Public Opinion*
LIPPMANN, WALTER, *The Phantom Public*
OLDER, FREMONT, *My Own Story*
OWEN, ROBERT LATHAM, *The Russian Imperial Conspiracy*
RAFFALOVITCH, ARTHUR, *L'Abominable Venalité de la Presse*
RUE, LARRY, *I Fly for News*
SELDES, GILBERT, *The Years of the Locust*
SINCLAIR, UPTON, *The Brass Check*
VILLARD, OSWALD GARRISON, *The Press Today*
VILLARD, OSWALD GARRISON, *Some Newspapers and Newspapermen*
WILKERSON, M. M., *Public Opinion and the Spanish-American War*
WINKLER, JOHN KENNEDY, *W. R. Hearst*

Advertising

CHASE, STUART AND SCHLINK, F. J., *Your Money's Worth*
PHILLIPS, MARY CATHERINE, *Skin Deep*
RORTY, JAMES, *Our Master's Voice: Advertising*
SCHLINK, FREDERICK JOHN, AND KALLET, ARTHUR, *100,000,000 Guinea Pigs*

The Classics

It is taken for granted that all persons interested in the problem of free speech, free press and freedom of the individual are acquainted with Milton's *Areopagitica, Speech for the Liberty of Unlicensed Printing,* James Mill's *Liberty of the Press* and John Stuart Mill's *On Liberty,* Bentham's *On the Liberty of the Press,* etc.